D1599382

YALE JUDAICA SERIES

VOLUME XXVIII

Gersonides on Song of Songs

COMMENTARY ON SONG OF SONGS

Levi ben Gershom
(Gersonides)

Translated from the Hebrew

with an introduction and annotations by

Menachem Kellner

Yale University Press

New Haven and London

Designed by James J. Johnson and set in Sabon Roman type by G & S Typesetters, Inc., Austin,
Texas. Printed in the United States of America by BookCrafters, Inc., Chelsea, Michigan.

Library of Congress Cataloging-in-Publication Data

Levi ben Gershom, 1288–1344.
Commentary on Song of songs / Levi ben Gershom (Gersonïdes);
translated from the Hebrew with an introduction and annotations by
Menachem Kellner.
p.   cm. — (Yale Judaica series ; v. 28)
Includes bibliographical references and index.
ISBN 0-300-07147-7 (alk. paper)
1. Bible. O.T.   Song of Solomon—Commentaries—Early works to
1800. I. Kellner, Menachem Marc, 1946–   . II. Title.
III. Series: Yale Judaica series; 28.
BS1485.L39   1998
223'.907—dc21   97-37385

A catalogue record for this book is available from the British Library.

1   3   5   7   9   10   8   6   4   2

CONTENTS

PREFACE

It is widely acknowledged that Levi ben Gershom, Ralbag, or Gersonides (Provence, 1288–1344) is one of medieval Judaism's most interesting figures. Philosopher, exegete, halakhist, he was also a first-class astronomer and mathematician who made historically significant contributions to both fields. With the exception of portions of the *Wars of the Lord*[1] and his commentary on Job, however, almost none of Gersonides' works have been translated into any European language. In many ways his commentary on Song of Songs is an ideal vehicle for entering into his thought: short enough to be translated, explained, and introduced in one volume, it nonetheless draws together many important strands and elements of his work—philosophical theology, philosophy of science, biblical exegesis, and commentary on Averroës.

Gersonides stands at the intersection of three worlds. A learned and devoted Jew, his major philosophical-scientific teachers were Muslims, although he worked in close scientific (astronomical and astrological) cooperation with Christians and was, at the very least, aware of some developments in Latin philosophy. He is almost a perfect case study in the acculturation of mid-fourteenth-century Provençal Jews, providing a window into the life and thought of his Jewish contemporaries. Gersonides interpreted the Bible as a philosophic text for a clearly defined audience; analysis of his interpretation allows us to encounter and come to know that audience.

Gersonides applied his learning, brilliance, and penetration to the Judaism he had inherited from his teachers, transforming it and thus passing on to his own students a Judaism that bore the stamp of his unique personality and of the Jewish-Muslim-Christian symbiosis he both represented and helped create. For Gersonides, Song of Songs was unique: the only book in the Bible written to teach the ultimate truths of the universe to the elite while being of no outward benefit to the masses. His commentary on Song of Songs thus serves as a prism, shattering the light of his philosophized Judaism into its constituent colors.

In general, Gersonides had two philosophical masters: Maimonides and Averroës. Indeed, Gersonides' philosophical magnum opus, *Wars of the Lord,* may be best understood as a work designed to correct the views of Maimonides where Gersonides thought that they needed correction (divine knowledge, creation) or to interpret those views where he thought they needed explication (human immortality, prophecy, providence). Rare are the places where Gersonides clearly rejects views held jointly by Maimonides and Averroës. My introduction emphasizes those aspects of Gersonides' thought that find expression in his commentary on Song of Songs and in which he expresses his independence from his two teachers. The introduction and annotation to the translation also emphasize the fact that Gersonides saw Song of Songs as one of three biblical books written by Solomon, and frequent reference is therefore made to Gersonides' commentaries on Ecclesiastes and Proverbs. Similarly, the commentary on Song of Songs is a commentary on a biblical book, and I have sought to make as much use as possible of Gersonides' other biblical commentaries (especially the commentary on the Torah) in elucidating the commentary on Song of Songs.

Recent scholarship has emphasized Gersonides' links to Arabic and Latin thought. This has led to a rather remarkable phenomenon: the treatment of Gersonides more in terms of Arabic and Latin philosophy than Jewish philosophy in particular and Jewish sources in general.[2] In my introduction and annotation I attempt to redress this scholarly imbalance by emphasizing Gersonides' links with previous Jewish thinkers, especially Maimonides and the whole school of Jewish philosophers influenced by Maimonides, while not ignoring his obvious dependence on Arabic thought and the possibility of his having some awareness of contemporary Latin thought. I do not mean to parochialize Gersonides; rather, I want to draw attention to something that should be obvious: Gersonides wrote in Hebrew for a Jewish audience. Attempts to understand his work should keep that audience in mind.

NOTE ON THE HEBREW TEXT
AND THIS TRANSLATION

The Institute for Microfilmed Hebrew Manuscripts at the Jewish National and University Library (JNUL) in Jerusalem houses more than thirty micro-films of manuscripts of Gersonides' commentary on Song of Songs. Seven are catalogued as dating from before 1400; they are the ones I examined. Having decided, in line with common sense and current scholarly practice, to create not an eclectic but a diplomatic text (that is, a text using one manuscript as a basis), I chose Ms. Vatican Urbino 17/1 (JNUL 656) as the root manuscript for the edition and translation. By virtue of its clarity, readability, complete-ness, and comprehensibility, it is the best of the seven. It is, however, far from perfect. In the first place, it was copied by two different scribes. The change-over takes place near the end, in the commentary on Song of Songs 7:1. The second scribe was much more careless than the first, often interchanging vav and yod. Second, the manuscript suffers from not a few cases of homoeote-leuton. It was necessary, therefore, to compare the manuscript to another, and I chose Ms. Hebr. Paris 257 (JNUL 4238). On the whole, the readings of Vat. 17/1 were superior, making more sense, but the copyist of Paris 257 skipped fewer lines, so I was able to use it as a source for most of the lines missed by the copyist of Vat. 17/1. The editio princeps (Riva di Trento, 1560) preserves readings not found in either of the manuscripts; I have used that text as a third source. Of the other two printed editions, that found in Moses Frankfurter's rabbinic Bible, *Kehillot Mosheh* (Amsterdam, 1724–27), is so full of mistakes as to be nearly incomprehensible, and the second (Koenigs-berg, 1860) is a faithful copy of the Riva edition. There still remained passages where the text seemed to me corrupt, and in attempting to understand them I consulted a third manuscript, Vatican 83 (JNUL 201). This manuscript is also catalogued as having been copied in the fourteenth century and is very close to but not identical to the one used as the basis of the Riva edition.

Modern translators of Gersonides into English have, it seems to me, largely chosen one of two options: faithfulness to the original Hebrew or faithfulness to the needs of modern English. Each approach has its advantages and disadvantages. When one makes the Hebrew text dominant, the ensuing translation is, of course, very faithful to the original but often involves gross sins against the English language. When taken to the extreme, this approach sometimes results in translations that are intelligible only to those who understand the original. Making the needs of English dominant, when done well, results in a readable and graceful text but runs the risks of rounding off sharp edges found in the original and of making the text appear less problematic than it sometimes is.

In the case of Gersonides, the temptation to follow in the footsteps of the legendary Yiddish translators of Shakespeare, who advertised their works as *verteitcht und verbessert* ("translated and improved"), is considerable. Even when judged by the standards of medieval philosophic Hebrew, a graceless language if ever there was one, Gersonides' style is particularly wooden, dry, and difficult. It is heavily Arabicized and in some passages hardly seems to be Hebrew at all.[1] Gersonides proves himself again and again to be the master of the ambiguous antecedent. His is a very limited vocabulary, the same word often serving for several different meanings within the space of a single paragraph. Indeed, some words, notably *'inyan,* seem to have an almost limitless range of reference.

In the translation here presented, I have largely tried to choose literalness over grace while still remaining as faithful as I could to the canons of reasonable English style. In this I follow Gersonides' own advice to translators: "If a text is translated from one language to another, word by word, without any change in order, the passage will be incomprehensible; this is clear to anyone who translates from Arabic to Hebrew [lit.: the holy language]."[2] I have thus in many places added words only implicit in the original Hebrew without drawing attention to that fact.

I italicize direct quotes from the biblical source; where I translate passages based on but not accurately reflecting the biblical source, I do not italicize. I have used the original Jewish Publication Society translation of the Bible, altering it on rare occasions to make it fit Gersonides' interpretations. In general, honorifics are simplified: "Moses, our Master" becomes "Moses," and "the rabbi, the guide," is simplified to "Maimonides." Where Gersonides writes "The Lord, May He be Praised," and so on, I write "God." This approach causes something of the flavor of the original to be lost but leads to a translation that is much easier to read.

ACKNOWLEDGMENTS

I am grateful to the staff of the Institute for Microfilmed Hebrew Manuscripts at the Jewish National and University Library in Jerusalem for their unfailingly courteous and knowledgeable assistance.

I had the privilege of presenting part of the text and some of the ideas that follow to a series of seminars at the Ecole Pratique des Hautes Etudes in Paris. I am grateful to my distinguished colleague, Charles Touati, for making that marvelous experience possible and to the students in the seminar for their comments and questions.

A number of long-suffering colleagues have cheerfully shared their knowledge and insight with me, making my work on this book easier and certainly more fun. Gad Freudenthal and Charles Manekin have made themselves available to me again and again and have saved me from errors and pointed me in the right direction at crucial intersections. For help with specific points or with discrete parts of what follows, I am also deeply grateful to Robert Eisen, Seymour Feldman, Avner Giladi, Bernard R. Goldstein, Giora Hon, Raphael Jospe, Howard Kreisel, Tzvi Langermann, Daniel J. Lasker, Avraham Melamed, and Marc Saperstein. Jesse S. Mashbaum was kind enough to place at my disposal his as-yet-unpublished critical edition of Gersonides' supercommentary on Averroës' *Epitome of Aristotle's* De Anima; I am very grateful to him for his exemplary collegiality.

I should like to thank a number of people who have helped me in the establishment of the text underlying the translation presented in this book. Rivka T. Kellner and Breindl B. Kellner, my daugher and niece, respectively, were most gracious in helping me to compare manuscripts. I had the pleasure of "learning" the text with my friend Nisan Arrarat, whose keen eye caught many a typo and incongruity. Amir Wind looked for errors with an eagle's eye. Last, Shula Haver provided me with cheerful and efficient assistance in formatting the Hebrew text. For their assistance in bringing this book to its home in the Yale Judaic Series and in pruning a much longer manuscript to its present proportions, I am grateful to David Ruderman, Sid Z. Leiman, and Ivan Marcus.

My wonderful wife, Jolene, and deeply appreciated children, Avinoam and Rivka, had to put up with many profoundly boring (to them) conversations about my friend Ralbag, and I appreciate their forbearance.

The Hebrew text of Gersonides' introduction to his commentary was published in *Da'at* 23 (1989): 15–32 and an earlier version of the English translation in J. Neusner (ed.), *From Ancient to Modern Judaism: Essays in Honor of Marvin Fox*, vol. 2 (Atlanta: Scholars Press, 1989), 187–205. It was my hope originally to publish a critical edition of the Hebrew text of Gersonides' commentary on Song of Songs with this translation, but that proved impossible within the framework of the Yale Judaica Series and, according to the decree of God, as Gersonides would have written, I shall publish it elsewhere.

Portions of my introduction have appeared as "Gersonides' Commentary on Song of Songs: For Whom Was It Written and Why?" in G. Dahan (ed.), *Gersonide en son temps* (Louvain: Peeters, 1994). My thanks to Professor Dahan and to Peeters Publishers for permission to reprint.

NOTE TO THE READER

I have occasionally emended cited translations slightly without noting the fact. For instance, I prefer "Active Intellect" to Feldman's "Agent Intellect." References to the Pentateuch commentary will be to *Perush ʿal ha-Torah ʿal Derekh ha-Beʾur* (Venice, 1547); passages from the Genesis commentary will also be referenced to *Perushe ha-Torah le-Rabbenu Levi ben Gershom, Sefer Bereshit,* edited by Yaʾakov Leib Levy (1992) and *Ḥamishah Ḥumshei Torah ʿim Beʾur ha-Ralbag, Bereshit,* edited by Baruch Braner and Eli Freiman (1993). Citations from the commentary on Genesis are according to page numbers of the three editions as follows: 1547/1992/1993. References to Gersonides' commentaries on Ecclesiastes cite page numbers from the 1860 Koenigsberg edition of *Perush ʿal Ḥamesh Megillot.*

TRANSLATOR'S INTRODUCTION

In June or July 1325, at the age of thirty-seven, Levi ben Gershom wrote his commentary on Song of Songs. He had already written a large number of works, beginning with his *Wars of the Lord* (parts of which were completed in 1317), continuing through independent works on logic, mathematics, and astronomy, and culminating in a long series of supercommentaries on many of the commentaries of Averroës on Aristotle.[1] In 1325, Gersonides completed his first biblical commentary, on the book of Job.[2] Hereafter, biblical commentaries became a regular part of his work; the second, on Song of Songs, appeared only six months after the first.[3] Indeed, if in his first thirty-seven years Gersonides published almost exclusively what we today would call philosophical and scientific works, the last nineteen years of his life were devoted almost exclusively to what can be called more narrowly Jewish works. With the admittedly notable exceptions of a supercommentary on Averroës on the *Metaphysics, Wars of the Lord,* Treatise V, and some smaller works, all of his later productions involved commenting on the Bible or the Talmud.

The commentaries on Job and Song of Songs, then, mark what may have been a turning point in Gersonides' life: the attempt in his maturity to present the classical texts of Judaism in light of the philosophic and scientific work of his youth. In his commentaries on Job and Song of Songs a striking characteristic of his approach to the Bible becomes clear: "Philosophical allegory is the *peshaṭ* [literal, contextual meaning][4] and it serves not only to refute and remove wrong opinions but to delineate a complete, correct cosmology (though pedagogically attuned to lesser minds) and metaphysics."[5] We will see this point made explicitly by Gersonides when we turn to his commentary on Song of Songs itself. That is not to say that Gersonides ignored the historical, legal, and moral teachings of the biblical books. In his commentaries he goes to great trouble to make sense of the historical narratives and to derive moral and halakhic teachings from the texts. He was, however, convinced that the Torah was a scientific treatise and ought to be approached as such. This was certainly his approach to Song of Songs.

Before turning to a discussion of Gersonides' commentary on Song of Songs, note should be taken of other commentaries on that text written by individuals close to Gersonides in space, time, and outlook. Gersonides was certainly not the first Jew of his time and place to write a commentary on Song of Songs in the spirit of Maimonides' comments on that text.[6]

In the *Mishneh Torah*[7] and the *Guide of the Perplexed*[8] Maimonides introduces a new and unprecedented understanding of Song of Songs. The scroll is presented as expressing not the love between God and the House of Israel but the love between God and individual human beings.[9] Maimonides, so far as I know, is the first thinker to take the innovative step of reading the poem in terms of the love between God and the human who seeks God.[10]

Several commentaries on Song of Songs in a Maimonidean mode were written before that of Gersonides.[11] The first appears to be that of Joseph ben Judah ben Jacob ibn 'Aknin, a younger contemporary of Maimonides'.[12] There is no evidence that Gersonides was familiar with this commentary. This is hardly surprising, since ibn 'Aknin wrote his commentary in Arabic in North Africa. It was not translated into Hebrew in the Middle Ages; it would have been surprising had Gersonides been aware of it.[13]

Samuel ibn Tibbon (d. c. 1232), in the introduction to his unpublished commentary on Ecclesiastes, maintains that all of Solomon's books (Song of Songs, Proverbs, Ecclesiastes) "expound the problem of the human soul and the Active Intellect."[14] Samuel was followed in this approach by his relation, Jacob Anatoli, and by his son, Moses ibn Tibbon.

Moses ibn Tibbon of Montpellier, whose writings date from the period between 1244 and 1274, wrote a complete commentary on Song of Songs.[15] Moses' commentary follows in the direction laid down by Maimonides and adopted by Samuel ibn Tibbon and Jacob Anatoli: the text describes the love of the human intellect for the Active Intellect.

A similar approach is taken by Immanuel ben Solomon of Rome (c. 1261–1328), an older contemporary of Gersonides'.[16] Joseph ibn Kaspi (b. 1279/80), who wrote a very short introduction to Song of Songs based on Maimonides' comments in *Guide of the Perplexed* 3:51, reads the text as an allegorical account of the conjunction (*devekut*) between the material intellect and the Active Intellect.[17] There is no evidence that Gersonides was aware of any of these other commentaries. This in itself is surprising, but I have examined the issue in detail elsewhere and it need not detain us here.[18]

Gersonides' commentary is divided into an introduction (*haṣa'ah*) and a running explanation of the text. The introduction takes up three issues. The first consists of an apologia in which Gersonides explains why he wrote the commentary. It is simply the case, he claims, that no previous commentary is adequate since all of the commentaries with which he is familiar follow the midrashic approach of the talmudic rabbis. He hastens to assure us that midrashim are fine in and of themselves—he even promises to write a book devoted to them—but they ought not to be taken as attempts to explicate the intended meaning of the text. Gersonides emphasizes the importance of distinguishing between the straightforward explication of a text and the erection of midrashic structures on the text. Failure to make this distinction can only result in the reader's despising the text, because of the prolixity this combined approach involves and because it involves the confusion of substantial and accidental matters. It is his intention, Gersonides announces, "to write what we understand of this scroll without mixing with it other things which vary from the author's intention" (text at note 7). He will not attempt to interpret the rabbinical midrashim on Song of Songs since they are deep and the task of interpreting the text itself is burden enough. Furthermore, the proper interpretation of the text is a prerequisite for understanding the midrashim.

The bulk of the introduction is given over to a discussion, in very basic terms, of various epistemological issues. This discussion is made necessary by the fact that Gersonides here defines the ultimate felicity of a human being as "cognizing and knowing God to the extent that that is possible for him" (text at note 14). Song of Songs, it will turn out, is an attempt both to describe the stages of this cognition and to guide the individual seeking ultimate felicity by its achievement.[19]

The narratives and commandments of the Torah generally hint at such information, but there is only one text in the whole Bible that deals exclusively with it—Song of Songs. Since, unlike the rest of the Bible, this text is meant to guide only selected individuals to their felicity, its outward, literal meaning teaches nothing to the masses.[20] This, it seems, is Gersonides' solution to the problem of how a text such as Song of Songs, with its outward meaning of frank carnality, came to be included in the Bible. It also points up an interesting fact: Gersonides chose to interpret the one book in the Bible in which passionate physical love is extolled as an argument for the need to overcome all physical passions.[21]

How do we cognize and know God so far as we are able? We achieve this, Gersonides informs us, through the observation of the order and harmony evident in all beings. Since an agent's activity indicates something about the agent, detailed examination of the world demonstrates aspects of God's wisdom. This being the case, the question of how we know becomes crucial. Although Gersonides does not allude to this explicitly, the reason for this is evident: unless we know how to know, so to speak, we will never achieve cognition of God so far as we are able and thus will never achieve ultimate felicity.

In order to understand this, it is necessary briefly to summarize the major features of Gersonides' epistemology. Despite its importance, Gersonides, like many other medieval Jewish and Muslim philosophers, presents no systematic account of his epistemology.[22] One of the epistemological problems with which he does grapple, and which is a central issue in his commentary on Song of Songs, is as old as the debate between Plato and Aristotle. Following the Aristotelian tradition, Gersonides was convinced that knowledge must have an empirical basis. But Aristotle himself had admitted that true knowledge was of unchanging universals.[23] For Gersonides, it is particularly important to protect the claim that true knowledge consists of universals, for it allows him to affirm that although God knows everything that can be known, God does not know—indeed cannot know—particulars, since mutable entities cannot be objects of knowledge.[24] This allows Gersonides to aver God's comprehensive knowledge (of what can be truly known) while protecting human freedom.[25] Gersonides is thus faced with an important problem: the process of coming to know must have an empirical basis, but it must result in trans-empirical knowledge of universals.

Before I turn to Gersonides' solution to this problem, a word must be said about the different ways in which he uses the term *intellect*.[26] Gersonides, along with most other medieval Aristotelians, distinguishes between the material intellect, the acquired intellect, and the Active Intellect.[27] His doctrine of the material intellect is sketched out in *Wars* 1 : 5. As he presents it on the basis of an extended philosophical debate with Alexander of Aphrodisias, Themistius, and Averroës, the material intellect is really nothing other than the human capacity to learn. *Material intellect* is the name given to the ability humans have to receive properly abstracted sensory data and, with the assistance of the Active Intellect, transform it into universals, the proper objects of knowledge. In Gersonides' words, "the body is the subject of this disposition via the imaginative faculty."[28] The material intellect, however, even though it is a disposition, "is not on the level of privation and absolute potentiality; it is, rather, a form to which this potentiality is attached."[29] Gersonides defines the acquired intellect succinctly as "the intelligibles that accrue from abstracting material forms from their matter."[30] The acquired intellect, in other words, is really nothing other than a collection of ideas. It is not just any ideas, however, that constitute the acquired intellect, but only those ideas found in a systematic fashion in the "mind" of the Active Intellect. The Active Intellect in Gersonides' view is the lens through which the other separate intellects influence the sublunary world, the giver of forms in that world, and the cause of human knowledge. It is also the transmitter of prophecy and the immediate agent of miracles.

We may now turn to Gersonides' solution of the problem of how transempirical knowledge of universals can be based on experience. He solves this problem (to his own satisfaction, at least) by appealing to the role of the Active Intellect in human intellection. Human knowing involves a process of abstraction in which the material aspects of the sensory data presented to the intellect are stripped away in a series of stages; the end result of this process is subjected to certain influences of the Active Intellect, in consequence of which knowledge of universals is obtained.[31]

Having explained these matters, we may return to the description of Gersonides' commentary on Song of Songs. After establishing the importance of learning, Gersonides launches into a detailed account of how it is done. This is the most elaborate discussion in his writings of how we form concepts through a process of abstraction from the material provided by our observations of the world around us. After describing the techniques by which we learn, he informs us that even knowing how to know is no guarantee of successful knowing. Learning is so difficult a process that its consequence, human felicity, is only rarely achieved. This for two reasons: (a) it is extraordinarily difficult to observe and learn about existent beings and (b) there are many impediments (Gersonides lists eight) to our properly cognizing the existent beings of the universe.

The Torah guides us to this cognition in the best possible fashion.[32] Gersonides distinguishes between two levels of guidance in the Torah. The first concerns ethics (a prerequisite for cognitive perfection), is geared to the masses, and is thus taught by the Torah publicly. The second deals with speculative (that is, philosophical and scientific) matters, is aimed at philosophers,[33] must be kept secret from the masses, and conveys that information required by philosophers seeking their own perfection: information concerning the speculative roots with which the philosopher typically has great difficulty and concerning the issues about which mistakes are particularly dangerous since they distance an individual from perfection.

Having brought us this far, Gersonides now shows how the structure of Song of Songs reflects its intent. The major topics dealt with in the book are the following: (a) the overcoming of the impediments to cognition (and thus to felicity) related to immoral behavior; (b) the overcoming of the impediments caused by failure to distinguish between truth and falsity; (c) the need to engage in speculation according to the proper order; (d) the division of the sciences (mathematics, physics, metaphysics) and how nature reflects that division; and (e) characteristics of these types of sciences.

The overall structure of the book now clear, Gersonides provides us with a detailed table of contents. When the intent of its author is properly understood, Song of Songs is seen to fall into the following sections:

1. Introductory material concerning the book, its name, its author, his position, the book's form of exposition, its subject matter, and its purpose; refutations of the objections that throw doubt on the possibility of achieving felicity (1:1–8).
2. The necessity of overcoming impediments relating to moral imperfection (1:9–2:7).
3. The necessity of overcoming impediments relating to imagination and opinion so that one can distinguish truth from falsity (2:8–2:17).
4. The study of mathematics (3:1–4:7).
5. The study of physics in the proper fashion (4:8–8:4).
6. The study of metaphysics (8:5–8:14).

The third issue taken up in Gersonides' introduction is an explanation of many of the symbolic representations (*ḥiqquyim*) out of which the book is constructed. A few examples here will suffice to give the flavor of the whole: Jerusalem stands for man. Just as man, among all the compounded entities, is set apart for the worship of God, so is Jerusalem set off from other cities. Furthermore, the name *Jerusalem* is derived from the Hebrew word for perfection; man is the most perfect of all the sublunary entities and thus called Jerusalem. The faculties of the soul are the daughters of Jerusalem, whereas *Solomon* refers to the intellect. Since Zion is the worthiest part of Jerusalem, *daughters of Zion* refers to the faculties of the soul closest to the activity of the intellect. Gersonides interprets in this fashion many of the expressions found in Song of Songs.

These are some of the major points in Gersonides' introduction. The text of his commentary contains few surprises, explicating in detail the position put forward in the introduction. In stylistic terms, it is unusual in two respects: (a) unlike his other commentaries on biblical books, it is not divided into sections (commentary on terms; on import; *to'aliyot*); (b) it quotes heavily from the philosophical literature available to Gersonides but only lightly from classical Jewish literature.

In his commentary Gersonides reads the text not as a dialogue between two physical lovers nor, as the talmudic rabbis had read it, as a dialogue between God and the House of Israel, but as two dialogues. In Gersonides' view the first dialogue is between the human material intellect and the Active Intellect, a kind of conjunction with which is a human being's highest perfection and greatest felicity. The second is between the faculties of the soul and the material intellect. These are not dialogues in the true sense, since in most instances Gersonides construes the participants in this discussion as talking about and not to each other. In any event, the main thrust of these discussions relates to the overwhelming desire of the material intellect to approach the Active Intellect and its attempts to enlist the (willing) aid of the other faculties of the soul in this quest.

The most amazing thing about this commentary, at least so far as this reader is concerned, is the way in which Gersonides' approach, absurd on the face of it as an attempt to explicate the true meaning of the text as intended by its author, becomes more and more convincing as one goes along.

There are a number of ways in which Gersonides' commentary on Song of Songs is unlike his other biblical commentaries. In the other commentaries he cites biblical and rabbinical sources extensively, philosophical and scientific writings relatively rarely. In the commentary on Song of Songs Gersonides cites the Bible only twenty-nine times;[34] of these citations, twelve are of verses used to explain terms in the text, three are simply worked into the text for their stylistic contribution, and fourteen are explicitly cited in order to make or support a point in the commentary. He explicitly cites rabbinical texts seven times, and I found two places where rabbinical statements were incorporated into the text without comment. He cites Maimonides twice, once from the *Guide of the Perplexed* and once from his commentary on the Mishnah. Gersonides cites himself eight times: four times to the *Wars of the Lord,* thrice to his supercommentary to Averroës' *Epitome of Aristotle's* De Anima, and once to his supercommentary on Averroës' *Epitome of Aristotle's* Parva Naturalia.

Turning to non-Jewish authors, we find Gersonides citing Aristotle forty-nine times. Five of these references are to Aristotle generally, the rest being to specific Aristotelian books (eight in all). Ptolemy's *Almagest* is cited three times; Epicurus, Ghazzali, and Averroës are each mentioned one time. In the few places where Gersonides cites at the same time both philosophic sources and the Bible and the talmudic rabbis, he cites the Jewish sources first. In this he varies from his custom in *Wars of the Lord,* where he generally quotes from Jewish sources—to the extent that he does at all—only after he has completed his philosophical discussion.

We usually find Gersonides' other Bible commentaries divided into three or sometimes four parts: explanations of individual words and phrases; explanation of the sense of each passage; discussion of the philosophic import of the passage (where appropriate); and in the commentary on the Pentateuch, lists of the moral, political, halakhic, and philosophic lessons (*to'aliyot*) to be derived from each section of the text. None of this is to be found in the commentary on Song of Songs. Here we are presented with a running commentary, moving along verse by verse. In this commentary Gersonides generally tells his reader who the speaker of the verse is (the Active Intellect, the material intellect, or the faculties of the soul, usually represented by the faculty of imagination), to whom the statement is addressed or about whom it is made, and the way in which the words and phrases of the verse advance the needs of the allegory. Occasionally Gersonides will alert the reader to the fact that a particular verse is to be interpreted as relating only to the allegory or only to its intended meaning; this, however, is relatively rare since he construes most of the verses as having significance for both, as one would expect in a well-constructed allegory.

We thus find a text structurally unlike any of Gersonides' other commentaries, one in which there is almost no separate attention paid to the meanings of individual words; the text, although divided into sections, is not treated in a section-by-section fashion; and there is no attempt to draw moral, political, halakhic, or even philosophic lessons from the text under discussion. It is, furthermore, a commentary on a biblical book in which citations from non-Jewish (that is, philosophic and scientific) sources far outnumber citations from Jewish ones. This last point becomes even clearer when note is taken of the fact that most of the biblical citations relate to the explication of *peshat* in what is, after all, a biblical book (Song of Songs); what we have here is not so much an appeal to Jewish sources as the use of an entire literary unit (the Bible) in the explanation of words and phrases in part of that unit. Furthermore, the eight citations to Gersonides' own writings all refer to his philosophic and scientific works, not to his Job commentary, and relate exclusively to philosophic issues. The preponderance, then, of philosophic and scientific citations in this commentary over those of what may be called a strictly Jewish character (primarily citations from the talmudic rabbis) is overwhelming.

The commentary is thus clearly aimed at an intellectual elite and not at the masses of the Jewish people. That it was Solomon's intent to keep the ideas taught in Song of Songs from the masses is a point Gersonides makes on a number of occasions.

It might be thought that this last is a trivial point. After all, once we admit that Solomon did not compose Song of Songs with the intention of exalting carnal love, it is immediately obvious that it has a meaning beyond that conveyed by the plain sense of the words. But that does not mean that the secondary meaning was intended to be hidden from the masses. This is evidenced by the fact that the talmudic rabbis did not construe the poem as describing a love affair between a man and a woman. They insisted that the poem had a level of meaning beyond that of the *peshat* and did everything in their power to bring that higher level of meaning to the attention of the masses. Gersonides' point, therefore, is hardly trivial.

This does not prove, however, that Gersonides aimed his own commentary on Song of Songs at an intellectual elite. Perhaps like the talmudic rabbis he was eager for or at least unconcerned by the prospect of the masses reading and understanding his commentary. But this is not the case: explaining why some of the verses relate to the allegory only and not to its intended meaning, Gersonides says, "This was done for the perfection of the text and its betterment, combining the hidden and the open, for this adds obscurity to his words, perfecting them as they ought to be in such cases, namely, keeping them hidden from those who are not fit for them and open to those who are fit" (text between notes 101 and 102). He tells us not only that Solomon sought to obscure the meaning of his words but also that he approves that intent, at least with respect to the subject matter of Song of Songs. We may safely conclude therefore that Gersonides addressed his commentary on this text to some sort of intellectual elite.

But when we examine the nature of the material addressed to them we find it surprisingly basic, introductory, and elementary.[35] For a work ostensibly designed to guide its reader to intellectual enlightenment, we find next to no philosophic argumentation or proof. In fact, nothing at all is taught about God, very little about God's activities, and almost nothing about the nature of the world around us, from the examination of which we are supposed to abstract conceptual knowledge that will lead us to the cognition of God. In place of this we find detailed discussions of the process of learning and constantly reiterated emphasis on the importance of approaching the process of learning in a properly structured fashion.

A large portion of the introduction is given over to a discussion of the division of the sciences, a proof that this division mirrors reality, and a passionate plea for studying these sciences in their proper (that is, natural) order. The division of the sciences is repeated at least twenty times in the commentary proper.[36] This last point is worthy of note since generally Gersonides does not repeat in the commentary points made in the introduction; rather, he refers his readers to his earlier discussion. Furthermore, the text takes very little for granted, citing chapter and verse in Aristotle and other scientific and philosophic writers in support of almost all its claims, including those with which we would expect any philosopher to be perfectly familiar. The elementary character of Gersonides' teachings here becomes even clearer when we compare our text with his commentaries on Job and Genesis, with their detailed and often difficult philosophical discussions.[37]

On one hand, then, we have a text ostensibly addressed to an intellectual elite, to whom it is appropriate to reveal the secrets concerning humankind's ultimate felicity taught by Solomon in Song of Songs.[38] On the other hand the text is clearly addressed to beginners in philosophy, takes very little in the way of philosophical erudition for granted, deals with the most basic issues in an elementary fashion, presents no philosophical proofs concerning the existence and nature of God, and propagandizes unceasingly for the proper approach to the study of science and philosophy. To whom, then, does Gersonides address his commentary on Song of Songs?

There is a related point concerning the content of Gersonides' commentary on Song of Songs to which I must draw attention before answering the question just raised—the question of esotericism. Gersonides, as we have seen, makes no bones about the fact that Solomon wrote Song of Songs for a restricted elite.[39] But beyond that, and as we saw above, Gersonides approves Solomon's intent, agreeing that the ideas taught in Song of Songs are not really appropriate for consumption by the masses. Furthermore, Gersonides himself time after time takes note of the subtle and sophisticated way in which Solomon constructed his allegory so as to arouse those for whom it was intended while keeping somnolent those for whom it was not intended.[40]

Fine and good; there is nothing new or surprising here. What needs to be answered, however, is the following question: If Solomon constructed Song of Songs as a poem with a meaning hidden by the outward sense of the words, and wanted that meaning to be understood by a restricted elite only, by what right does Gersonides publicly reveal that secret doctrine? All this, of course, assumes that he recognized Solomon's authority and would feel the need to justify behavior that went against the king's express wishes. This is a safe assumption: Gersonides, as we have seen, asserts that Solomon wrote Song of Songs as one who speaks by virtue of the holy spirit. Even if that is a low level of prophecy, it is still worthy of respect![41] But even in the unlikely eventuality that Gersonides saw no need to justify his revelation of what Solomon sought to keep secret, he would still have to justify such behavior in the light of Maimonides' strictures against it. (Maimonides' position will be discussed below.) Furthermore, at the beginning of his introduction (text at note 11) Gersonides indicates that his philosophic interpretation of Song of Songs will make the rabbinical midrashim on it understandable. The clear implication is that the interpretation of Gersonides accords with that of the talmudic rabbis, which interpretation the rabbis sought to keep secret by casting it in allegorical fashion. That being the case, Gersonides must justify making public not only what Solomon sought to keep secret, and what Maimonides insisted must not be made public, but what the rabbis of the Midrash actually did try to keep hidden.

It is surely odd that Gersonides should at one and the same time admit that Solomon meant to keep hidden the doctrines taught in Song of Songs and cheerfully and enthusiastically reveal those doctrines to all and sundry.

It may be objected that Gersonides himself rejects esotericism. In his introduction to *Wars of the Lord* he implicitly criticizes Maimonides for his

esotericism and in his commentary to Song of Songs further intimates his opposition to it.[42] All this is true; but the fact that Gersonides criticizes esoteric
writing in Maimonides and rejects it as an option for himself in *Wars of the
Lord* does not mean that he must reveal what the Bible kept hidden. No one
forced him to write a commentary on Song of Songs! He could have kept
silent on the issue or communicated it privately to a select group of colleagues
or disciples. Thus, our question remains: How did Gersonides justify revealing to anyone with a reading knowledge of Hebrew, secrets that Solomon,
wisest king of Israel, preferred to keep hidden?

We thus find ourselves faced with two interrelated questions: Why did
Gersonides publicly reveal the secrets hidden in Song of Songs, and for whom
did he write the commentary?[43]

In order to answer the questions it is necessary to examine the way in
which Gersonides' Maimonidean predecessors dealt with the question of revealing the secrets of the Torah in general and of Song of Songs in particular.
Note must also be taken of an event that occurred when Gersonides was
seventeen years old and that must surely have had a more than trivial impact
on him: the ban in 1305 against persons under the age of twenty-five studying philosophy. This ban was issued by the greatest halakhic authority of the
age, Rabbi Solomon ibn Adret of Barcelona.[44]

Maimonides' ideas concerning the proper approach to the interpretation
of biblical texts are well known if hardly uncontroversial.[45] Many biblical
texts have two meanings—an external, or public, sense and an internal, or
esoteric, meaning. Texts having both senses are parables but are not always
recognized as such. It is one of the purposes of the *Guide,* then, to specify
certain biblical texts as parables. Maimonides so identifies Song of Songs in
Guide of the Perplexed 3:51 (626) and 3:54 (636).

Generally speaking, however, Maimonides is loath to reveal these matters
directly and clearly: "Hence you should not ask of me here anything beyond
the chapter headings. And even those are not set down in order or arranged
in coherent fashion in this Treatise, but rather are scattered and entangled
with other subjects that are to be clarified . . . so as not to oppose that divine
purpose which one cannot possibly oppose and which has concealed from
the vulgar among the people those truths especially requisite for His apprehension."[46] This is a very important passage. According to Gersonides, Song
of Songs does guide us to "those truths especially requisite for His apprehension," and it is precisely Gersonides' intent to lay out the teachings of

Song of Songs in the clearest possible fashion, thus laying himself open to the charge of opposing "that divine purpose which one cannot possibly oppose."

The conflict between Maimonides and Gersonides surfaces in another fashion as well. Maimonides apparently maintained that the external meaning of all biblical parables contains wisdom and utility.[47] For Gersonides, however, the external meaning of Song of Songs does not contain wisdom that is useful in any respect; on the contrary, its external meaning is crude. Rejecting the idea that its meaning could be in its external sense, Gersonides writes (in his commentary to 1:1): "It is not characteristic of those who speak by virtue of the holy spirit to write poems crafted so as to attract one to despicable behavior or to write poems of vanity and falsehood." Comparing Maimonides and Gersonides briefly, we may say that although the latter appears to have agreed with Maimonides on the inner meaning of Song of Songs, he certainly disagrees with him on the value of the outer meaning of the poem and on the obligation to keep its inner meaning secret.

Having looked at these issues we are in a somewhat better position to understand the background against which Gersonides wrote his commentary on Song of Songs but not much closer to an answer to our two questions—why he was willing to reveal Solomon's secrets and to whom he addressed the commentary.

In a number of important studies Aviezer Ravitzky has drawn attention to the existence of a self-conscious school of Jewish philosophers founded by Samuel ibn Tibbon, the translator of Maimonides' *Guide of the Perplexed*.[48] Members of this school saw themselves as engaged in a joint project: furthering Maimonidean values and teachings. One of the issues that exercised them all was the question of the extent to which it was legitimate to give public expression to the secret teachings of the Torah. In one sense, their deliberations on the issue have an almost insincere flavor since they all wrote books in which these secrets were publicly revealed, and some of them were even active and enthusiastic propagandists for the philosophical interpretation of the Torah.

Samuel ibn Tibbon, for example, whatever his hesitations on the matter, did much to aid the public spread of philosophical ideas and interpretations of the Torah. He translated the *Guide of the Perplexed* into Hebrew, composed a glossary of philosophical terms printed in most editions, explained some of the esoteric meanings of Ecclesiastes in a commentary,[49] and wrote an independent work of philosophical Bible exegesis, *Ma'amar Yiqqavu ha-*

Mayim.[50] The twenty-second and final chapter of that book serves as a kind of apologia for it in which ibn Tibbon explains that if he has revealed more than he ought of those things "which the Sages commanded to keep hidden," he did it only for "the sake of Heaven." He offers a compound justification: "the secret is out," so to speak, because the gentile nations know some of it, because previous Jewish authors have revealed portions of it, and because Maimonides revealed more of it. Ibn Tibbon is implicitly using the authority of Maimonides to justify his own behavior: Maimonides' public (or semi-public) teaching of the secrets of the Torah made the project respectable for others.

Samuel ibn Tibbon was faced with a cruel dilemma. Convinced, like his teacher Maimonides, that the Torah was the ultimate repository of all truth, including most emphatically philosophic truth, and stung by the barbs of the gentiles who mocked the Jews for their lack of philosophic sophistication, he naturally desired to publish the philosophic teachings of Judaism in the clearest possible fashion. Doing so would not only salve his injured pride, but it would also acquaint those Jews capable of understanding it with their philosophical heritage. On the other hand, there existed a long tradition, he thought, of keeping these very teachings hidden from the masses, a tradition emphatically endorsed by his teacher Maimonides in word and deed.

This tension between the desire to reveal the true teachings of the Torah and the perceived necessity of keeping them secret from the masses is typical of all thirteenth-century Jewish philosophers in the Tibbonian school. That they resolved this tension in favor of revelation is evidenced by the fact that they ultimately wrote the books by which we know them.[51]

The activities of these philosophers did not go unnoticed. They were criticized by those who rejected the philosophical interpretation of the Torah for their falsification of the teachings of Judaism and even by those who accepted those teachings but objected to their being revealed wholesale to the uninitiated. Of particular interest is the criticism of would-be philosophers (*mithakmim*)—individuals, apparently, who study philosophy without being ready for it.[52]

The opposition to these activities culminated in the ban of 1305. The ban forbade the study of physics and metaphysics by individuals under twenty-five years of age; it also forbade the teaching of these subjects to such individuals. Questions concerning the areas in which the ban was applied and its actual efficacy need not detain us here. As a resident of Provence, Gersonides may not have been directly affected by a ban issued in Barcelona (even though it was aimed directly at individuals such as Gersonides, who, as we know, was only seventeen at the time), but it strains credulity to suggest that he was unaware of it. Furthermore, he was a brilliant and innovative halakhist;[53] it seems unlikely that he would cavalierly ignore a stand taken so decisively by a rabbinical figure as eminent as ibn Adret.

Given the background here briefly surveyed we can now answer the questions posed above. First, why was Gersonides willing to oppose what Maimonides had called the "divine intention" of keeping the secrets of the Torah hidden from the masses by revealing in his commentary the secrets of Song of Songs? Second, for whom did he write his commentary, dealing as it does with philosophic themes in so elementary a fashion and emphasizing as it does questions of pedagogy and the proper order for the study of the sciences?

The background we have provided, it seems, makes the answers to these questions almost obvious. Once Maimonides and the Tibbonian school had published their writings, there was no longer any point in keeping hidden the secrets of the Torah. The material was already in the public domain.[54] When Samuel ibn Tibbon used that claim to justify his philosophic activities, its legitimacy was questionable at best. By the time of Gersonides, just a bit more than a generation later, the claim was entirely legitimate, as is evidenced by the ban of 1305. The danger lay not in revealing the philosophic secrets of the Torah but in risking their being misunderstood and misused.[55] Thus, in revealing the secrets of the Torah generally and of Song of Songs in particular Gersonides was not opposing God's intent. That intent had already been opposed—successfully, I might add—by Maimonides in a hesitant, partial fashion and by Samuel ibn Tibbon and his school in a more straightforward way (although they would, of course, have denied that they were opposing God's will). The secret having been revealed, Gersonides had no reason to continue keeping it under wraps. In his own fashion and, I am sure, without being explicitly aware of it, Gersonides was continuing the Tibbonian project of spreading philosophic erudition and sophistication among the Jews.

If so, why was his commentary on Song of Songs framed in so curious a manner, treating allegedly of the highest questions of human perfection without actually taking substantive steps to guide the reader any closer to that perfection by teaching him or her and proving the truth of philosophic conceptions of God? Furthermore, why does Gersonides frame the commentary as if it were addressed to tyros in philosophy, spelling out basic ideas in elementary form, citing chapter and verse for commonly accepted philosophic notions and emphasizing again and again the importance of studying the sciences in their proper order?

Once again the historical background provided above suggests an answer. The critique of the would-be philosophers noted above (a criticism later to be leveled against Gersonides himself),[56] coupled with the very issuance of the ban of 1305, indicates that there existed a not insubstantial class of would-be philosophers who apparently confused enthusiasm for the subject with the hard work of philosophic study and argument.[57] Assuming the existence of such a class answers our question. Gersonides' commentary on Song of Songs is a polemical work, addressed to philosophic amateurs unaware of their amateur status. It is designed to convince them that philosophic perfection can only be achieved through hard, well-organized work and study and that the sought-after goal is worthy of the effort.

If the attitude of many of our contemporaries is any guide, then Gersonides was wise to go about his task in the way he did. By teaching this material in the form of a commentary on the Bible, he indicates to the "sophisticated" that the Torah is not to be despised as unsophisticated since it is the repository of philosophic truth. Thus, too, we can explain the relative wealth of "academic" references and the relative dearth of Jewish ones in what purports to be a Bible commentary. Many "sophisticates" today and, one supposes, in the Middle Ages, would be more impressed by references to Aristotle than to Rabbi Akiva. On the other hand, by teaching this material in the form of a commentary on the Bible, Gersonides accomplishes the secondary goal of indicating to more conservative Jews (such as those who promulgated the ban of 1305) that philosophy ought not to be despised since it is taught in the Torah.

This last point is of some importance. Those of Gersonides' contemporaries who opposed the teaching of philosophy were not by and large entirely ignorant of the discipline; rather, they were deeply suspicious of its potential for causing damage to the Jewish community. Convincing such individuals that Solomon was a philosopher can be seen as a vitally important enterprise. We may have here a further explanation of why Gersonides chose to take up the issues he discusses in his commentary to Song of Songs precisely in that commentary and not in an independent treatise.

Addressed as it is, then, to overeager philosophic amateurs, Gersonides' commentary on Song of Songs quite rightly teaches basic philosophic conceptions, refers the reader to the relevant classical discussions of these issues (and occasionally to Gersonides' own contributions to these discussions in *Wars of the Lord*), and, most important, urges the student time and time again to take these things in their proper order and not to rush ahead to metaphysics before achieving proper grounding in the mathematical and physical sciences. This, too, might explain why Gersonides emphasizes the importance of the cooperative nature of scientific progress and the need to take advantage of what has been accomplished by previous generations of scholars.[58] Persons studying together in a group under the guidance of a seasoned tutor are less likely to go astray and follow their fancies than those who pursue their studies alone and without guidance.

GERSONIDES' COMMENTARY ON
SONG OF SONGS

INTRODUCTION TO THE
COMMENTARY ON SONG OF SONGS
COMPOSED BY THE SAGE
LEVI BEN GERSHOM

Said Levi ben Gershom: We have seen fit to comment on this scroll, the scroll of Song of Songs, as we understand it, for we have not found any other commentary on it which could be construed as a correct explanation of the words of this scroll.[1] Rather, we have seen that all the commentaries which our predecessors have made upon it and which have reached us adopt the midrashic approach, including interpretations which are the opposite of what was intended by the author of Song of Songs.[2] These midrashic explanations, even though they are good in and of themselves, ought not to be applied as explanations of the things upon which they are said midrashically. For this reason one who wishes to explain these and similar things ought not to apply to them the midrashic explanations regarding them; rather, he should endeavor to explain them himself according to their intention.[3] He also ought not to combine those midrashic explanations with his explanations, for this will either confuse the reader and cause him to misunderstand what he intended, most especially with deep things such as these, or bring the reader to despise the words of the author.[4] This latter is so for two reasons: [a] the excessive length of the matter,[5] or [b] the confusion in them of substantial and accidental matters, for all this causes things to be despised.[6]

For this reason we have set as our intention to write what we understand of this scroll without mixing with it other things which vary from the author's intention.[7] We have made no attempt in our commentary to mention what the sages have said about some of the words of this book. This is so because it has already been made clear that what they said midrashically ought not to be cited in this commentary, despite their being very good things in and of themselves.[8] Further, that which was reported from the sages which does not accord with the intention of the scroll is so deep that it needs more of a commentary than all that upon which they commented. The weight and burden of commenting on the words of this book—because of their depth themselves and even more from the fact that they were expressed in symbolic representations[9] and deep allegories[10]—is enough for us without adding a burden to our burden, especially when we add to this what it would involve in the matter of length! Furthermore, the meaning of those statements will not remain hidden after the intention of the book is made clear.[11]

We will devote a separate treatise to the explanation of the statements by the sages in connection with this scroll and others whether by way of midrash or by way of commentary if God wills and decrees that I live.[12] This appears to us as the most appropriate way: to explain those statements all together in their proper places.

We shall begin by laying down the following premise, which encompasses everything included in this book. It is evident from the perspective of the Torah and the prophets and from the perspective of philosophic speculation that man's ultimate felicity[13] resides in cognizing and knowing God to the extent that that is possible for him.[14] This will be perfected through the observation of the state of existent beings, their order, their equilibrium,[15] and the manner of God's wisdom in organizing them as they are.[16] This is so because these intelligibles[17] direct one to knowledge of God to some extent, for an activity gives some indication concerning its agent; that is, absolutely perfect activity indicates that its agent is absolutely perfect, insofar as it is an agent.

From this perspective we can cognize and know God, that is, from the perspective of his actions, these being the things which are consequent upon him for he has no antecedent causes at all; rather, he is the first cause of all existent beings. It is thus evident that he has no antecedent causes better known than him.[18]

This is even more evident according to what Aristotle thought concerning his apprehension,[19] that he is the *nomos* of existent beings, their order, and their equilibrium. This is so because it is necessary according to this position that he who knows the nomos of some of the existent beings apprehends God's essence to some extent. We have already made the truth concerning this clear in *Wars of the Lord;* its investigation does not concern us here.[20] However it may be, God's existence and perfection are clearly, evidently, and strongly shown by what can be seen of the magnitude of wisdom in the existence of all existent beings as they are, since it cannot be said of these things—in that they are found in the state of utmost possible perfection for them and in constant order—that their existence could have come about by accident, without an efficient cause, as Epicurus and his followers maintained. Aristotle explained this in the *Physics*.[21]

It has been shown in *On the Soul* that our passive intellect is without intelligibles at all at the beginning of its creation and it is thus possible for it to cognize them all, as glass can become all colors since it lacks them all.[22] The matter being so, all the intelligibles which we cognize are acquired.

It has been shown in the *Posterior Analytics* that in order to acquire any intelligible a person needs prior knowledge.[23] This [prior knowledge] is of two types: primary intelligibles and secondary intelligibles,[24] the latter being acquired syllogistically from the primary intelligibles. We acquire the primary intelligibles through our sense by way of repetition.[25] This is carried out by our faculties of memory and imagination,[26] for the imagination acquires for us the sensed notion upon its being revealed by the senses, and the faculty of memory perfects the repetition by virtue of which the universal statement is completed.[27] Thus these two faculties are to some extent a cause of our acquiring all the intelligibles which we acquire. There is another, worthier agent which plays a role in the process of our acquiring intelligibles: this is the Active Intellect, as was shown in *On the Soul*.[28] No intelligible can be acquired without it, for only through it can we determine whether the repetition which is presented by the senses is essential to those things or not. We then make an infinite judgment[29] on the basis of this limited multiplicity, apprehension of which comes from the senses; that is, on this basis we judge the extension of the judgment concerning each individual member of that species and in every particular time, without end.[30]

It has already been shown in *On the Soul* and in *Parva Naturalia* that there are different levels of spirituality among the impressions which reach the soul from the senses, the latter being outside of the soul.[31] The first of these is the impression[32] which is presented by the sensation of any of the individual senses. The second level is the impression presented by the form in the sensation of any of the individual senses to the common sense. The third level is the impression which is presented by the sensations in the common sense to the faculty of imagination. The fourth level is the impression which is presented by the impression in the imagination to the faculty of discrimination. The fifth level is the impression which is presented by the faculty of discrimination to the faculty which preserves and remembers. These impressions are more spiritual than all the others because the other faculties have already abstracted from them many of the material attributes of the sensed object by virtue of which it was distinctively particular. Thus the impressions in the faculty of memory are potentially the sensible form. So also with the impressions in the imagination, that is, that they are potentially in the sensible form, since these impressions reach the soul through these faculties from the sensed objects, after many of the material attributes of the sensed object outside of the soul were abstracted from them. So also each of these faculties of the soul ought to be considered in connection with the faculty of the soul which precedes it; for example,[33] the imaginative forms are potentially in the impressions, which are in turn potentially, not actually, in the common sense since they are more abstract and more spiritual.

You ought to know that the intelligible form is also potentially in those forms which are in these faculties, even if the potentiality is more distant. For example, after the intellect abstracts the material attributes—by virtue of which this apprehended thing was distinctively particular—from the imaginative form, that form becomes itself universal;[34] that is, it is the universal nature common to the infinite individuals of that species. In this manner one may solve the problem which prompted the ancients to posit forms and numbers or to deny the possibility of knowledge, as was made clear in the *Metaphysics*.[35]

One ought not to ignore the fact that there is great difficulty in acquiring this stupendous felicity toward which we are disposed; so much so that its ultimate acquisition is very unlikely for any particular human being; indeed, only very few individuals can acquire even a large measure of it. This is for two reasons: first, the difficulty in perfectly apprehending the states of existent beings; second, the multiplicity of impediments which impede our attempts properly to achieve this apprehension.[36]

The first of these impediments is the effervescence of our natures while we are young, which causes us to be drawn after our physical desires.[37] The second is the misleading nature of imagination and opinion, which brings us to confuse substantial and accidental matters and to think that what exists does not and vice versa.

The difficulty in perfectly apprehending the states of existent beings has many causes. First [is] the difficulty in finding the method which will correctly bring us to the apprehension of each subject which we investigate; for example, moving to it on the basis of the essential matters specific to that subject matter.

Second [is] our ignorance, ab initio, of the method which will cause us perfectly to apprehend the states of existent beings—because there is here a definite and unique order by virtue of which this apprehension can be perfected; for example, that one should study first what ought to be studied first.[38] There is a difficulty about this which is not easily overcome,[39] especially when we take into account the great desire which humans have to achieve the end, for this brings them to break through[40] and enter first what should be last in order of study. In this manner, not only do they not acquire perfection, but, rather, they add deficiency to their deficiency.[41]

Third [is] our ignorance of many of the things which ought to be investigated, which makes it such that we cannot even strive to reach the truth concerning them,[42] for one who does not know the subject under discussion certainly does not know the method which will bring him to the acquisition of the truth concerning it.[43]

Fourth [is] the difficulty in acquiring from the senses what is needed for the apprehension of many of the existent things.[44]

Fifth [is] the subtlety[45] of the matters themselves, and their depth.

Sixth [are] the many objections which may be raised concerning each of the possible alternatives in a contradiction.

Seventh [is] the confusion of conventional truths concerning it[46] with the truth itself, for much of what we believe is what we have grown accustomed to hearing from our youth.

Eighth [are] the great differences of opinion concerning the subject which are found among those who have studied it, each of them bringing many arguments in support of his position.[47]

Generally, acquiring felicity is inordinately difficult because of the reasons just mentioned and others like them. Therefore, the prophets and sages never ceased guiding individuals to the way in which they could acquire felicity, each according to his ability. With respect to this guidance the Torah is absolutely the most perfect among all the guides because it contains absolutely perfect guidance for both the masses and for individuals. If we wanted to make this clear on the basis of the words of the Torah, we would need a long treatise; but we will be brief and adduce proofs concerning this only sufficient to our intention in this place.

We say that since what we ought to be guided toward first is moral perfection, the Torah guides us toward this perfection through many of the commandments.[48] However, that which it contains concerning the improvement of the soul was kept hidden because of its irrelevance for the masses.[49] Most of what the Torah guides us toward concerning speculation deals either with the speculative principles the apprehension of which for the scholar is very difficult or with the great principles, mistakes concerning which greatly distance a man from human perfection.[50] Since it is fitting that every activity directed toward some end should be so directed from its beginning, so that the activity altogether may be directed by its end, and since this is impossible for the masses with respect to what the Torah commanded concerning moral perfection, for they do not know what the human end is, the Torah cunningly collected both things together.[51]

It hinted at this end and commanded it—it being cleaving to God—and referred to many of the wonderful speculative matters in some of the narratives and commandments and in describing the sanctuary and its implements as if guiding the elite to the realization that the rest of the Torah commandments are for this end.[52] It said for the multitudes, concerning many of the commandments, that they who observe them will thereby achieve length of days and many other fanciful felicities, and the opposite concerning those who do not observe them, even though the Torah commandments are not for this purpose.[53] This is so since the multitudes cannot picture the purpose of the Torah commandments and since a man will not desire to perform some action if he cannot picture its advantage for him; thus the Torah guided the multitudes to fulfill these commandments first for this purpose, and through performing this worship first not for its own sake they will be guided to doing it afterwards for its own sake.[54] The Torah did not strive to teach us these things perfectly according to their methods, because this is not the objective of a prophet in his capacity as a prophet but rather in his capacity as a savant.[55] And thus the prophets and those who speak by virtue of the holy spirit[56] never ceased from guiding men to perfection, either to the first perfection, or to the final perfection, or to both. This will be accomplished when what is understood by the multitudes from the words of the prophets guides one to moral perfection and what is understood by the elite guides one to conceptual perfection.[57] The book of Proverbs is of this latter type.[58]

But this book, Song of Songs, guides only the elite to the way of achieving felicity, and thus its external meaning was not made useful to the masses. According to our understanding of its words, it first referred to the overcoming of impediments consequent upon moral deficiency, for this is what ought to come first, as was noted above. After this, it referred to the overcoming of impediments consequent upon the failure to distinguish between truth and falsehood. After this, it referred to the procedure[59] for speculation according to the proper order of three kinds, as Aristotle mentioned in many places: one kind deals with body and what is abstracted from body in speech only, not in reality, as you will find concerning mathematical things; one kind deals with body and what is not abstracted from body in speech, as in the case of physics, for the study there of form deals with it insofar as it is a perfection of matter, and matter is studied in physics insofar as it is a substratum for form; one kind does not deal with body at all, neither in speech nor in reality, as is the case with metaphysics.[60]

Now the nature of things in themselves necessitated that the stages in the study of existent beings follow this order. This is so because what the mathematical sciences investigate is body qua absolute body, not as some body or other; for example, heavy or light, or, not heavy and not light.[61] Physics investigates a particular body insofar as it is body; for example, changing body, or heavy or light, or not heavy and not light.[62] Now the investigation of the attributes of absolute body must precede the investigation of the attributes of some body or other, for the general matters ought to be studied before the specific matters, especially since the general matters are better known to us, as was made clear in the first book of the *Physics*.[63]

In general, that which many things have in common is better known to us than what is particular, and thus the study of this science precedes the study of physics; this is all the more the case when we add to this consideration the strength of our knowledge of this science, since it is not entangled in matter.[64] Further, it trains our intellect, actualizes it,[65] and causes it to acquire the proper mode of speculation, thus guarding it from error in other sciences due to the strength of the demonstration[s][66] based on this science, since most of the demonstrations in it are absolute demonstrations.[67] Further, the mathematical sciences guide one to some extent to physics and metaphysics, as was made clear in the first part of the *Almagest*.[68]

Physics necessarily precedes divine science, which is metaphysics, since metaphysics goes further than it on the path of perfection and purpose.[69] It also assumes the existence of the separate causes, which are neither physical things nor physical forces, something which is established in physics.[70] The level of verification which can be reached in physics is below the level of verification which can be reached in the mathematical sciences, since most of its demonstrations are a posteriori,[71] and it is not the way of causes discovered through a posteriori demonstrations to affirm existence if it was unknown. For this reason, this science requires a more settled mind than do the mathematical sciences.[72] Thus, of those who wish to plunge deeply into this science and will not believe something unless it is impossible to disagree with it, many fall by the way and do not achieve perfection in this science.[73]

The verification we achieve with metaphysics, despite its [higher] degree, is weaker, in that it is taken from remote commonly accepted premises.[74] In particular this is so with respect to its investigations concerning those things which are neither a body nor a physical force, this being the fruit of that science and its end.[75] The verification we achieve in physics, on the other hand, is based upon particular appropriate premises. It is the way of commonly accepted premises that they lead to two contraries or contradictories. Thus this science[76] is impossible for one who is not strongly settled on the true views from the perspective of the Torah and speculation, and for one the effervescence of whose nature has not quieted, lest his yearning to follow after his desires brings him to make his views in this science accord with what he sees fit, as is well known concerning Elisha Aher when he entered Pardes.[77] Moreover, the smallest mistake which occurs in this science is great from the perspective of the degree of the subject matter and since the object of this science is the utmost human felicity.[78]

Because the object of this book is to make known the way to achieve felicity, and since there are great doubts concerning whether it is possible to achieve it, it was necessary that these doubts be resolved at the beginning. This is what concerned the author, as we see it, from the beginning of the book to the beginning of the third paragraph,[79] where it says, To a steed (1:9). Included here also is the name of the book, the name of the author and his rank, his method of approaching the subject, the subject under investigation, and its purpose.[80]

From the beginning of the third paragraph to the beginning of the fifth paragraph, where it says, Hark! My beloved! (2:8), he[81] indicates the effort necessary to overcome the impediment [to perfection] caused by moral deficiency.

From the beginning of the fifth paragraph to the beginning of the eighth paragraph, where it says, on my bed (3:1), he indicates the effort necessary to overcome the impediments [to perfection] caused by[82] imagination and thought, so that one will know how to escape from error and distinguish between truth and falsehood.

From the beginning of the eighth paragraph to the beginning of the thirteenth paragraph, where it says, *Come with me from Lebanon, my bride* (4:8), he indicates the attainment of the mathematical sciences.

From the beginning of the thirteenth paragraph until *Who is this who cometh up from the wilderness, leaning upon her beloved?* (8:5), he indicates the attainment of physics in the order appropriate to it.

From the statement *Who is this who cometh up from the wilderness . . .* to the end of the book, he indicates the attainment of metaphysics.

This is what we wish to offer here. We have seen fit to preface it to our commentary on this book. It is a great gateway for what we want to accomplish here, since the difficulty in explaining this book arises from one of two perspectives: the depth of the matters themselves and the depth of the symbolic representations found in this book. Having first guided the reader to an understanding of these matters, what remains is the understanding of the depth of the symbolic representations.[83] This is not something which is exceptionally difficult for us. But if we had burdened ourselves with both matters at the same time, it would have been exceptionally difficult for us. The activity here is of the type of one who found his burden too heavy to carry all at once and therefore divided it into two parts, making it easy for him to carry those parts, one after the other. Furthermore, in this way it will be easier for the reader of our words to understand them and determine their truth; they will not confuse him because of their length or because of their combining the understanding of the two matters together.

From this point we will begin to explain generally many of the symbolic representations and allegories found in this book so that we will not have to explain them separately in each place where they occur. This is also a valuable guide toward the understanding of the words of this book.[84]

We say that it is self-evidently clear that this sage used Jerusalem (6:4) as an allegory in this book for "man," for man alone among all compound entities[85] is distinguished by worship of God, as Jerusalem was distinguished by this from other cities and places. There is another reason for this: the word *Jerusalem* is derived from *shelemut* [perfection], and thus it is called *Shalem*, as it says, *king of Shalem* (Gen. 14:18) and *In Shalem also is set His taber-*

nacle (Pss. 76:3). Since man is the most perfect of all the existents in the sub-lunary world, so much so that he is like a microcosm,[86] he is called Jerusalem allegorically.

For this reason the faculties of the soul were allegorically called *daughters of Jerusalem* (1:5, etc.). The intellect was allegorically called Solomon (1:5, etc.) since he was the king of Jerusalem as the intellect is ruler of the man.[87] So much [is the intellect ruler of the man] that he used *Solomon* to indicate the perfection of this part since it is derived from *shelemut*.

Since Zion was the worthiest part of Jerusalem, the temple and the king's palace being there, he allegorically called the faculties of the soul most closely related to the activity of the intellect *daughters of Zion* (3:11).

It is known that the temple was *in the forest of Lebanon* (1 Kings 7:2, etc.), and thus the temple is called Lebanon, as it says *Lebanon is ashamed, it withereth* (Isa. 33:9).[88] You will thus find that in this book, in an allegory connected to this one,[89] he calls that which originates in an activity of the intellect *of the wood of Lebanon* (3:9) and *flowing streams from Lebanon* (4:15) and [says] *Come with me from Lebanon, my bride* (4:8). The repetition of this allegory was intended to stimulate the reader of his words to understand his intention in this wonderful allegory according to his ability,[90] while understanding that despite this the intended meaning of the allegory was to remain hidden from the masses by virtue of the symbolic representations and allegories which he used.

We also say that he allegorically compares the beginning of the time when a person prepares himself to move in the direction of one of the speculative perfections to the time when plants begin to bear fruit or to the time when the shadows of the night begin to pass.[91] The allegory in this is clear, for then the darkness of ignorance passes and the light of wisdom begins to be seen. Then the soul strives to bear its fruit when it acquires this perfection to which it has been directed by those premises on the basis of which one can grasp the matters of that science. Allegories of this sort are found repeatedly in this book.

Since he allegorically compares scientific perfection[92] to fruit, he allegorically compares that which potentially is that fruit to flowers and lilies because flowers and lilies are potentially the fruit or the seed, which is the primary end. They are also that which the plant puts forth first in its attempt to bear its fruit or its seed.[93] Thus he says of the intellect concerning that which reaches it from the imagination that it *feedeth among the lilies* (2:16, 6:3), for the intelligible form is found in potential in the imaginative forms. The imagination is also called that which feedeth among the lilies with respect to that which reaches it from the senses for this very reason itself, as we mentioned above.[94]

Connected to this allegory, he allegorically compared beneficial speculative, physical, and metaphysical matters to spices and distilled oils because of their merit and because they stimulate one to grasp their truth from what one smells of them at first. These are matters which are posterior to them in that they wonderfully show the perfection of their cause, just as a person is stimulated to pay attention to a spice when he senses the goodness of its fragrance. This is so because his sensing the goodness of its fragrance causes him to pay attention to the place where the spice is found, and stimulates in him a desire to search for it until he reaches it. This is also repeated often in this book.

Since perfection of the intellect comes from the Active Intellect by way of those imaginative forms which the imagination emanates upon it,[95] and this is perfected—that is, the presentation to the intellect by the imagination of what it[96] needs from the senses in each subject of study—when it[97] so wonderfully desires to be subservient to the material intellect that it places all of its activities in the service of the intellect so far as it can. He allegorically compared this desire to the desire of the male and female who desire each other, in order to indicate the great extent of this desire. He allegorically compared the intellect to the male since it is on the level of form relative to the imaginative faculty.[98] This is something which continues throughout this book.[99]

He likened the influence of [the imagination on] the material intellect to suckling from breasts [8:8] because this is a very appropriate allegory concerning the female influence and also because milk is potentially the very substance of that which is nourished and is on the level of material relative to it. So it is also with respect to the imaginative forms relative to the intelligible forms.[100]

You must not fail to note that some of the attributes with which the lovers described each other relate both to the allegory and to its intended meaning; of these there are many. Some of them relate only to the intended meaning, as when it says, *thy hair is as a flock of goats* (4:1, 6:5), for this is not a fitting indication of beautiful hair if it were according to the allegory. So also *thy belly is like a heap of wheat* (7:3) and *we have a little sister [and she hath no breasts]* (8:8). After that it says, *and if she be a door, we will enclose her with boards of cedar* (8:9), *if she be a wall [we will build upon her a turret of silver]* (8:9),[101] for this does not fit the allegory at all. This is also found often in this book. This was done in order to indicate the hidden meaning, so that one would not mistakenly think that the statements in this book should be taken according to their external sense.

In a small number of places, as we see it, those attributes relate to the allegory only. This was done for the perfection of the text and its betterment, combining the hidden and the open, for this adds obscurity to his words, perfecting them as they ought to be in such cases, namely, keeping them hidden from those who are not fit for them and open to those who are fit.

We must not fail to note that this beloved man[102] is first called Solomon (3:7) and after that King Solomon (3:9)—it says, *behold, it is the litter of Solomon* (3:7), *King Solomon made himself a palanquin* (3:9), *upon King Solomon* (3:11)—for this is the sort of thing which ought to have significance, certainly in so wonderfully crafted[103] an allegory.[104]

We ought to be aware of the different names by which this beloved woman is called and their various degrees. Thus, in the beginning, he called her *my beloved* (1:9); after that he called her *my beloved, my fair one* (2:10, 13); after that he called her *bride* (4:8, etc.);[105] after that he called her *my dove* (2:14); after that, *my dove, my undefiled* (5:2); after that he called her *Shulammite* (7:1) and *prince's daughter* (7:2). For this also ought to have significance.[106]

We ought to be aware that in her adjuration of the daughters of Jerusalem the first and second time (2:7, 3:5) she said, *by the gazelles and by the hinds of the field that ye awaken not* and the third time (8:4) she did not say *by the gazelles and by the hinds of the fields* and she did not say *that ye awaken not;* rather, she said, *why should ye awaken.*[107]

We ought to be aware of the different orderings in which the praise of this beloved woman and her beauty are described in this book. Thus, the first time he began his praises from her head and descended with them gradually to her breasts.[108] The second time he began his praises from her head and the praises never left her head, that is, they never descended below her head.[109] The third time he began his praises with her legs and did not cease ascending with them until he reached her head.[110] This could not possibly be without significance in so perfectly structured an allegory.[111]

We ought to be aware of the wisdom expressed in the allegorical expression of the perfection which one passes through at the beginning of one's approach to perfection in the sciences as *the ascent upon the mountains of* spices (2:17): *Until the day breathe, and the shadows flee away, turn, my beloved, and be thou like a gazelle or a young hart upon the mountains of spices* (2:17); and in the allegorical expression of the perfection which one passes through afterwards as his arriving at the ascent upon *the mountain of myrrh* and *the hill of frankincense*: it says, *Until the day breathe, and the shadows flee away, I will get me to the mountain of myrrh and to the hill of frankincense* (4:6); and in the allegorical expression of the perfection which one passes through at the end as the ascent *upon the mountains of spices* (8:14). What is intended here relates to the differences concerning the mountains: why the first and last were expressed in the plural—it says, *upon the mountains of spices* (2:17) and *upon the mountains of spices* (8:14)— whereas the second was in the singular—it says, *mountain of myrrh and hill of frankincense* (4:6). Further, why did it designate specific spices in the second description while in the third referring to *spices* generally? For this is also something which ought to have significance.[112]

We ought to be aware of that which we have found to be unique in the passage *come with me from Lebanon, my bride* (4:8) with respect to this beloved woman's garden and what the beloved plucked from his garden concerning the word *with*—indicating combination and generality—which is repeated here often. It says, *a park of pomegranates with precious fruits; henna with spikenard plants; spikenard with saffron, calamus and cinnamon, with all trees of frankincense; myrrh and aloes, with all the chief spices* (4:13– 14); *my myrrh with my spice; I have eaten my honeycomb with my honey; I have drunk my wine with my milk* (5:1). See how the word *with* is repeated here; you will not find it repeated so in this book except in this passage. It is as if to awaken the somnolent with this wonderful repetition so that they will be aware of what is intended by this. This reflects his[113] perfection and his desire that his words be both understood according to the ability of those fit to understand them and kept hidden from the masses, as he must do.[114]

This is what we have seen fit to present as an introduction concerning the symbolic representations and allegories found in this book. Through this, coupled with the previous introduction,[115] the content of this book has almost been made perfectly clear. Having completed this we commence the explanation of this scroll as we intended.

I:I − I:8

As the object of this book is to make known the way to achieve felicity, and since there are great doubts concerning whether it is possible to achieve it, it was necessary that these doubts be resolved at the beginning. This is what concerned the author, as we see it, from the beginning of the book to the beginning of the third paragraph, where it says *To a steed* (I:9). Included here also is the name of the book, the name of the author and his rank, his method of approaching the subject, the subject under investigation, and its purpose.

The Song of Songs, Which Is Solomon's (I:I)

It is known that Solomon[1] *crafted* many *proverbs*[2] (Eccles. 12:9) and poems *to find out words of delight* (Eccles. 12:10), as it says, *And he spoke three thousand proverbs, and his songs were a thousand and five* (1 Kings 5:12). It is as if it said in this verse, as it appears, that this poem is the choicest of the poems crafted by Solomon. There is no doubt that all of them guided one toward the perfection intended for man, whether to the first perfection or to the ultimate perfection,[3] or to them both together, for it is not characteristic of those who speak by virtue of the holy spirit[4] to write[5] poems crafted so as to attract one to despicable behavior or to write poems of vanity and falsehood which do not attract one to the things which ought to be loved or to the rejection of things which ought to be rejected. For this reason the sages said, "All the poems are holy, but the Song of Songs is the holy of holies."[6] They meant by this that all of Solomon's poems are holy, because it is to his poems that the verse refers.[7] It is in accord with this intention[8] that he[9] indicated—as is his wont[10]—the name of the author by saying *which is Solomon's*.

However, according to the symbolic representation which he adopted in this book, his saying *which is Solomon's* refers to the material intellect. It is as if he said that this poem is the choicest of those poems which direct one to what is fitting for the intellect and its felicity. His saying *which is Solomon's* indicates the subject which he will investigate in this book, the material intellect. He also refers by this to that felicity which is the ultimate perfection of the material intellect, for the acquired intellect is also called Solomon in this allegory; indeed, it deserves this name more than does the material intellect because of its perfection. This, because *Solomon* is said of the material intellect by virtue of its disposition to receive perfection. Thus, his saying *which is Solomon's* indicates both the subject of this book and its benefit,[11] for the letter lamed is used in our language in both senses, as is clearly evident.[12]

The matter being so, in this verse this sage referred to this book, Song of Songs; to its exalted degree, by saying that it is the most worthy of those poems the end of which is guidance to perfection; to the subject of the book, the material intellect; to its benefit, which is reaching felicity, which in turn is the emanated acquired intellect;[13] and to the form of speech in it, that is, poetry as opposed to discourse and narrative couched in clear words and speech.[14] He also made us aware, as is his wont, of the name of the author. These matters to which he made reference in this verse are those matters with which every author ought to begin, before taking up the subject matter of his book itself.[15]

Their statement that this poem is the most wonderful and choicest of the *songs which are Solomon's* is very clearly true because there are two types of worthy poems. The first type is the poem which presents a representation[16] of deep things which are difficult to represent, through the use of symbolic representations and allegory. The second type is the poem crafted to draw one to love what ought to be loved and to reject what ought to be rejected. It is clear that the more the poem represents worthy matters which are ever more useful to the attainment of felicity, it is itself more worthy. So, too, with the second type: the more a poem is crafted to draw one to love worthier things and those things useful for the attainment of felicity, the worthier it is itself. In this book these two types of poems have been combined together in the worthiest fashion, for it presents a representation of the ultimate felicity and attracts one to draw near to it and to strive for it with every possible form of striving.[17]

> Let him kiss me with the kisses of his mouth
> For thy love is better than wine (1:2)

In that the acquisition of this perfection is so unlikely that for many reasons it is thought to be impossible, this sage began his book by making the possibility of its acquisition clear, since that is the object of inquiry[18] in this book, that is, how it is possible for a man to acquire this perfection. It is not possible to investigate the way which will bring one to it if he does not first make known that it is possible to acquire [it].

Of the reasons which bring one to think that the acquisition of this perfection is impossible for us, one is that it is thought that it is not possible that a man do any activity unless he first represented that action to himself and desired it. For example, one who never represented to himself the activity of building will not desire it in any fashion. Even if he had represented to himself the notion of building, he would not attempt to build a building unless he had an antecedent desire to build. The matter being so, it is clear according to this supposition that it is not possible for a man to actualize the potential in his intellect. This is so because ab initio[19] he cannot represent to himself his ultimate perfection and thus will not desire it. If he does not desire it, it is not possible that he will strive to do this activity.

Second, ab initio, man's desire is for that which renders the acquisition of his ultimate perfection impossible, that is, his desire is for the satisfaction of physical cravings. The more he holds on to them, the more they attract him and increase his desire for them constantly, as it says, *Woe unto them that rise up early in the morning that they may follow strong drink; that tarry late into the night, till wine pursue them!* (Isa. 5:11). This means that they seek wine in the morning and after they accustom themselves to that behavior the wine will seek them out and pursue them; or the wine will arrange matters such that they will be pursued by others—and his saying *pursue them* refers to a third party.[20] Similarly, the sages said, "This is the way of the evil inclination. Today it says to one, 'do this!' and on the morrow it says to him, 'do this!' and on the morrow it says, 'worship idolatry!'"[21] Such being the case, it is highly improbable that a man would desire the perfection intended for him.

Third, it is still the case that even if one admits that it is possible for a man to represent to himself his ultimate perfection ab initio,[22] it is still unlikely that he will acquire it because the route to its acquisition is unknown to him. In truth, it is so largely unknown that even if a man could know the essence of his felicity ab initio—for example, knowledge of the goodness of the order and the equilibrium found among existent beings—reaching this perfection is still very difficult since he does not know ab initio the route which will bring him to it.[23] It[24] is that he choose the correct path in his investigations into the state of existent beings, by attending to first things first; and also that in his investigations he investigate each thing in the way appropriate to it—for example, that he move toward it from the essential matters specific to that inquiry, and preserve himself from the fallacies of the imagination and the faculty of supposition, and preserve himself from mistaking accidental matters for substantial ones, and other things of which he should be wary in his investigation of each existent matter. There is great difficulty in all of this.

Further, since some of the principles in a scientific investigation are derived from sense only with great difficulty,[25] and if we do not apprehend through the senses all that ought to be apprehended in that investigation, we will err and think that what is accidental is substantial, as in the case of one who thinks that every living being has a head, because every living being of which he was aware had a head.[26]

Further, some of these principles derived from sense can only be apprehended through the senses over a very long time, exceeding the span of human life.[27]

It is all these things which bring one to think that man cannot possibly achieve his perfection.[28] For this reason this sage began by making clear the extent to which Divine Wisdom providentially furnished the instruments prepared for man to bring him to his perfection and through which we may overcome those factors which render the acquisition of our felicities impossible.[29]

This, in truth, is the point of the passage from this verse until *I have compared thee, O my love, to a steed in Pharaoh's chariots* (1:9). First it explained that God placed in our natures, we the community of human beings, a stronger desire to know the states of existent beings than our desire for physical pleasures.[30] That this proposition is incontrovertibly true has been made clear by Aristotle in *Metaphysics* 1, in the new translation.[31] Solomon presented a wonderful explanation for this; it is that every man, ab initio, can see God's wisdom and greatness in created things by virtue of the perfection found in the way in which they were created. From this perspective every man has a wonderful desire to know the goodness of the order and the equilibrium found among created things, all of which wonderfully indicate the perfection of the agent, as stated above.[32]

This explanation which Solomon gave here is very perfect; it is almost of the rank of explanations which account for existence, these being the most perfect explanations.[33] Aristotle explained this as follows: since we are more greatly attracted to the sense impressions of sight and sound than we are to those of smell, taste, and touch, notwithstanding that these sense impressions relate more to the pleasures of our bodies, as is clear from their natures, it is thus seen that in truth nature has given us a stronger desire for the sense impressions of sight and sound, notwithstanding their slighter relation to physical pleasures, because of their greater relation to that through which we acquire knowledge.[34] For this reason these two senses alone were mentioned in this book, in his saying, *Let me see thy countenance, let me hear thy voice* (2:14).

Some of the moderns have brought another demonstration for this.[35] They said that any entity should desire its perfection. Indeed, true knowledge[36] is our perfection. From this they infer that we desire true knowledge. This demonstration is weak: it would indeed be correct if we admitted that we know our perfection ab initio, for then we could say that it is necessarily the case that our desire is always for the good. But, ab initio, it is unknown to us whether or not we have any perfection other than physical perfections.[37] But even if we admit that ab initio we know that we have another, better perfection, we do not know, ab initio, what this perfection is; and we do not always desire the good.[38]

That which appears correct to me is that this desire is, as we see, spread among all members of the species—that is, that every one of them naturally desires his perfection—but that some or most of them do not go beyond the preliminaries and thus abandon the matter and remain with the desire only, as it says, *The desire of the slothful killeth him; for his hand refuses to labor* (Prov. 21:25).[39] The reason for affirming the presence of this desire in us is that nature, having given us this disposition, must have necessarily given us the instruments through which this disposition can be actualized. Otherwise, this disposition in us would be for naught, and nature does nothing for naught.[40] The matter being so, and since it would be impossible for us to achieve the perfection for which we are disposed without this desire, nature must have endowed us with this desire.

How could it be otherwise? You see that nature endowed animals with a desire for the activity whereby they give birth, so that the intended action will be achieved, in order to stabilize the existence of the species. Similarly, nature placed a desire for food when it needs it in every animal, so that it

would move towards the food, this oy secreting the black bile which stimulates the stomach.[41] So, too, the matter of the ejection of excrement, through
the intermediation of the red bile, which brings the animal to desire to evacu-
ate its bowels, as is mentioned in the book *On Animals*[42] and in the art of
medicine.[43]

And if nature endowed animals with desires concerning these dispositions, which are so inferior with respect to the human intellect, so that their
purpose be actualized by their functions being known ab initio, how much
more so is it fitting that it endow us with a desire for this worthy disposition,
through which man is man,[44] even if the manner of its functioning is unknown to us ab initio. In sum, this desire is one of the instruments which God
created for us to bring us to our ultimate perfection.[45]

Solomon mentioned the existence[46] of another instrument which God
gave us to direct us to our felicity. This is the existence of perfected individuals in every generation, who naturally desire to direct others to perfection,
whether through speech or writing, as if it were natural to imitate God—
who emanated from Himself this perfect existence not in order to achieve
anything useful for Himself—so far as possible.[47]

In this fashion the overcoming of the impediments which have been mentioned is fully explained. Thus, the first impediment, our ignorance of the
essence of felicity, will be overcome in this fashion: either because these perfected individuals will make it known to us so far as possible or they will
direct us to it.[48] Once they have directed us to it, the fact that we have no
representation of felicity will no longer render us incapable of achieving it.
For one who is moved by himself to do any action necessarily must know the
purpose of the action at its beginning, or he will not accomplish that purpose
except by accident. However, when one guides another to do a certain action, it is not actually necessary that he represent the end for which that action is done.[49] On the other hand, it is necessary that he who directs him to
do the action represent the end to himself; this is self-evidently clear. Thus
you will find that every practical craft has crafts subservient to it which serve
it and that none of the serving crafts fully apprehends the end for which they
are crafts. In truth, however, the primary craft apprehends it perfectly, and it
directs the crafts subservient to it to do what they do in the fashion in which
they do it.

For example, the craft of carpentry serves the craft of boatbuilding and is
guided by it with respect to how to cut the planks out of which boats are built;

it is not necessary that the craft of carpentry know the reason for which it is necessary that the planks be cut in such a fashion. However, this is necessary with respect to the primary craft, which directs carpentry to this action.[50]

The second impediment—our desire ab initio to follow our physical lusts—will also be overcome in this fashion, for these perfected individuals will employ stratagems to lead people away from being attracted by their lusts so far as possible, in a way which will cause them to perfect their endeavors to reach human felicity.

The third impediment—our ignorance of the way that leads us to perfection—will also be overcome in this fashion. This is so because whereas each of those who endeavor to achieve this apprehension by themselves will apprehend either nothing or very little, when what all of them has apprehended is gathered together, a worthy amount will have been gathered, either in and of itself or by virtue of its directing those who see their words toward the achievement of the truth in this. Therefore, one must always be aided in one's research by the words of those who preceded him, especially when the truth in them has been revealed to those who preceded him, as was the case during the time of this sage,[51] for the sciences were then greatly perfected in our nation.[52] The matter being so, our perfected predecessors guide us in speculation in a way which brings us to perfection, through either their speech or writing, by virtue of the natural desire they have for proffering this influence,[53] and will make known to us concerning each thing the way in which it should be researched and what they have understood concerning it, together with the assistance concerning it which they have derived from their predecessors.[54]

And that for which we need sensual apprehensions which can be accomplished only with difficulty and over a long time, surpassing the span of a human life, will also be completed in this fashion, for these perfected ones will make known to us what they and their predecessors apprehended concerning this through sensation over time, so that we arrive at the complete truth in this matter in this fashion.

This, then, is what this sage prefaced to his book: before speaking of how we may achieve this perfection, he resolved those objections on the basis of which one might think that our achievement of this felicity is impossible. Before mentioning these objections, he first confirmed the existence in us of a desire for our perfection.

Having posited this, we return to explain it out of the words of this sage.

With reference to our material intellect's desire *ab initio* to cleave to God—
the material intellect being called Solomon in this book, as we said above—
the material intellect said, expressing its desire, "Would that God would *kiss
me with the kisses of His mouth!*" that is, that it cleave to Him so far as possible, for "kissing" indicates cleaving and coming close, and thus the sages
said of Moses, Aaron, and Miriam that they "died by a kiss," that is, that at
the time of their deaths they cleaved to God.[55]

He said *Let him kiss me* and not "I will kiss him" because in truth God is
the Actor in this matter, for what we know is an emanation emanating upon
us from God, through the intermediation of the Active Intellect.[56]

He said *with the kisses of his mouth* because a kiss on the mouth indicates
a cleaving of great strength, since it is like a spiritual attachment, that is, that
they kiss each other with their mouths indicates that it were as if they were
attached by their breath, which they inhale one from the other.[57]

His saying *for thy love is better than wine* means that the intellect reck-
oned *ab initio* that love of God is more desirable and worthier than physical pleasures. He mentioned wine because it is the best known of all physical
pleasures and most delectable to the masses, and the one which brings one
to be drawn after the other pleasures, such as intercourse and gluttony. Thus
he mentioned wine alone,[58] as when in Ecclesiastes he used wine to indicate
the physical pleasures, as he said, *to pamper my flesh with wine* (2:3).

> Thine oils have a goodly fragrance
> Thy name is as oil poured forth
> Therefore do the maidens love thee (1:3)

He said, giving a reason for our natural desire to cognize and know God
so far as possible, that even with our weak apprehension *ab initio* of the order
and equilibrium of existent beings and the manner of the wisdom manifest in
them, we see very clearly the greatness of God's degree.[59] And therefore *do
the maidens* love him—these maidens being the young girls who had not
been with a man,[60] that is, the rational souls before their dispositions have
been actualized—for one's natural desire is for worthy things, and the worthier the object of desire, the greater the desire.

With respect to his saying *thine oils have a goodly fragrance*, you know
already how the sages and prophets compared knowledge to liquids, as it
says, *Ho, everyone that thirsteth, come ye for water* (Isa. 55:1), *And drink*

of the wine which I have mingled (Prov. 9:5), *And let thy head lack no oil* (Eccles. 9:8). The sages have already given an explanation for this symbolic representation and allegory.[61]

In sum, in that the terms *eating* and *drinking* have been used in a borrowed sense to mean "learning"—as Maimonides made clear and explained in his worthy book, *Guide of the Perplexed,* maintaining that *food* and *drink* are used in a borrowed sense for the sciences[62]—he here compared the worthiest of apprehensions to oil, which is the worthiest of liquids, superior to them all.[63] You know already that the worthiest type of apprehension is the intelligibles. Because of the abundant wisdom of God apparent in existent beings ab initio, due to the goodness of their order and equilibrium, and the greatest possible perfection in them, and because they stimulate one to examine them[64] until he knows the manner of the wisdom manifested in their existence as it is, he called them *goodly oils,* that is, processed oils, since processed oil is called good oil, as it says, *It is like the goodly oil upon the head, coming down upon the beard, even Aaron's beard* (Ps. 133:2).[65] He therefore called them *goodly oils* for these two reasons, that is, because of their degree themselves and because they stimulate one to study them until he knows them perfectly, as when a man would desire to acquire myrrh upon sensing its good fragrance.[66] He said further that first we "smell" these wonderful intelligibles before we cognize them; we therefore know that *thy* worthy *name* is like goodly oil which is poured from vessel to vessel so that its fragrance be strongly sensed, so *thy* worthy *name* is very clearly revealed like the fragrance of these goodly oils. This is so because the enduring perfection found in them is one of those things which emphatically teaches your existence and your perfection, since it is impossible that they could have caused their own existence or come into existence by accident, especially given their perfection as they are, all this in enduring order.[67]

The intended meaning of *Thy name is as oil poured forth* could be to teach the fact of God's emanation, as if he said that since *thine oils have a goodly fragrance*—and that is what we "smell" ab initio from these orderings of existent beings—we know that *thy name* is the ordering from which all of these orderings are emanated. This is so because it is evident from the goodness of the wisdom and order of these existent beings that their existence emanated from thee. Thus, *the fragrance of* these oils stimulates us to admit that there exists one existent from which is emanated these existent beings and that this existent is of the ultimate degree and perfection, as is shown by the fact that what has been emanated from it was emanated in so perfect a fashion.

Therefore *do the maidens love* him, they being the young girls who have not known men,[68] that is, the rational souls before their dispositions have been actualized; they desire to apprehend thee and something of the goodness of the order and equilibrium of the existence of these existent beings as they are. This desire is the reason we strive to achieve our perfection.

> Draw me, we will run after thee;
> The king hath brought me into his chambers
> We will be glad and rejoice in thee
> We will find thy love more fragrant than wine!
> Sincerely do they love thee (1:4)

This verse is addressed to God, in order to indicate the passionate desire and many motivating factors which directs it[69] to him and which draws it so much that it runs after him, it and the other faculties of the soul. This will occur when the other faculties of the soul are subordinated[70] to the service[71] of the intellect.[72]

Or, by *we will run after,* he and others like him—that is, other rational beings—may be meant, in that this desire is naturally found in all men; this interpretation makes more sense.[73]

Either way he attributed the activity in this to God because man cannot achieve his perfection without that which is emanated upon him from God. Further, because of the multitude of impediments, one needs divine assistance in order to be drawn to him.[74]

With respect to this desire he said that if we reach this end, that is, that God bring us *into his chambers,* this will constitute the ultimate pleasure and joy. This is true, because there is so much rejoicing and joy in this that physical joys cannot be compared to it;[75] perfect pleasure and joy occur when a worthy thing is apprehended correctly, as has been made clear in the appropriate places.[76] Thus David said, *In thy presence is fullness of joy* (Ps. 16:11), and the sages said, "in whose abode is happiness,"[77] meaning that the ultimate joy is found at God's degree.[78] By this they meant that the end intended for us is that we long after him with a wonderful longing; this is among those things which direct us to achieve the end, as was explained above.[79]

It further said that the strength of the rejoicing and joy of one who achieves this end is evident already ab initio because of what we "smell" ab initio of *thy love,* that is, we prefer those things which bring us to long for you more *than wine,* that is, more than physical lusts.[80]

In the statement *sincerely do they love thee,* a noun replaces an adjective, something which is found often in our language.[81] He means by this that it is the sincere individuals who love God, that is, those who aroused themselves to see the equilibrium[82] in the existent beings and the manner in which wisdom is found in them, who will prefer what they "smell" of *thy love* more *than wine.*

We have explained *we will find* as "we will sniff" according to the meaning of *its memorial part* (Lev. 2:2) and *in every place where I cause my name to be mentioned* (Exod. 20:21) according to the correct interpretation.[83]

> I am black, but comely
> O ye daughters of Jerusalem
> As the tents of Kedar
> As the curtains of Solomon (1:5)

The material intellect said to the other faculties of the soul that ab initio she is *black* since she lacks any intelligibles but is nonetheless *comely* because of her disposition to receive every intelligible when she will be stimulated to do this.[84] She said that in addition to all the blackness which was essentially hers because of her ignorance of things at first she also has *curtains* which impede[85] her from looking upon what should be looked upon and philosophically studied.[86] These curtains are her material impediments, which add blackness to her blackness. He[87] compared the blackness of her materiality to *the tents of Kedar,* which are very dark because of the excessive heat there;[88] that is, they try to cover the tents exceptionally well because of the excessive heat, so much so that the name *Kedar* came to indicate blackness. It is as if he said, "like the tents of Kedar, which are as dark as the curtains of Solomon." This is so because occasionally in the Hebrew language two kaffin[89] are used in a comparative sense, as it says, *my people as thy people, my horses as thy horses* (1 Kings 22:4) and *as with the maid, so with her mistress* (Isa. 24:2), and others like them.[90]

> Look not upon me that I am swarthy[91]
> That the sun hath tanned me

> My mother's sons were incensed against me,
> They made me keeper of the vineyards
> But mine own vineyard have I not kept (1:6)

She said to the other faculties of the soul, explaining the origin of these curtains which she mentioned in the previous verse, that they[92] not demean her on account of her magnified swarthiness, for that swarthiness is not hers essentially, but comes from outside, like the swarthiness of someone tanned by the sun. This is according to the allegory.

However, according to the intended meaning of the allegory he meant that she was made swarthy by the physical things under the sun,[93] these being things subject to generation and corruption, the longing for which things impedes her attainment of perfection. He attributed them to the sun because its activities are made clear through them.[94] Similarly, he said in the book of Ecclesiastes, *wherein he laboreth under the sun* (1:3).[95]

She explained who they were who attracted her to these physical matters and said that the other faculties of the soul brought it about that she would not keep her vineyard, by which is meant doing the specific activity which would cause her vineyard to bear its fruit, but induced her so to behave that her endeavors related to the physical actions connected to them.[96] She called these faculties which attract her to the physical desires her *mother's sons,* because the soul, insofar as it is one,[97] is the mother of all these faculties which branch out from it. She called them sons because they are active faculties. The faculties which in turn are affected by them, that is, which obey them, are *the daughters of Jerusalem* (1:5).[98] It is clear to one who knows the soul and its faculties that among the faculties of the soul are some on the level of mover and cause and others on the level of moved and caused.[99]

However, our saying that by *swarthy* he means magnified swarthiness is clearly correct since occasionally doubling[100] is used to indicate enhancement, as in *thou art fairer*[101] *than the children of men* (Ps. 45:3).

> Tell me, O thou whom my soul loveth
> Where thou feedest
> Where thou makest thy flock to rest at noon
> For why should I be as one that veileth herself
> Beside the flocks of thy companions? (1:7)

This is the speech of the material intellect to the Active Intellect, which perfects it and actualizes it.[102] It is said allegorically, like *And the Lord said unto Satan* (Job 1:7), and those verses like it.[103] It said this by way of protest, because in addition to [the] impediments mentioned in the previous verses,[104] there are also other impediments, which prevent it from attaining perfection: it does not know in what felicity consists, nor does it know the way by which it can arrive at its perfection and felicity.[105] Therefore, it said, "Tell me what is the thing which my soul ought to love, that for which I naturally desire and long, that is, felicity, for this is unknown to me ab initio." Also, "Tell me how my soul can feed, that is, how it can receive its nourishment, these being the intelligibles." The meaning of this is that he should let her know the way to arrive at this perfection.[106]

Where thou makest thy flock to rest at noon, that is, where she can rest having achieved[107] her fate, it being the ultimate light related to her, as at noon the sun's light is at its strongest.[108] The meaning of this is that with her apprehension of the intelligibles, and that is what is cognized from these things,[109] there is achieved an apprehension which goes part of the way toward perfection—for example, metaphysics and the way of apprehension in it, from doubt and perplexity.[110] For this reason she said that he should make known to her how this is.[111]

Or, *where thou feedest* could mean, "How will you guide the other faculties of the soul?" for the intellect is the shepherd of the other faculties of the soul and their leader.[112] Or it could mean that it was given this sovereignty at the root of creation.[113] It is clear that this proper leadership, that is, that the intellect lead the other faculties of the soul according to what is fitting, is a necessary preliminary for man to reach his ultimate perfection. According to this explanation, then, the meaning of *where thou makest thy flock to rest at noon* is that he make known to her the way whereby she can achieve and arrive at perfection, because this is unknown to her ab initio, as was explained above.[114]

For why should I be as one that veileth herself means "as one who coils"[115] in accordance with *Yea, he will wind thee round and round* (Isa. 22:17)[116] or "as one who covers himself" in accordance with *and he shall cover his upper lip* (Lev. 13:45) as one who has shame and sorrow and covers his face.[117]

By saying *thy companions* he meant the other active faculties.[118] Not that they are equal to him,[119] but their relation to the *daughters of Jerusalem* (1:5) is the relation of the Active Intellect to the material intellect,[120] and from this perspective he called them "his companions."[121] In addition to this is the fact that man cannot reach his first perfection if all of these faculties are not companions of the intellect, that is, that they all intend to facilitate the achievement of perfection and that their activities are solely directed to what will lead to this perfection.[122] The meaning here is "Why should I be as one that veileth herself, leading the flocks of thy companions?"—that is, why should I be as one who busies herself with the activities related to those faculties which are not properly mine[123] and impede those activities which are properly mine,[124] they being the true perfection? This is so because if I do not know the intended end, and the way which leads to it, it is not possible that I will endeavor to achieve my perfection, and all of my activities will be according to the ways of *the flocks of thy companions,* given also that they attract me to their activities, as she said, *they made me keeper of the vineyards* (1:6).

> If thou know not, O thou fairest among women
> Go thy way forth by the footsteps of the flock
> And feed thy kids
> Beside the shepherds' tents (1:8)

The Active Intellect responded to her that nature has already provided for the overcoming of all of these impediments which she mentioned in that it has brought into existence in every generation perfected individuals who direct others to the intended felicity, through either their speech or their writing, because of the natural longing for this influence given them by nature.[125] We have already explained above how all these impediments can be overcome in this fashion.[126] Thus he said, "If thou know not what thy soul loveth, and know not how thou will feed my way, which is the way of sheep which have a shepherd and leader, then nourish thy faculties beside the shepherds' tents," they being the perfected individuals who guide other men and direct them to the places from which the soul takes its nourishment, that is, its perfection, just as the shepherd guides the sheep to the place where they can graze. The comparison of leaders to shepherds and those who receive their admonition to sheep is often repeated in the words of the prophets.[127]

He called her *the fairest among women* because among the passive faculties of the soul there is no faculty as worthy as she.[128]

PART TWO

1:9 – 2:7

From the beginning of the third paragraph to the beginning of the fifth paragraph, where it says, *Hark! My beloved!* (2:8), he indicates the effort necessary to overcome the impediment [to perfection] caused by moral deficiency.

> I have compared thee, O my love
> To a steed in Pharaoh's chariots (1:9)

It is known that many choice horses are found in Egypt, as it says, *Nor cause the people to return to Egypt to the end that he should multiply horses* (Deut. 17:16); *And a chariot [came up] and went out of Egypt for six hundred shekels of silver, and a horse for a hundred and fifty* (1 Kings 10:29). There is no doubt that *in Pharaoh's chariots*—he being the king there[1]—are found the choicest horses, swift, and decorated with varieties of ornaments, such as *circlets of gold* (1:11) and *beads* (1:10).

The Active Intellect said to the material intellect, the female in this passage, which was compared to a mare *in Pharaoh's chariots,* that she was disposed by her beauty to receive the decoration and ornament with which they[2] are decorated and that she was also disposed to run to the desired place. For this reason he compared her to the horses *in Pharaoh's chariots* for it is not their[3] custom to lead them from place to place until they have been decorated and ornamented. With respect to this it is clear concerning the material intellect that it cannot possibly go to the place of its desire if the man[4] had not previously decorated himself with praiseworthy moral qualities and divested himself of the *filthy garments,*[5] that is, inferior moral qualities.[6] This has been made clear and referred to by the prophets and those who speak by virtue of the holy spirit, the sages have made reference to this, and

31

the philosophers have made reference to this as well. Abu Hammad already said in his book about intentions,[7] making an allegory about this matter, that the intellect is similar to a mirror; just as a dirty, unpolished mirror will not receive the impression of things seen, but will receive them when its dirt is removed and it is polished, so the intellect will not apprehend things if it is not cleansed first of the filth of inferior moral qualities and if their dirt is not removed from it.[8] This is the intention of his[9] words, even if he did not phrase them in this fashion.

In truth, he compared her to a mare and not to a stallion because in this passage he allegorically presents it[10] as a female, since the female is passive, whereas the male is active. We have found a second reason concerning this in a midrash of the sages. It is that a mare while running will not interrupt its running to perform its bodily functions, unlike the male.[11] Thus, according to their statement, she is compared to a mare, for the material intellect, once decorated with appropriate decorations, will not interrupt its running progress toward its felicity, while taking what it needs for the maintenance of its body from time to time. This is possible with respect to the material intellect, even if its actual occurrence is very unlikely, that is, that there will be found a man who constantly studies the ways of God even while taking what he needs for the maintenance of his body.[12]

> Thy cheeks are comely with circlets,
> Thy neck with beads (1:10)

He meant by this that she is fit to receive the decoration and ornament and absolutely disposed for it. He said *thy cheeks* and *thy neck* because they are the places where it is customary to put these decorations in that land.

> We will make thee circlets of gold
> With studs of silver (1:11)

He said *we will make* and did not say "I will make" because for this decoration he needs the help of another besides the Active Intellect. This is the help which he[13] will receive from the shepherds mentioned above who will direct him to this decoration.[14] Further, he needs the help of the other faculties of the soul; moreover, their mutual agreement to abandon physical desires and pleasures must be complete.

It may be that the meaning of this "decoration" is her apprehension of the intelligibles and her being perfected by them;[15] his comparing her to a mare would then be from the perspective of her uninterrupted racing toward the desired place, as above.[16] He then means to say that she is disposed to receive this perfection.[17]

He compared it[18] to circlets and beads because they bring the limbs upon which they are customarily placed to completion and perfection.

His saying *we will make* refers to the fact that the actualization of this potentiality is not attributed to the Active Intellect alone, other assistance being needed as stated above, this being provided by the perfected ones who guide one to this perfection. Further, there is no way of acquiring the primary intelligibles from the Active Intellect[19] without sense, imagination, and the faculty of memory, as above.[20]

> While the king sat at his table,
> My spikenard sent forth its fragrance (1:12)

In that, as has already been established, this perfection can be achieved only with the assistance of others beyond the Active Intellect, these being sense, imagination, and the faculty of memory; and in that the intention of this book is to indicate the way for us to achieve this perfection, and what must be done first in order to necessitate our achieving it, and how it may be achieved so that the matter end with the accomplishment of our ultimate perfection; he therefore proceeded here by referring to the first step in the order of steps which bring us to our felicity when we long for it, this being perfection of morals. This is the meaning of every fruit mentioned in this passage[21] until *Hark! My beloved! Behold, he cometh* (2:8).

He placed the faculty of the soul which stands in the relation of matter[22] to the material intellect[23] at the level of the female lover and the material intellect at the level of the male beloved.[24] This is something which continues throughout the rest of this book.[25] This faculty stands in the relation of matter to the material intellect from one aspect and from another aspect stands in the relation of actor, as was mentioned in *On the Soul*.[26]

In order to stimulate the material intellect to proceed toward perfection by perfecting itself so much that it would become *the king sitting at his table*—he the king being the material intellect—this faculty of the soul[27] said, "My spice will give forth its fragrance and will stimulate it[28] to acquire the intelligibles." In truth, this is so because these imaginative forms through their repetition stimulate one to draw general propositions and the infinite judgment.[29]

By saying *at his table* he meant those things apprehended by the intellect, for they are a rotating circle:[30] existent things exist on various levels; some of them stand in the relation of form and perfection to others and some of them stand in the relation of matter to others.[31] Since the intellect investigates the essence of sensible things—which is matter and form—as it investigates matter, it will sometimes occur that it moves from the worthy to the inferior until it reaches that matter for which no matter precedes it, that is, the most remote matter.[32] And when it investigates form the opposite occurs, that is, it moves from the inferior to the worthy, until it reaches the form which is the first form for all existence, that is, God.[33] And the issue returns as if it were rotating.[34] Apprehension with respect to most natural matters is also by way of "rotation." This, because with respect to most of them we go from the posterior to the anterior; we further return and go from the anterior to the attributes posterior to it.[35] This is evident to those who study physics, for we apprehend many things in this fashion.

Or, he means by his saying *at his table,* "in his place." He means by this that he should begin to strive to cognize the intelligibles. The meaning is the same whichever of these explanations is chosen.[36]

According to this explanation, the male beloved mentioned already in this allegory would be the Active Intellect, whereas the female lover would be the material intellect.[37] From this verse to the end of the book, the male beloved would be the material intellect and the female lover the faculty of the soul which stands to the material intellect in the relation of matter, for example, the faculty of imagination or the imaginative forms impressed upon it[38] by the sensible things through the senses and the faculty of memory. Although this is a bit odd linguistically,[39] it fits the matter itself very well, that is, that in this allegory concerning a male beloved and female lover, he[40] will intend by the male beloved now the material intellect and now the Active Intellect; so, too, with respect to the meaning of the female lover, intending now the material intellect, now the faculty of the soul which stands to it in the relation of matter.[41]

Perhaps we can say that the male beloved, in his saying *to a steed in Pha-*

raoh's chariots (1:9), is the material intellect and the female lover is the faculty of the soul which stands to it in the relation of *matter*. He said, by way
of recounting the degree of her great desire, that he compares her to a mare
in Pharaoh's chariots because of her fleetness. He said that before being ornamented in this fashion she needed the important moral qualities and that
she is greatly disposed toward this ornamentation. However, he said, *We will
make thee circlets of gold* (1:11) because this ornamentation cannot be attributed to the intellect alone without the assistance of the shepherds mentioned above and the assistance of the rest of the faculties of the soul, which
must act in concert and subjugate themselves to the service of the intellect.
This fits the language very well. On this approach the entire allegory in this
book refers to one male beloved and one female lover.

But the passage *I am black but comely* (1:5) is not an allegory concerning
the male lover and the female lover, and therefore it is not odd if this statement refers back to the intellect. Withal, it is also possible to explain it such
that the statement refers back to the faculty of the soul which stands in the
relation of matter to the intellect. The swarthiness of this faculty will then
relate to its being ab initio without those forms which bring the material intellect to its perfection. It is comely despite this from the perspective of its
being disposed to receive them. He[42] said that the impediments which keep
it apart from its perfection, themselves impeding the intellect from achieving
its perfection, bring darkness like *the tents of Kedar* (1:5); that is why he
called them *the curtains of Solomon,* because it is a screen separating the
material intellect from its perfection.[43] He said that the other faculties of the
soul *were incensed* (1:6) against it,[44] seeing it as striving to do what is best
for them;[45] they did not permit him to strive to do the activity particular to
him, on the basis of which he would reach perfection. He said to the material
intellect, *tell me* (1:7) what is that thing which my soul desires so that I may
become corrected[46] through the provision of the imaginative forms which are
needed for its achievement. [He further said to the material intellect, tell me]
how my soul *can feed* (1:7),[47] that is, what is the order which it must follow
in its investigation of each of the existent things, and how can it achieve its
destiny?[48] In sum, that which follows this can be interpreted according to the
preceding fashion in the preceding explanation; there is no difference in it.
Only, the speaker here is this faculty of the soul and its interlocutor is the
material intellect. In the preceding explanation the speaker was the material

intellect and its interlocutor the Active Intellect. This[49] fits the language very well, whereas the previous explanation fits the meaning very well.[50]

> My beloved is unto me as a bag of myrrh
> That lieth between my breasts (1:13)

This faculty of the soul said that the material intellect which *lieth between* her breasts and which she nurses and nourishes so that it begins to progress toward its perfection is similar to *a bag of myrrh*. This is so because myrrh does not give forth its scent unless it be placed in fire, as Aristotle remarked.[51] Thus, it needs assistance from without in order to give forth its scent; it does not itself give forth its scent actually, only potentially.[52] Myrrh gathered together in a bag is even less likely to give forth its scent because of the outside impediment.[53] Similarly, the material intellect's perfection is, ab initio, only potential, and it needs outside assistance to actualize that potential; but the outside impediments must first be removed before it can progress towards its perfection.

> My beloved is unto me as a cluster of henna
> In the vineyards of En-Gedi (1:14)

This faculty of the soul said that the material intellect is similar to *a cluster of henna,* which is an imperfect existent,[54] that is, it is the beginning stage of the making of the fruit. *En-Gedi* is in the hills, as may be seen in the book of Joshua.[55] It is clear that *a cluster of henna* takes much longer than other fruits to perfect its generation. In the hills it needs a longer time for the perfection of its generation than what is needed by other fruits in the valley and in the Sharon;[56] but its being in the hills makes it choicer and of a higher degree. In this way he says that the material intellect is an uncompleted perfection the actualization of which is difficult, but when it is actualized, it is choicer and of a higher degree than other perfected faculties.[57]

> Behold, thou art fair, my love
> Behold, thou art fair
> Thine eyes are as doves (1:15)

The material intellect allegorically said concerning the beauty of this faculty of the soul's preparation and the natural longing between them to cooperate in order to proceed toward perfection that this female beloved is very fair and that her eyes *are as doves,* that is, that her eyes are as fair as the eyes of doves, as it says, *his eyes are like doves beside the water-brooks* (5:12). Fair eyes are among those things which strengthen the longing of the lover for his beloved. This matter is well known concerning lovers, and it relates to the allegory alone.[58]

> Behold, thou art fair, my beloved, yea, pleasant
> Also our couch is fresh (1:16)

She[59] replied that, just as the intellect desires her because of her beauty and the excellence of her preparation to provide that which will bring it to perfection, so she desires the intellect and yearns to unite with it and provide[60] it with what it needs to progress toward perfection. She said that her beloved, along with being fair and handsome, is also good and pleasant and that the couch on which they will be joined together *is fresh* and their pleasure will be enhanced upon it.[61] By saying *is fresh* he[62] also referred to the fact that their joining together is fruitful, because freshness and moistness are together the cause of the tree's giving fruit, whereas dryness is the cause of its not giving fruit; this is true of both plants and animals. Thus, her desire for him grows because of his handsomeness and pleasantness and because of the good end achieved through her being joined together with him.

> The beams of our houses are cedars
> And our panels are cypresses (1:17)

She said that the beams and the panels which nature prepared for them to use in the building of the house in which they would be joined together are very strong, and thus the building which they will build will be very strong. The beams and panels are the sensory apprehensions[63] from which are built the imaginative forms and the intelligibles. It is clear that when these apprehensions are used as tools for that for which they are designated the results will be correct and without error since errors are not caused by the senses insofar as they are used for that for which they are uniquely qualified to apprehend. For example, we do not make mistakes relative to the sense of vision when we judge on its basis that some thing is black or white; we will, however, err if we judge on its basis that, for example, black is bitter because of our having perceived of allowin[64] that it is bitter and that it is black, since it is not necessary that every black [thing] be bitter.

Perhaps we can say that the meaning here is that this building which they will build to guard themselves from the impediments without and in order to be joined together within ought to be very strong; thus she said that *the beams* of this building will be *cedars* and its panels *cypresses* such that that building will be very strong. It serves them as a shelter and hiding place from wind and rain and other things outside. This is necessary for them before they perfect the bond between them, that is, that they be guarded from the impediments which they have from the perspective of inferior moral qualities and the mistakes caused by the imagination and by the mixing together of accidental and substantial matters.

> I am a rose of Sharon
> A lily of the valleys (2 : 1)

It is known that the rose and the lily need much moisture in order to be nourished. In the Sharon and the valleys there is much moisture, and thus the rose and the lily blossom there and maintain their freshness. And thus this female lover says that as the *rose of Sharon* and the *lily of the valleys* find their nourishment prepared for them easily, so is perfection prepared for her easily in the other faculties of the soul and in the acquisition of the imaginative forms through her.[65] He[66] connected the lily to *the valleys* because it needs, I think, moisture more, and one finds more moisture in the valley than in the Sharon.

The nature of the wisdom found in his allegorically comparing this faculty to a lily has already been made clear in our introduction to this book.[67] We will expand that discussion here: it is clear that the lily is one of the choicer flowers in and of itself. Flowers are of the class of things which are produced first by the plant before the production of the fruit or the seed, which was the original intention.[68] The attainment of imaginative forms in the soul is the perfection which precedes intellectual apprehension, and thus this matter was allegorically compared to the lily. Further, the lily is potentially the fruit or the seed which comes from it. So the imaginative forms are potentially the intelligibles apprehended by the intellect; but the intellect abstracts from them the material attributes through which they were individuated,[69] as was made clear in *On the Soul* and in the *Metaphysics*.[70]

> As a lily among thorns
> So is my love among the daughters (2:2)

You ought to know that the faculties of the soul, when they obey the intellect, all turn toward it and intend its perfection. And when they do not intend this object they distance the intellect from its perfection and turn toward the physical desires, *for the inclination of man's heart is evil from his youth* (Gen. 8:21). Thus, as we said at first, one who wishes to progress toward the intelligibles must subordinate all the faculties of his soul to the service of his intellect. This will happen when he discards and abandons his material desires and takes from them only what he needs for the maintenance of his body. Since this is the matter which must be striven for first, the intellect pointed out the existence of these impediments and called them thorns because they are thorns and brambles which inflict pain and destruction upon themselves and others.[71] He compared his beloved from among these animative faculties to *a lily among the thorns*.[72] The reason for his allegorically comparing her to the lily has already been stated.

There is more wisdom to be found in this allegory. It is that the thorns impede the growth of the lily because they dry out the earth and interfere with [the lily's] nourishment. So, too, these faculties of the soul, when they turn to material desires, impede this female lover from performing her proper function.

> As an apple-tree among the trees of the wood
> So is my beloved among the sons
> Under its shadow I delighted to sit
> And its fruit was sweet to my palate (2:3)

She replied to the intellect that it, among the other guiding faculties of the soul, is like the apple tree—which produces a fruit very beautiful with respect to its appearance, scent, taste, and feel—among the other trees of the forest, trees which do not produce fruit. In truth, fruit is ascribed to the intellect alone among the other guiding faculties of the soul[73] because it alone can achieve the condition of eternity in an individual.[74] This is the entire fruit of these sublunary[75] existents and the final perfection with respect to which the first matter exists in potential.[76] Of the other perfections which may be acquired by first matter, some are acquired through others and they all exist for this perfection.[77]

There is more wisdom to be found in this allegory. It is that the apple tree, when it is among other trees, is prevented by those trees from growing and producing its fruit.

With respect to the strength of the longing she said that she greatly delights to sit *under its shadow* and that its fruit would be sweet to her palate were this possible,[78] in accordance with her estimation of the sweetness of that fruit. All this comes to indicate the strength of her longing to be joined with him.

Perhaps we can say that the meaning of this is that she determines with her palate that his fruit ought to be very sweet and this is the reason for her desiring him, that is, because she deems that his perfection is very good.[79]

> He hath brought me to the banqueting-house
> And his banner over me is love (2:4)

She said, "Would that the intellect would force me to abandon my desires, and would force me to strive to serve him, and bring me to the banqueting-house where he drinks"—and that is what God emanates upon him[80]—"then his cup which he lifts over me will draw from me wonderful love for him." [81] She ascribed this activity to him,[82] however, because he motivates the other faculties of the soul to progress toward this perfection and help him *with a strong hand* (Isa. 8:11) because of the natural longing which he has for its achievement.

Or we can say that her saying *he hath brought me* is missing the actor[83] and does not refer to her beloved.[84] The meaning of this would then be that even though my innate nature[85] or my will *hath brought me to the banqueting-house*—these[86] are the physical desires—the *banner* of the material intellect, which will be *over me* to draw me after him and to abandon my desires, is for me great *love*.[87]

> Stay ye me with dainties
> Refresh me with apples
> For I am love-sick (2:5)

In order to indicate the strength of the desire, she said that her heart had become enfeebled, as often happens with lovers. She asked the other faculties of the soul to give her delicacies which strengthen the heart such as dainties and apples. All this is in accordance with the allegory alone.[88]

> Let his left hand be under my head
> And his right hand embrace me (2:6)

This verse accords with both the allegory and its intended meaning. It accords with the allegory for this is customary behavior of lovers who join together. It accords with the intended meaning because to the left of the intellect are the *thorns* (2:2) and *the trees of the wood* (2:3) mentioned above. And thus the evil inclination is called "left" and "Satan."[89] This is so because he[90] causes one to turn from the path of the healthy intellect.[91] His right is the intellect, which is good. She mentioned that all of the faculties of the soul have already subordinated themselves to the service of the intellect and that they are under her head and that the right of the intellect is the female.[92] For this reason the impediments to the intellect caused by these faculties, that is, from the perspective of their turning to the physical desires, retreated. This is what must be done first by one who wishes to progress toward perfection.

> I adjure you, O daughters of Jerusalem, by the gazelles
> And by the hinds of the field
> That you awaken not, nor stir up love
> Until it please (2:7)

This adjuration is necessitated by the strength of the longing to achieve the end; perhaps they will break through and not progress toward this perfection in the right way. Thus she urged them not to awaken nor stir up *love until it please*. He mentioned *gazelles* and *hinds of the field* because they are so fleet, as if to say that they, because of their longing, run fleetly to achieve the end and ought to restrain themselves from this but go in the appropriate ordering, from level to level, allowing him to reach the desired end.[93]

PART THREE

2:8 – 2:17

From the beginning of the fifth paragraph to the beginning of the eighth paragraph, where it says, *on my bed* (3:1), he indicates the effort necessary to overcome the impediments [to perfection] caused by imagination and thought, so that one will know how to escape from error and distinguish between truth and falsehood.

Hark! My beloved!
Behold, he cometh
Leaping upon the mountains
Skipping upon the hills (2:8)

After their attainment of moral perfection, as explained in the preceding part of this allegory, he here begins to proceed by making reference to knowing how to distinguish truth from falsehood so as to be preserved from being misled by the imagination and faculty of estimation,[1] because this must precede research on the characteristics of existent things. This was his intent in this section until his statement *By night on my bed* (3:1) according to one of the explanations of this text which appears correct to us, or until *Who is this that cometh up* (3:6)[2] according to another explanation.

He referred to their proceeding toward those perfections which are not desired for themselves,[3] as if ab initio he strives to attain the final perfection with respect to that which he mentioned concerning their speeches one to the other, not to these perfections alone[4] but also to that which will bring them to strive to attain the final perfection for which they have longed from the beginning.[5] It is clear that stammering and perplexity will occur to one who does not know how truth may be distinguished from falsehood such that he will *leap* and *skip*[6] from one alternative in a contradiction to the other,[7] his intellect not resting on either of them, because of his consideration of the ob-

jections to each at first estimation. He has nothing with which he can determine which of the objections are correct and which are simply adopted on
the basis of first estimation or imagination, so that he can distinguish from
among them the substantial from the accidental matters and the correct from
the incorrect. For this reason she said that her beloved was *leaping upon the
mountains, skipping upon the hills* because of his perplexity concerning the
things he was researching.

We can possibly say that the meaning of this verse is that her beloved
came to her running as fast as possible to stimulate her to attempt to attain
perfection and for this reason he *leaps* and *skips,* because of the strength of
his running.

> My beloved is like a gazelle
> Or a young hart
> Behold, he standeth behind our wall
> He looketh in through the windows
> He glimpseth through the lattice (2:9)

She allegorically compared him to *a young hart* because of the fleetness
of his running toward and his longing to attain the end. She said that he was
behind her *wall* to indicate that the connection between them was not yet
such that this apprehension could be perfected; rather, there was a partition
and screen between them. Because the partition is between them, she said
that he *glimpseth* and *looketh* through the small openings, which are so small
that it is not possible that she go out to him through them, nor that he come
to her, until the connection between them be perfected.

> My beloved spoke and said unto me
> Rise up, my love, my fair one
> And come away (2:10)

She said that her beloved, reckoning that she would not perfect this apprehension for him without the assistance which she ought to get from him,
called to her and *said unto* her that she should arise and go on the way appropriate to bring her to this longed-for perfection. Here, however, he called
her *my love, my fair one,* whereas in the previous passage he called her *my
love* (1:15) only because of the beauty and ornamentation which she has by
now acquired, this being moral perfection.[8]

> For, lo, the winter is past
> The rain is over
> And gone (2:11)

The meaning of this is that the period when perfection with him was impossible has passed. This was the period when the faculties of the soul turned toward the physical desires. He allegorically compared that time to *the winter* and *the rain* since at that time most plants do not produce fruit because of the great cold. *The winter* and *the rain* are synonyms since winter is the time of rain in nature, as was made clear in the *Meteorology.*[9]

> The buds appear on the earth
> The time of singing is come
> And the voice of the turtle-dove is heard in our land (2:12)
> The fig-tree putteth forth her green figs
> And the vines in blossom
> Give forth their fragrance
> Arise, my love, my fair one
> And come away (2:13)

He said to her that the time has already come when nature will begin to try to produce fruits, this being the time when the plants have put forth buds and the time when some of the birds which went south because of the great cold of the winter come back. The *fig-tree* has begun trying to produce fruit, that is, it has already *put forth her green figs;* and *the vines* are *in blossom* and *give forth their fragrance.* All this is according to the allegory, whereas [according to its intended meaning][10] the time has already come when they ought to begin to strive to progress toward the intended perfection. For this reason he stimulated her that she rise and come away on the route by which this will be perfected for him.

> O my dove
> That art in the clefts of the rock
> In the covert of the cliff
> Let me see thy countenance
> Let me hear thy voice
> For sweet is thy voice
> And thy countenance is comely (2:14)

He called her *my dove* because the dove has a unique characteristic which distinguishes it from other animals: it only mates with a male with which it was born. So also this female beloved, now that all of her striving is for his service, and now that she is also more disposed to mate with him, will not turn aside from him at all.

This verse fits both the allegory and its intended meaning. It fits the allegory because it is the custom of lovers to join themselves together in hidden places like *the clefts of the rock* and *the covert of the cliff;* there he will first desire to see her countenance and hear her voice and then will he be aroused to join together with her. And thus he says now, since that which will perfect their joining together has not yet been perfected, that he desires to see her countenance and hear her voice there.

It fits the intended meaning of the allegory for he says that in the hidden places he must be shown what she apprehended through the senses, so that he [will] be enabled to arrive at a universal statement on the basis of repetition.[11] He mentioned here sights and sounds alone because these two senses are more disposed toward speculation than other senses;[12] it is clear that this is of their nature. Therefore, one who has lost one or both of these senses is very poorly prepared.[13] The other senses are more disposed to serve the needs of the body.

> Take us the foxes
> Little foxes that spoil the vineyards
> For our vineyards are in blossom (2:15)

Since, in addition to attraction to the physical pleasures, there exist other impediments to apprehension, these being the mistakes which occur because of estimation and imagination which bring us to think the accidental to be substantial or the nonexistent to exist, or vice versa, these additional impediments ought first to be removed. This is done with the art of logic, which guides the intellect so as to preserve itself from these mistakes and to adopt the order and way by which the truth is determined with respect to each thing.[14]

The intellect said that they ought first to take away these impediments lest they destroy that which they worked at. Such destruction would be easy for them because they are still at the beginning of estimation.[15] He allegorically said that they should take away these *foxes* which, despite their being *little,* still *spoil the vineyards* and destroy their fruit-bearing capacity. They must especially take away these *foxes* since their vineyard is *in blossom,* that is, since it already started delicately producing its fruit and could be destroyed by the least of causes.[16]

> My beloved is mine, and I am his
> That feedeth among the lilies (2:16)

She said that these impediments have already been removed also. Thus, she can be her beloved's and her beloved can be hers without impediment. She called him *that feedeth among the lilies* since, after all these impediments were removed, it was his way that he be nourished by that which is potentially in the fruit and seed through which the imaginative forms are directed to him, as above.[17] But before this it was not possible for her.

> Until the day breathe
> And the shadows flee away
> Turn, my beloved, and be thou like a gazelle or young hart
> Upon the mountains of spices (2:17)

Drawing attention to the strength of her obedience to him and to her desire to perfect him, as he requested of her, she said to him that while the wind of *the day* still *breathes* and until *the* nighttime *shadows flee away,* she will strive with the greatest energy to ascend *upon the mountains of spices,* because the darkness of ignorance is already being removed and the light of wisdom is beginning to be seen. This is because they have the instruments through which she can acquire perfection in that the impediments have already been removed. It is thus necessary that they begin studying those things which are first in order.

By *mountains of spices* he meant division[18] and abstraction,[19] which are the mathematical sciences. This is so because with them one renders abstract in speech that which is not abstract in existence.[20] He used the plural here because the mathematical sciences are many.

He used the singular with respect to physics and said *[Until the day breathe and the shadows flee away] I will get me to the mountain of myrrh, and to the hill of frankincense* (4:6) because physics is one science even if it has many parts, since it has a specific subject matter, namely, mutable existent[s];[21] [but since, withal, it has many parts] he ascribed it to specific spices.[22] The reason for relating it to spices is that most of its demonstrations are a posteriori,[23] that is, they are taken from posterior matters from which we derive proofs concerning antecedent matters.[24]

He used the plural, however, with respect to metaphysics and did not relate it to specific spices because of the multiplicity of different subjects of research in metaphysics. This is so because it speculates concerning the principles of demonstration, and the principles of substance, and the essences of the subjects of specific sciences; in sum, the subjects of research in this science and its parts are many. This is clear to anyone who looked into this science and saw the subjects of inquiry which Aristotle counted in it.[25] But this is not the case with respect to the parts of physics. This is so because some of the parts of physics encompass others; for example, the first part is more inclusive, moving in this fashion from the inclusive to the more specific. This is not the case in metaphysics. Thus metaphysical science are many [sic] because of the multiplicity of its subjects of research.[26] He related it to spices in general for the same reason which we mentioned concerning physics and did not relate it to specific spices, since this science investigates absolute existence, not specific existent[s].

This is what we understand with respect to these mountains, and it fits both the language and the intended meaning very well. He allegorically compared the sciences to mountains because they are very high and can only be ascended with great difficulty.[27]

PART FOUR

3 : 1 − 4 : 7

From the beginning of the eighth paragraph to the beginning of the thirteenth paragraph, where it says, *Come with me from Lebanon, my bride* (4 : 8), he indicates the attainment of the mathematical sciences.

> By night on my bed
> I sought him whom my soul loveth
> I sought him, but I found him not (3 : 1)

The meaning of this is that notwithstanding her being in the darkness of ignorance, she nonetheless sought to investigate the final perfection which her *soul loveth* because of the strength of her desire for it; she did not find it because it is impossible to achieve the end except in the proper order.

> I will rise now and go about the city
> In the streets and the broad ways
> I will seek him whom my soul loveth
> I sought him but I found him not (3 : 2)

The meaning of this is that there is no effort by which she will be able to find him now but that it is proper that she do this in a step-by-step way and in the proper order.[1]

> The watchmen that go about the city found me:
> Saw ye him whom my soul loveth? (3 : 3)

You ought to know that the senses are *the watchmen,* for they were put in the body of the animal to preserve it from injury and to direct it to fitting things; they *go about* the body to protect it. That this is their meaning is clear to the reader of this book.

She said they *found me* because it is not the custom of the faculty of imagination to seek them out; rather, they find it and meet it when the impressions
of the senses have reached the common sense and it rests,[2] for then these impressions which are in the common sense reach the imagination.[3] They do
not reach the imagination until the senses stand still, since they are otherwise
preoccupied with sense impressions.[4] For this reason, it is fitting that it says
that they *found me.*

She asked them if they saw *him whom* her *soul loveth,* since everything
which reaches him[5] from the imagination ultimately reaches him from sense
perception. All this comes to indicate the strength of the longing in the quest
for this perfection.

> Scarce had I passed from them
> When I found him
> Whom my soul loveth
> I held him and would not let him go
> Until I had brought him into my mother's house
> And into the chamber of she that conceived me (3:4)

She said that because of the strength of her desire she almost did not agree
to pass *from them* unless she first achieved the object of her search. She said
that if it [were to] occur that she hold him and find him, she would not let
go of him until she brings him *into* her *mother's house and into the chamber
of she that conceived* her, it being the faculty of memory, for it is a repository of sensed things.[6] There[7] is the last stage of the stages of the sensible soul
which is his *mother* and *she that conceived* him.[8]

> I adjure you
> O daughters of Jerusalem by the gazelles
> And by the hinds of the field
> That ye awaken not, nor stir up love
> Until it please (3:5)

This oath comes here because of the great longing to seek out the end: it
urges that one approach the different species of speculation in their order, *lest
they break through*[9] and the end be withheld from them. It was thus necessary that speculation begin with the mathematical sciences, even though the
desire for physics and metaphysics is greater. This is the explanation which
seems fitting to us in this passage.[10] Nothing is intended here beyond the

adjuration to save oneself from breaking through. Thus, he first told of her desire to break through and enter first into the final perfection, so much so that she strove in every possible way to achieve this without accomplishing anything.

According to the second explanation which we mentioned,[11] however, he begins at the beginning of the passage to tell of her inquiries in the mathematical sciences, and the explanation of this passage will be as follows: she said, "while in the darkness of night—the darkness of ignorance—I was *on my bed* (3:1) and I sought by myself, without the assistance of the senses, to seek the principles which the intellect needs from me for these mathematical sciences with which I am now striving, and I did not find them." In truth, he said this because many think that with respect to these principles we do not need the senses in order to determine them, for example, the premise which says that different things equal to the same thing are equal to each other and that the whole is greater than a part of it, and the other first premises similar to these upon which are built many of the mathematical theses.[12] But this interpretation, when investigated, is seen to be false.[13] This is so because these primary intelligibles in these mathematical sciences can be but one of two things: either we possess them[14] from the time we are formed or we acquire them. If they were with us from the time we were formed, it would be impossible for us to acquire any other intelligible. This is so because the intellect in truth can receive all of the intelligibles only because it is without all of them, as was made clear in *On the Soul;*[15] this[16] is clearly false.

If it be, on the other hand, that we acquire them, then we must acquire them from the sense and the imagination or from the intellect—since every learning or study requires earlier knowledge, as was made clear in *Posterior Analytics.*[17] It is false that we acquire them from the intellect alone, for if the matter were so, they would be acquired by syllogism from premises better known than them and prior to them, thus making the primary intelligibles not primary; this is false and untrue. No option remains but that they be acquired from the sense and imagination as is the case with the other primary intelligibles; due to the ease with which we acquire them from sense—since there is no need for repetition in their acquisition we do not know when they reached us from sensation—we think that they reach the intellect without the senses.[18]

She also said that she went about the city[19] to discover if she could find these principles from herself without sensation. When she saw that she did not find it from herself, she asked the senses, when they found her,[20] if they had acquired anything which would help her to find these principles. She said, due to the ease with which what is needed of these premises reaches the senses, since there is no need for repetition, that she *almost* (3:4)[21] did not agree to *pass from them* (3:4) without first finding perfectly everything which the intellect needed with respect to these premises. She said that she did not let go of that which she held[22] from them, so that it would not be forgotten until she brought it to the faculty of memory, that being the *house* of her mother *and into the chamber of she that conceived* her (3:4). It is also possible that she said *I held him and would not let him go* (3:4) because of the ease with which one forgets the sense impressions from which these first premises are derived.[23]

In this passage the intellect does not acquire any speculative perfection; rather, the principles are prepared which the intellect makes into the first premises of the mathematical sciences. The adjurative form is used here because of the strength of the longing for the search for the end;[24] she adjured the *daughters of Jerusalem* (3:5) that they not break through by attempting to study physics and metaphysics, but, rather, that their entry into the scientific investigation of existent beings be in the proper order, and it was thus necessitated that they commence the investigation[25] with the mathematical sciences.

> Who is this that cometh up out of the wilderness
> Like pillars of smoke
> Perfumed with myrrh and frankincense
> With all powders of the merchant? (3:6)

After her having achieved perfection in morals and in the ability to distinguish truth from falsehood, he commenced mentioning here the perfection of the intellect through the mathematical sciences because they precede the other sciences in order, continuing through his statement, *until the day breathe* (4:6). This accords with each of the explanations which we made in the previous comment[26] because according to each of those explanations the intellect had not achieved perfection in this science in the previous section.[27]

He commenced and said, indicating the perfection of apprehension to be had in the mathematical sciences, *Who is this that cometh up out of the wilderness*—it being a place which cannot be traversed—since not much effort is needed to arrive at these first premises.[28] He said that she *cometh up out of the wilderness directly*[29] *like pillars of smoke* because only in this science will order and equilibrium be found in the study of most of it, going directly from prior to posterior. Thus, in most of it will be found absolute demonstrations.[30] He said *perfumed with myrrh and frankincense, with all powders of the merchant* because there is to found in this science that which comes very close to physics,[31] and it also directs one to astronomy, and also wonderfully directs one to metaphysics, as has been made clear in *Wars of the Lord*[32] and in the *Almagest.*[33]

> Behold, it is the litter of Solomon
> Threescore mighty men are about it
> Of the mighty men of Israel (3:7)

He said that the litter is Solomon's when he conjoins with his beloved in order to proceed toward perfection in this desired science,[34] and *about it* were prepared a large number of guides which steer one to equilibrium and preserve one from error so that one[35] [may] not suffer from anything, and thus they were called *mighty men of Israel.* He said *threescore* by way of example, since it is a complete number. Thus, in some places, it is made the end of counting by tens.[36]

He said this because here[37] part of this science requires much help from the senses for repetition. This part is astronomy, which is the fruit of the mathematical sciences and their purpose.[38] Further, the making of the observations which steer one to what is correct in it has elements of difficulty; this was unknown to[39] the ancients, as was mentioned in the *Almagest.*[40] For this reason, he anticipated and said that the guards were already prepared *about* Solomon's litter, as already mentioned, that is, that he already prepared the arrangements and the ways which will steer him to that which is correct in this science and preserve him from error.

> They all handle the sword
> And are expert in war
> Every man hath his sword upon his thigh
> Because of dread in the night (3:8)

He told, concerning these guards, that they *are expert in war,* negating the mistakes which occur in research in this science, saying that they had anticipated and prepared for themselves weapons with which these mistakes which occur in this science could be negated before they occur. This is the proper approach,[41] since it is not proper that a person seek two things at the same time, that is, the negation of error and the way in which it is to be negated. Rather, of necessity first the ways in general in which error be removed from this science[42] should be known to the scientist; afterwards, he can strive to negate them should they occur. Aristotle already mentioned this matter indirectly[43] in *Metaphysics* I.[44]

He said *because of dread in the night* in order to indicate that the cause because of which he was forced to prepare these guards is his fear of mistakes, which are caused by our darkness and ignorance in those subjects of study.[45]

> King Solomon made himself a palanquin
> Of the wood of Lebanon (3:9)
> He made the pillars thereof of silver
> The top thereof of gold
> The seat of it of purple
> The inside thereof being inlaid with love
> From the daughters of Jerusalem (3:10)

It is known that *a palanquin* is a special place for a bridal canopy, wherein the groom begins to conjoin with the bride. He said that he built it strongly and beautifully: this building was made *of the wood of Lebanon; he made the pillars thereof of silver, the top thereof of gold,* and *the seat of it of purple,* so that it be perfectly constructed and *the inside thereof being inlaid with love from the daughters of Jerusalem,* they being the faculties of the soul collectively which all subordinate themselves to the service of the intellect in this subject of study, and do it from love and wondrous longing. That is why he is called *king* here.

He said of this building that it was made *of the wood of Lebanon* to draw attention to the fact that the order of this building is ordered by the intellect, as we explained at the beginning of this commentary.[46]

This building, according to what I think, is an allegory for the pursuing of the paths and arrangements according to which one who engages in this craft ought to pursue his research. Following this one ought to investigate what is necessary for achieving knowledge according to those paths and arrangements in each subject of inquiry. To indicate that this science has many parts, the last of which is worthier than those which precede it because of its being closer to physics, he first mentioned *silver,* after it *gold,* and after it *purple.*[47]

> Go forth
> O ye daughters of Zion
> And gaze upon King Solomon
> Even upon the crown wherewith his mother hath crowned him
> In the day of his espousals
> And in the day of the gladness of his heart (3 : 11)

We have already stated that he allegorically compared the faculties of the soul in their generality to *the daughters of Jerusalem* (1 : 5).[48] For this reason he allegorically compares those faculties of the soul which have a stronger relation to the intellect to the *daughters of Zion* because the house of the king is found there and that is the choicest of all places in Jerusalem, for there is the temple.

By *the crown wherewith his mother hath crowned him* he means the soul generally,[49] for it is the mother of each of its faculties and he meant by this it causes him to reign over the rest of its faculties.[50] We can possibly say that he called his female beloved *his mother* from the aspect of his nursing from her breasts; this is because the imaginative forms, in a certain fashion, have the status of agent vis-à-vis the apprehension of the intellect, as above.[51] But the first explanation seems more correct to us.

He said, *in the day of his espousals,* because it is the day of his conjunction with his beloved.

He said, *and in the day of the gladness of his heart* because the happiness of the intellect and its pleasures are its perfection through the intelligibles.

> Behold, thou art fair, my love, behold, thou art fair
> Thine eyes are as doves behind thy veil
> thy hair is as a flock of goats
> That trail down from Mount Gilead (4 : 1)

He began recounting her beauty, which brings him to desire her. He recounted with this the above-mentioned assistance from the mathematical sciences for this apprehension, and thus some of the aspects of her beauty which he mentioned accord with the allegory alone and some accord with the intended meaning of the allegory. He said *thine eyes are as doves* according to

the allegory alone to indicate her beauty. He said *behind thy veil* to indicate
her adornment and her modesty because a veil is a mask which she places
on her face, her eyes being seen through the mask. So also, he said that her
temple appeared like *a pomegranate split open* (4:3); this is all according to
the allegory.

According to me, however, what he said about her hair relates to the intended meaning of the allegory, because it is not of the nature of beautiful
hair in a woman to be praised in this fashion. So, too, concerning what he
said about her teeth.[52] The allegorical aspect of this is that the strands of hair
of *goats* which *trail down from Mount Gilead* are conjoined and lie altogether one upon the other. It may be said thus about those places in which
repetition from the senses is necessary in these mathematical sciences, as is
the case with astronomy, which needs great repetition from the senses.[53] That
which she prepared for him from this repetition is a repetition which is consistent and conjoined one with the other and is thus appropriate for reaching
the intended end.[54] I think that this was also his intention with respect to his
descriptions of her eyes and teeth, as we will explain below.[55] By specifying
hair and teeth from among her other parts, he hinted at this consistent repetition, because there is nothing among animals so emphasized and multiplied
as this abundance of hair and teeth; this is self-evidently clear.

> Thy teeth are like a flock of ewes all shaped up
> Which are come up from the washing
> Whereof all are paired
> And none faileth among them (4:2)

Below he mentioned the characteristic of the *flock of ewes* (6:6)[56] which
are *all shaped up,* that is, which have one size and march with one step. He
said *which are come up from the washing* to indicate their beauty. By *whereof
all are paired* he means that their repetition is consistent. By *and none faileth
among them* he means that not one of them will fail to bring forth fruit.[57]
By this he indicates that these imaginative forms which she prepares for his
knowledge all have consistent repetition and bear fruit. This must be said because not every repetition which comes from the senses in a subject investigated by a science causes one to acquire knowledge which bears fruit in that
science; this is self-evidently clear.

Perhaps we can say that *whereof all are paired and none faileth among them* means that every one of these imaginative forms has one imaginative form which conjoins with it, and not one of them is single and alone. Or, by *faileth* he means "deficient," that is, that not one of them is missing any virtue, but that they all are consistent together. All come to the same thing, whichever of these explanations is chosen.

> Thy lips are like a thread of scarlet
> And thy mouth is comely
> Thy temples are like a pomegranate split open
> Behind thy veil (4:3)

This entire verse, according to me, indicates her beauty, which brings him to desire her; it accords with the allegory alone.

> Thy neck is like the tower of David
> Builded with turrets
> Whereon there hang a thousand shields
> All the armour of the mighty men (4:4)

This entire verse accords with the intended meaning of the allegory alone. Its meaning is that what she produced for him in this science is as strong as it can be, like *the tower of David* which is *builded with turrets* for strength. Thus, *whereon there hang a thousand shields, all the armour of the mighty men,* and therefore he fears no disputant or confuser. This is something which is clear concerning the mathematical sciences, that is, that no mistake at all can befall concerning the truth produced by them through mathematical demonstrations.

> Thy two breasts are like two fawns
> That are twins of a gazelle
> Which feed among the lilies (4:5)

Since breasts serve to nurse he compared that which emanates to breasts. He allegorically compared her to *two fawns that are twins of a gazelle* because of their fleetness. He said this because of her diligence to prepare for him what he needs from her in these sciences. His statement *which feed among the lilies* is clear on the basis of what we said in our introduction.[58] This verse accords with the allegory alone.[59]

He began praising her from her head and descended step by step to her breasts since in this science one always proceeds from the prior to the posterior when we judge the existence of one thing because of the existence of another thing. This is clear. On the whole, few things escape this.[60]

It might be thought that the opposite obtains in astronomy. For we judge the shapes[61] of the heavenly bodies and their number from the[ir] motions,[62] but when the matter is examined it will be seen that in it, too, we proceed from the prior to the posterior. This is so because the form of every effect[63] necessary to produce its effect is posterior to that effect. For example, the assimilation of the visual image by the eye[64] is posterior to the visual image, for this shape exists for the sake of the visual image.[65] When we say that the heavenly bodies have a certain characteristic because of their effects, as is clear to those who carefully study this issue, it is because knowledge of their shapes is posterior to their motions. Similarly, whoever determines the spherical shape of the moon by a demonstration from the increasing and diminishing of the light of the moon has taken the increase and diminution of its light as prior to its spherical shape, because determining its shape in this fashion is in order to account for the change in the light proceeding from it, and this is a reason to strive to attain it, because its effects vary in this sublunary world in this way.[66] However, one who determines the arrangement of motions in general from the motions specific to them is like one who understands on the basis of our sensing concerning one whole that is greater than the part that the whole is always greater than the part, because it is necessary that we acquire from particulars, which we understand from sense-perception, all the premises that we acquire.[67]

> Until the day breathe
> And the shadows flee away
> I will get me to the mountain of myrrh
> And to the hill of frankincense (4:6)

After telling what she prepared for him from the mathematical sciences, these sciences not being intended for themselves but are intended in order to direct one to physics and metaphysics, the intellect said that since the darkness of the night—an allegory for ignorance—was beginning to pass, he would strive to pursue research in physics, and since he would need in the pursuit of this science much assistance from his beloved, the intellect began to draw her attention to this, asking for her assistance which he needed.[68]

It has already been made clear why this science, that is, physics, was related to one mountain and a particular spice.[69]

> Thou art all fair, my love
> And there is no spot in thee (4:7)

He said, praising her for what she presented to him from the mathematical sciences, that she is entirely *fair,* without *spot* or deficiency. This indeed is possible with those sciences because of their limited entanglement with matter.

PART FIVE

4:8 – 8:4

From the beginning of the thirteenth paragraph until *Who is this who cometh up from the wilderness, leaning upon her beloved?* (8:5), he indicates the attainment of physics in the order appropriate to it.

Come with me from Lebanon, my bride
With me from Lebanon
Look from the top of Amana, from the top of Senir and Hermon
From the lions' dens
From the mountains of the leopards (4:8)

By *Lebanon,* he hinted at the intellect, as we explained in the introduction to this commentary,[1] and meant that the beginning of the investigation[2] using the senses in this craft must come from the intellect because of the difficulty in attaining those things which must be apprehended from the senses.[3] He called her *bride* because this is the beginning of his joining together with her in an essentially fruitful joining. This is not the case with respect to the mathematical sciences. This is clear to anyone who has deeply researched the matter of the faculties of the soul. We have spoken on this at length in our commentary to *On the Soul*[4] and in *Wars of the Lord;*[5] this is not the place for this investigation.

Since the way of research in this science is to study first the general characteristics of mutable entities insofar as they are mutable, these being the remote principles of natural matters, for example, the remote mover, and the remote matter, and their general attributes; and since these are the loci of danger in the study of this science because mistakes which occur concerning principles are potentially the cause of mistakes in that which comes after these principles, he mentioned these principles first and compared them to the generalities by virtue of which he will get to the mountain called *Amana.*

The top of Senir and Hermon is also one mountain; some men called it *Senir* and some *Hermon,* as is mentioned in the Torah.[6] He called these mountains *the mountains of the leopards* and *the lions' dens* because of the danger involved if a mistake occurs with respect to them, as we explained.[7]

By *top of Amana* he hinted at the first mover, from which are emanated these natural matters as the waters of Amana emanate from *the top of Amana;* further, *Amana* indicates truth;[8] further, the First Mover is the cause of truth of every being other than himself for he is the cause of the existence of everything, and that which makes another thing exist is the cause of its being true.[9] The First Mover, however, has no cause which makes it exist and thus is true in and of itself. This is so because the degree of things with respect to truth is the degree of their existence. This has already been explained in *Metaphysics* 1.[10]

By *from the top of Senir and Hermon* he hinted at the remote matter, for these two principles alone[11] can be investigated in physics, as was made clear in *Physics* 2 and *Metaphysics* 3.[12] Thus, he called it *Hermon* to indicate the privation attaching to it.[13] He did not call it *the top of Hermon* alone so as not to mislead us by his allegory into thinking that the privation is the first matter,[14] as some of the ancients thought, bringing them to deny the existence of generation and sensible things.[15] On the other hand, he said *top of Senir* to indicate that it is something, even though privation attaches to it. But first he mentioned the remote mover, even though we arrive at our knowledge of it last, since the agent precedes matter.

> Thou hast ravished my heart, my sister, my bride
> Thou hast ravished my heart with one of thine eyes
> With one bead of thy necklace (4:9)

He said to her that his longing for her had grown because of the *one of* her eyes with which she had examined those things which she produced for him in the mathematical sciences.[16] This also is the meaning of his statement *with one bead of thy necklace* because the neck is doubled,[17] and it was the custom there to put one bead on each of its sides. In truth, he said this for two reasons: the first concerning that in which what is prior according to the senses is prior in nature, as is the case with most of the mathematical sciences; the second, the opposite of this. Thus he said that the greatness of his longing for her is proportionate to what she produced for him in this fashion;

that is, that which is prior for him according to the senses is prior according to nature.[18]

> How fair is thy love, my sister, my bride
> How much better is thy love than wine
> And the smell of thine ointments than all manner of spices (4:10)

He said, as one hyperbolizing concerning her, that none of the physical pleasures are as pleasant as the degree of that which she produced for him, because it is more pleasant *than wine*. The *smell* of what she produces for him from posterior things—as when a man concludes from the presence of a fragrance that there exists a source of the fragrance—is more pleasant than *all manner of spices*.

> Thy lips, O my bride, drop honey
> Honey and milk are under thy tongue
> And the smell of thy garments is like the smell of Lebanon (4:11)

He allegorically compared what she emanates to him, because of its pleasantness and sweetness, to *drop[ping] honey,* and to *honey* and to *milk*. He said that the smell of her dress is *like the smell of Lebanon* to indicate that what she produces for him from among the posterior things is absolutely correct[19] and beautiful, as if this ordering were ordered by the intellect itself; the truth is that it is the intellect which guides her to this.[20]

> A garden shut up is my sister, my bride
> A spring shut up, a fountain sealed (4:12)

He said to her that the *garden* which he gave her to work and to keep until she gives him its fruit is *shut up,* that is, that it has no gate by which he can enter it, and that the *fountain* which waters the *garden* is still blocked— it being the emanation of the Active Intellect, as it says, *And a river went out of Eden to water the garden* (Gen. 2:10).[21] This is the meaning of their statement "that no eye has ever seen it,"[22] since it was free of matter, as was made clear in *On the Soul*.[23] It is clear that the intellect cannot apprehend anything of this matter if there was no prior sense apprehension of it—by God!—unless it be by some wonder and very rarely, as is the case with prophecy, true dreams, and divination.[24] Even with respect to them there is room to inves-

tigate whether there is need of sense observation in some respect, as Averroës
remarked in his *Epitome of* Parva Naturalia,[25] and whether this form of emanation is possible with respect to speculative matters; we have already spoken
of this in our commentary on Averroës' *Epitome*.[26] However the case may
be, the natural ordering with respect to this, and that is what usually happens, is that that which is taken from sense first is, through repetition, made
by the intellect into a judgment. If the second form of emanation occurs with
respect to these speculative matters, it does not depend upon our choice and
striving.[27]

> Thy shoots are a park of pomegranates
> With precious fruits
> Henna with spikenard plants (4:13)
> Spikenard and saffron, calamus and cinnamon
> With all trees of frankincense
> Myrrh and aloes
> With all the chief spices (4:14)

These two verses come to indicate[28] the generality in these matters concerning which he asks of her first, in that they indicate generality and the
mixing of thing with thing. Thus he said, *a park of pomegranates with precious fruits, henna with spikenard plants . . . with all trees of frankincense . . .
with all the chief spices;* he further said that that which she can provide him
concerning these general matters is very good and *bears fruit* (Gen. 1:11,
etc.) for the intellect when mixed with the sweetness of these things for the
senses.[29]

> Thou art a fountain of gardens
> A well of living waters
> And flowing streams from Lebanon (4:15)

He said that what she emanates upon him is very good to water the *gardens* so that they bear fruit and that that *well* is *a well of living waters, whose
waters fail not* (Isa. 58:11). His statement *and flowing streams from Lebanon* means, however, that she is well prepared for this emanation and well
ordered by the intellect. By this he indicates continuance and continued existence; since waters which originate in the mountains are more constant because of the combination there of the causes of the generation of water, as

has been explained in the *Meteorology*.[30] It is as if he said that she is prepared to emanate upon him what he needs concerning this science without doubts so that he may achieve perfection in it.

> Awake, O north wind and come thou south
> Blow upon my garden
> That the spices thereof may flow out
> Let my beloved come into his garden
> And eat his precious fruits (4:16)

This verse accords with both the allegory and its intended meaning. It accords with the allegory in that the north wind greatly obstructs the growth of plants because of its cold and dryness, whereas the south wind helps the growth of plants due to its warmth and humidity.[31] It is as if he said, "Arouse yourself, O north wind, and turn and come, O south wind, *blow upon my garden that the spices thereof may flow out.*"

Its accord with the intended meaning of the allegory lies in the fact that the *north* is left and the *south* is right,[32] and he said this in order to remove that which might cause mistakes concerning these principles and that which causes one to veer from the path of truth, and will bring that which will necessitate the finding of the truth, and that is what is intended.[33] He did not speak in these terms concerning the mathematical sciences because of the rarity of finding these mistakes among them. She responded to him and said that she had already prepared for him what he asked of her, and therefore she said, *Let my beloved come into his garden,* for he will already find the gate which was closed open,[34] so that he will be able to eat its *precious fruits* (4:13) from what the Active Intellect will emanate upon him.

> I am come into my garden, my sister, my bride
> I have gathered my myrrh with my spice
> I have eaten my honeycomb with my honey
> I have drunk my wine with my milk
> Eat, O friends
> Drink, yea, drink abundantly, O beloved (5:1)

He responded to her that he had already done what he had intended to do, it being the apprehension of some of these principles and the general attributes of mutable existent things insofar as they are mutable, since the ap-

prehension of these necessarily precedes in nature the apprehension of the
remote mover, as will have become clear to anyone who has studied physics.
He made reference to the matter of his apprehension in language which indicates intermingling and generality because of the general nature of these
apprehensions, and for this reason said *my myrrh with my spice . . . with my
honey . . . with my milk.*[35] Indicating the pleasantness of what he had already
apprehended in this subject of inquiry, he said that the *friends* and *beloved*
who can do this should eat with him; these are those who have intellect.
Moreover, he said this further to indicate the natural desire of one who has
apprehended part of this science to emanate it upon others.[36] It is as if this
were one of the things which direct one to the acquisition of this apprehension, despite the difficulties in it which led all the ancient philosophers whose
works were known to Aristotle to err in it, as is mentioned in *Physics* 1 and
Metaphysics 2.[37] This is the error which they had concerning this principle.

> I sleep, but my heart waketh
> Hark! My beloved knocketh
> Open to me, my sister, my love, my undefiled
> For my head is filled with dew
> My locks with the drops of the night (5:2)

In that he is now investigating the apprehension of the first mover, concerning which there is tremendous difficulty, as has already been made clear;
and in that this apprehension and those similar to it involve the investigation
of deep things in physics, with respect to which there are many impediments,
because of the delicacy of these apprehensions themselves and because of the
difficulty of apprehending what we need of them with the senses, because of
its great dependence on the senses before we are able to take from it premises
useful for those investigations concerning everything which must be clarified
through them, it will thus happen to he who conducts research in these matters that when he gets close to apprehending the subject of inquiry, some of
the information which he needs from sense observation will be beyond his
reach, and the subject of inquiry will be lost to him.[38] He will also succumb
to inability because of the difficulty of the matters under investigation; the
truth will at one time peek [39] out at him and at another time become invisible.
Thus, one who studies the physical sciences must fulfill many conditions, as
the sages said.[40]

This passage comes to indicate these impediments and to instruct one to strive to remove them according to one's ability. This will indeed occur when the faculties of the soul wonderfully subordinate themselves to the intellect to the extent that its activity is not restrained at all because of them. This is as difficult as can be. He mentioned first these impediments and made clear that they occur with respect to the female lover and with respect to the male lover only from the aspect of the greatness of his cleaving to matter.[41] Therefore this female lover said that even though her heart's desire[42] is to satisfy her beloved's desire as much as possible, she was *sleep[ing]* because of the depth of these matters and the aspects of difficulty concerning what she has to prepare for the intellect in this science so that her beloved had to call her, but she was too lazy to get up and open the gate for him.

At his point he called her *my undefiled* because of the necessity that she conjoin with him continuously so that she [may] be able to prepare for him what he needs in each subject of inquiry and that all of her preparation be in his service.[43]

His saying *for my head is filled with dew, my locks with the drops of the night* accords with both the allegory and its intended meaning. According to the allegory, he is rushing her to open the gate so that the falling *dew* and *drops* [may] not hurt him.[44] According to the intended meaning of the allegory, he says to her that he has already begun to receive the emanation of the Active Intellect concerning what he was investigating, and he needs help from her to perfect that which was beyond his reach because she had not prepared for him that which would direct him to it.

> I have put off my coat
> How shall I put it on?
> I have washed my feet
> How shall I defile them? (5 : 3)

This verse accords with the intended meaning of the allegory and comes to indicate the laziness which she necessarily has with respect to doing what her beloved requested of her; this laziness is a consequence of the difficulty of acquiring what she needs for him from the senses; and because she needs her beloved for this, that is, that he direct her to what he needs from her and how she may be perfected so that she prepare for him what he needs from her in that subject of inquiry.[45]

My beloved put in his hand by the hole of the door
And my inmost parts were moved for him (5:4)

She said that when he *put in his hand by the hole of the door,* that being
the small entryway which he has in this inquiry, helping her and directing her
so that she [may] perfect the preparation of what he needs from the senses,
her heart was moved *for him* due to the strength of her longing to satisfy his
desire. We have interpreted *my inmost parts* according to *yea, thy Torah is in
my inmost parts* (Ps. 40:9), the meaning of which is "heart." [46]

I rose up to open to my beloved
And my hands dropped with myrrh,
And my fingers with flowing myrrh
Upon the handles of the bar (5:5)

She said that she rose to open for her beloved, that is, that she had already
prepared for him what he needed in this inquiry; this is what she meant by
and my hands dropped with myrrh, and my fingers with flowing myrrh.

I opened to my beloved
But my beloved had turned away and was gone
My soul went out when he spoke
I sought him but I could not find him
I called him but he gave me no answer (5:6)

She said that even though she had already opened the gate for him, her
beloved turned and passed her because [47] the bodily faculties [48] hid from him
what had been previously apprehended by him in this inquiry. Because of the
depth of the matter itself and the difficulty encountered by the faculties of the
soul in appropriately subordinating themselves to the intellect with respect
to these apprehensions, this will necessarily occur to him. [49]

Her saying *my soul went out when he spoke* means, I think, that *when he
spoke* to her what he did, calling her to open for him, her great longing to
satisfy his desire was aroused; therefore her soul *went out* to wander and to
seek here and there to see if she could find him.

The watchmen that go about the city found me
They smote me, they wounded me

> The keepers of the walls
> Took my mantle from me (5:7)

It has already been stated above[50] who these watchmen who smote and wounded her are—when the senses are engaged in their activities, her activity is rendered impossible, as has been made clear in *On the Soul*.[51] These smitings and woundings impede her from what she intends, and they are also the impediments of the intellect since in that the soul is one it cannot use these two activities together.[52] This is the meaning of her statement they *took my mantle from me* since they removed the mantle and the ornament with which she decorated herself in order to conjoin with her beloved.

> I adjure you, O daughters of Jerusalem
> If ye find my beloved
> What will ye tell him?
> That I am love-sick (5:8)

She said this to stimulate[53] herself to try with all her strength properly to subordinate all the faculties of the soul to the intellect according to the subject of its current investigation; she said to them *that I am love-sick* because of the strength of her longing to satisfy the desire of her beloved.

> What is thy beloved more than another beloved
> O, thou fairest among women?
> What is thy beloved more than another beloved
> That thou dost so adjure us? (5:9)

All this accords with the intended meaning of the allegory, recounting his praises and the greatness of his perfection, which is so great that all the faculties of the soul subordinate themselves to him absolutely because of their love for him.

> My beloved is white and ruddy
> Pre-eminent above ten thousand (5:10)

This entirely accords with the allegory.[54] She said that he *is white and ruddy* allegorically to indicate his beauty. Her saying *preeminent above ten thousand,* however, is according to both the allegory and the intended meaning. According to the allegory it indicates his greatness in that he is like a great king around whom many people gather. Its intention according to the intended meaning is that the group which congregates about him and apprehends him is something more wonderful than *ten thousand,* because the plural is without end.[55]

> His head is as the most fine gold
> His locks are curled
> And black as a raven (5:11)

This verse indicates his beauty and perfection and accords with the allegory alone.

> His eyes are like doves beside the water-brooks
> Washed with milk
> And fitly set (5:12)

This verse accords with both the allegory and its intended meaning. According to the allegory it indicates their beauty because the eyes of doves which are *beside the water-brooks* are beautiful because water is among those things which enhance the beauty of organs of vision and are appropriate to their nature because vision takes place through the medium of watery liquid, it being the vitreous liquid, and through the medium of the other liquids in the eye; also, washing them in milk enhances their beauty and improves vision.

By *and fitly set* he means their perfection: they neither bulge out nor are they sunken more than is fitting. This makes the organ more beautiful and its vision keen, as was made clear in *On Animals.*[56]

According to the intended meaning of the allegory, he makes reference to the "eyes of the intellect," which are absolutely perfected to apprehend what it apprehends, and this is because all of these things, as we noted, help toward good vision.[57]

> His cheeks are as a bed of spices
> As banks of sweet herbs
> His lips are as lilies
> Dropping with flowing myrrh (5:13)

Since the cheeks and lips are used for the ingestion of nourishment, he compared that by which the intellect receives this emanation to *a bed of spices* in a garden in which grow a variety of spices from which are made distilled potions and to the *lilies* which *drop with flowing myrrh,* all this to indicate his preparation to receive the intelligibles. It is possible that the meaning intended by *his lips are as lilies dropping with flowing myrrh* is that in *his lips* will always be found the *lilies* which are in potential the intelligibles toward which he intends, and thus it says *dropping with flowing myrrh.* The allegorical aspect of this is clear from what was said above at the beginning of the commentary.[58]

> His hands are as rods of gold
> Set with beryl
> His body is as polished ivory
> Overlaid with sapphires (5:14)

In that intellect is divided into the speculative and the practical, as was made clear in *On the Soul,*[59] she came to praise him in this verse concerning each of these activities.[60] *His hands* hints at the practical intellect since the hands are the most distinctive and most perfected of the organs for the accomplishment of all the practical arts. She said by way of allegory that he is endowed with this faculty in an absolutely beautiful way and compared them[61] to the beauty of *rods of gold* which are *set with beryl. His body*[62]— it is his heart—hints at the speculative intellect, and she said by way of allegory that he was endowed with this part in an absolutely beautiful way. She also compared these faculties with things which become corrupted[63] only with great difficulty[64] to indicate the everlastingness of the intellect.

> His legs are as pillars of marble
> Set upon sockets of fine gold
> His aspect is like Lebanon
> Excellent as the cedars (5:15)

Because the body's ability to stand depends upon the legs, as a building leans upon its pillars, she said, indicating the existence of these pillars and foundations[65] through which he exists, which pillars and foundations refer to the Active Intellect—through which he will become everlasting[66]—that they are like *pillars of marble* which are *set upon sockets of fine gold,* which are things of great endurance. She said, indicating his beauty and the elevated degree of his soul, that *his aspect is like Lebanon,* it being the temple which is of perfect beauty, and that his soul had a very high degree. Or, perhaps the reference here was to *the forest of Lebanon* (1 Kings 7:2), where there were great and very choice trees. In any event, her saying *excellent as the cedars* means that just as the cedars are distinguished from other trees by their beauty and great size, so is he distinguished from the other faculties of the soul.

> His mouth is most sweet
> Yea, he is altogether lovely
> This is my beloved and this is my friend
> O daughters of Jerusalem (5:16)

You ought to know that the step-by-step account of her beloved's praises, descending by degrees from his head, indicated that his apprehension went from prior to posterior. Since here[67] the intellect has another way of apprehending, that is, going from the posterior to the prior, as is the case with most of physics, which it is her concern for him to acquire now, she said that what the intellect apprehends in this fashion is perfectly sweet and pleasant. She allegorically compared this apprehension to a mouth because through the mouth one moves from taste to knowledge of the thing tasted. Perhaps the meaning of her saying *his mouth is most sweet* is that in his mouth will be found the sweetest and most pleasant food, since the pleasantness of the intelligibles is most wondrous. She said *he is altogether lovely,* meaning that there is nothing about him which is not very precious and desirable and thus all the faculties of the soul ought to cherish him and seek to serve him.

> Whither is thy beloved gone
> O thou fairest among women?
> Whither hath thy beloved turned him
> That we may seek him with thee? (6:1)

This accords with the intended meaning of the allegory,[68] indicating that all of the faculties of the soul perfectly subordinated themselves to the service of the intellect, and thus they all longed to seek him.

My beloved is gone down to his garden
To the beds of spices
To feed in the gardens
And to gather lilies (6:2)

She said that her beloved *is gone down* to work in his garden, to bring the *spices* in him [69] potentially to actuality, they being the intelligibles. Thus, he strove *to feed in* other *gardens* in order *to gather lilies* from them, they [70] being that which he acquires from the senses concerning this issue which he now strives to apprehend, that is, the first mover. This apprehension is acquired by way of the senses, the imagination, and the faculty of memory, and thus he needs to be assisted by all the faculties of the soul together, striving mightily not to impede him from his activity.

I am my beloved's and my beloved is mine
That feedeth among the lilies (6:3)

It has been stated above [71] that before this the intellect was obstructed from making these apprehensions because of two things: first, because of the difficulties in making his female beloved his own, that is, her difficulty in preparing what he needs for his apprehension; second, the difficulties in making him hers, since the bodily faculties hide the truth from him after he begins to look at it, since the necessary isolation of the intellect from the other faculties of the soul [72] with respect to these apprehensions involves tremendous difficulties. Because of this she mentioned now that all of the impediments which obstruct her becoming his and his becoming hers have already been removed because its reason [73] was, as above, the failure of the faculties of the soul perfectly to subordinate themselves to the intellect as is needed in this apprehension.

She called him *that feedeth among the lilies* because from the perspective of his feeding *among the lilies* he needs her. The allegorical aspect of this is clear, as above. [74]

Thou art beautiful, O my love, as Tirsah
Comely as Jerusalem
Terrible as an army with banners (6:4)

After these impediments had been removed from him, and his beloved prepared for him what he needs from the senses concerning the question under investigation, he now began to praise her with respect to these matters. He said that she was very beautiful because the faculties of the soul all together[75] had already perfectly ornamented themselves. He allegorically compared her to *Tirsah,* which was so beautiful a city that it became a royal city, as was recounted in Kings,[76] and so it is with Jerusalem. His saying *terrible as an army with banners,* however, indicates that what she acquires for him,[77] even if it is particular,[78] is very spiritual, since many of its material attributes had been abstracted from it, in particular what she takes for him from the faculty of memory.[79] Therefore, he said that she was *comely* like the intellectual faculties which apprehend multiplicity and the infinite aggregate,[80] not that she was terrible in this respect; but she has a marvelous degree of spirituality, as was made clear in *Parva Naturalia.*[81]

It is possible to say that the meaning of his statement *terrible as an army with banners* is that she is as terrible as the legions carrying banners, that is, those which have a flag and leader. This is because they all agree on one intention, and thus it is a most terrible legion. So it is with the other faculties of the soul, for the other faculties of the soul have already ornamented themselves appropriately and subordinated themselves to the service of the intellect, and thus they are all jointly agreed on this activity which this female beloved intends. This last explanation is most fitting according to my opinion.

> Turn away thine eyes from me
> For they have overcome me
> Thy hair is as a flock of goats
> That trail down from Gilead (6:5)
> Thy teeth are like a flock of ewes
> Which are come up from the washing
> Whereof all are paired
> And none faileth among them (6:6)

He said this to indicate the strength of his longing for her, as if he said that the beauty of her eyes amazes him and adds to his longing for her. He recounted her praises with respect to what she had prepared for him concerning this question and in general with respect to what she had prepared for him concerning the apprehension of the prime matter and the first mover and the general attributes of mutable existents insofar as they are mutable. For this reason he said, *thy hair is as a flock of goats that trail down from Gilead, thy teeth are like a flock of ewes, etc.* I mean, using the senses, she had already prepared for him those premises which are necessary for these investigations with consistent and appropriate repetition. The allegorical aspect of this has been made clear above.

> Thy temples are like a pomegranate split open
> Behind thy veil (6:7)

This verse accords with the allegory alone, indicating her beauty and modesty. The ordering of her praises in this place is different from the previous one; he did not move in a step-by-step fashion, ordering her praises below her head, as he did in the previous apprehension,[82] because in this apprehension one moves—in some fashion—from the prior, for example,[83] the study of physics.[84] This is so because that which is investigated first is prior in some fashion to that which is investigated later, for the general things[85] investigated first are prior to the specific things, whether it be material priority, as is the case with the remote matter, or priority by way of efficient cause, formal cause, and final cause as is the case with the remote mover, as has been made clear in the *Metaphysics*.[86] His praises of her did not pass below her head since movement in this science is not from prior to posterior, that is, that one investigates in it each of the actually existent, natural,[87] specific things, but rather the movement toward apprehending them is through the sense apprehension of things posterior to them, they being the accidents and attributes, as will be explained below.

> There are threescore queens
> And fourscore concubines
> And maidens without number (6:8)

You ought to know that the faculties of the soul in general are of three sorts: a primary kind; a kind which prepares for it[88] and is primary in some respect; and a kind which is neither primary nor preparatory. It is clear that the number of faculties of the soul is very great, what with each organ having its own specific activity, whether it be some movement, or nourishment, growth, attraction, storage, digestion, evacuation, and others of the abilities[89] which cannot be missing from any of the organs, unless it be by reason of illness or birth defect.[90] In that each of these activities, abilities, and movements is ordered by a particular faculty of the soul, the number of faculties of the soul will without a doubt be very great; this is clear to anyone who has studied anatomy even a little.[91] This is so because there are many muscles and each has many different movements. In general, each of these things has a specific instrument and a specific faculty of the soul, "since one angel does not perform two missions,"[92] that is, in that each is one, only one activity is ordered by it, for were this possible,[93] one matter could have more than one form, which is clearly absurd.

Examples of the preparatory kind of these faculties include the mouth and stomach, which prepare nourishment for the liver so that it can absorb it and turn it into blood. The liver also prepares in a certain fashion, since it is that whereby some of the blood is sent to the heart, there to be perfected and from thence to be sent to the other organs by way of the arteries, nerves, and muscles, this activity being perfected through them, as the mouth and stomach prepare for the liver. They[94] also prepare after a fashion, for they are the way whereby the element of air is conveyed to those organs which it reaches.

Examples of those which are primary in some fashion include the heart and the liver in that they send part of the blood to the organs without perfecting it in the heart, and the brain, spinal cord, and the nerve. This is true even though the absolutely primary is one alone, it being the heart, as was made clear in *On Animals*.[95] Despite this, these and things like them have some primariness.

Similarly, the apprehending faculties are either primary or prepare for the primaries. In general, each faculty produces an activity in one organ other than its subject, whether it be primary or preparatory. The last forces in each organ, from which are ordered no activities beyond themselves, are neither primary nor preparatory. It is clear that there are many primary forces, more preparatory forces, and even more last forces, they being neither primary nor preparatory.

He allegorically compared the primary forces to *queens* since they have a certain primariness but are subordinate to one head, he being the king, the preparatory forces to *concubines* because the concubine serves but has some primariness. Those forces which are neither primary nor preparatory he called *maidens* since maidens have no primariness in any fashion. He says that the number of forces which are *queens* is great, the number of forces which are *concubines* is greater, and the *maidens* are so multitudinous that, because of the difficulty of counting them, they are without limit.

> My dove, my undefiled, is but one
> She is the only one of her mother
> She is the choice one of her that bore her
> The daughters saw her, and called her happy
> Yea, the queens and the concubines, and they praised her (6 : 9)

He said, praising his beloved, that she is only *one,* there is no multiplicity in her. This is so because among the other forces one finds what has multiplicity in a certain way, as the nourishing force is in each limb in a manner which distinguishes it from similar matters. This faculty of the soul which stands to the intellect in the relation of matter is one, however; there is no multiplicity in it. It is closer to[96] form and perfection than all the other faculties of the soul but the intellect. Thus its says that she *is the choice one of her that bore her,* she being the soul, and that the other faculties of the soul, these being the *maidens*[97] (6 : 8), and the *queens,* and the *concubines, praised her* and *called her happy.*

> Who is she that looketh forth as the dawn
> Fair as the moon
> Clear as the sun
> Terrible as an army with banners? (6 : 10)

After perfecting the apprehension concerning things which in their generality pertain to mutable existents as such, he began to praise his beloved for that which she prepares for him concerning his research into specific natural things, for such research involves great wonder and difficulty. Progress in understanding them depends upon things posterior to them, and they are attributes and accidents.[98]

This allegory relates to things which are similar to the parts since we already understand their essence and nature from their taste, appearance, and fragrance, and their becoming congealed due to the heat or cold, and their becoming melted due to the cold or heat, and others of their attributes and accidents as some of this was made clear in *Meteorology* 4,[99] and some in the *Parva Naturalia*[100] and some in the books of medicine.

This allegory relates to creatures having souls, for we infer[101] from the activities the essence of the faculties from which are ordered these activities, and not from the activities themselves alone, but from the things concerning which the activities take place, since they are better known than the activities. For example, we infer from the food the faculty of nourishment, from perceived things perception, from the intelligible to the intellect, as was made clear in *On the Soul* 1.[102] It was made clear there the necessity which forces research in these matters to be carried out in this fashion, and afterwards the matter returns upon itself, as was made clear there, that is, that after we understand the relation of these attributes and accidents to the essence of the things they are accidents of, we return and move in a perfect fashion from the essence of those things to all the essential attributes and the specific accidents which they have.

Since deriving knowledge of the essence of things through perception of these attributes and accidents which direct one to such knowledge involves great difficulty and necessitates many stratagems—this because knowing from which of these attributes we should take demonstrations concerning the essence of things is difficult and something concerning which mistakes occur—we are led to think of something not specific that it is specific. Had we not determined the essential attributes which it is appropriate to determine in this investigation, this would have been a cause for mistakes concerning the essence of the things.[103] And because of the difficulty in the preparation of what he needs from perception for these [matters] which he investigates, as we mentioned,[104] he began recounting her praises concerning what she had prepared for him concerning these investigations and the wonder which there is in this method of acquisition.[105] He said that her looking out is *as the dawn* which is the beginning of the light, and after that he compared her to *the moon* and after that to *the sun* since the light which comes from her is weak ab initio, but it was of the sort which grew stronger *unto the perfect day* (Prov. 4:18),[106] that is, that which she prepared for him from among the posterior things among these things is perfectly prepared—so much so that he was enabled to move to the essence of the things in a perfect manner. Also, from the perspective of her receiving the emanation from others, he first compared her to *the moon,* which receives its light from another, and from the perspective that she emanated to him what she emanated to him, he compared her to *the sun.*

The meaning of his saying *terrible as an army with banners* was explained above, however.[107]

I went down into the garden of nuts
To look at the green plants of the valley
To see whether the vine budded
And the pomegranates were in flower (6:11)
Before I was aware
My soul set me
Upon the chariots of my princely people (6:12)

The intellect said, recounting her praises and expressing wonderment at the perfection of what she had prepared for him concerning these investigations into the garden *of nuts*—it being a special perfume[108]—*I went down . . . to look at* the trees of *the valley,* that is, to see if they had yet given forth their fruit. The meaning of this is that he descended in the investigation of these things which he now strives to investigate and came *to see* if he can in any fashion find premises which will bring him to the object of his desire, for there is great difficulty in this, as we mentioned. He said that he did not know how his soul *set* him from these sensed matters to ride *upon the chariots* of the infinite multiplicity, that is, the making of universal premises which will bring him to the subject of inquiry.[109]

He called this generality *Aminadiv*[110]—it being the name of a man[111]—to hide the matter. Despite this, it is as if he said *am nadiv,*[112] the yod being extra, extra yods like this being common in our language.[113] He called this aggregation "a princely people" for it is this aggregation which persists in these matters thanks to the princeliness of the agent, as Aristotle mentioned.[114] Destruction occurs because of matter; that is, in that the existence of an individual is not permanent, and this is so because the nature of matter necessitates its not being always obedient to the form, which strives to preserve its existence, and its defeating of it.[115] To draw our attention to that which he had hinted at by saying *Aminadav,* he called his beloved in this passage *prince's daughter* (7:2).[116]

In this verse he called his beloved "his soul," according to what I think, because of her great need of many of the faculties of the soul in this apprehension and since the faculties of the soul in their generality help her by subordinating themselves properly to the intellect. He attributed the apprehension of the universal premises to her because she prepared for him from the senses that which directs him to their acquisition. But in actuality, their acquisition will be from the Active Intellect, as was made clear in *On the Soul.*[117]

It is possible to say that he called his soul the Active Intellect, for it stands
to him in the status of form, as was made clear in *On the Soul*.[118] The meaning of this would then be that he did not know how the Active Intellect *set*
him to know these universal premises on the basis of these things which had
been prepared for him by his beloved, as if he expressed wonderment at the
perfection of the improvement in what she prepared for him, so that the intellect could move from them to these premises.

> Return, return, O Shulammite
> Return, return, that we may look upon thee
> What will ye see in the Shulammite?
> As it were a dance of two companies (7:1)

In that his beloved is now at the stage of the ultimate perfection possible
for her, he called her *Shulammite,* since it is derived from "perfection." [119] He
said to her that she should return and prepare for him what he needs for these
investigations. He expressed this in the plural and said *that we may look
upon thee* as if he said that he and the Active Intellect will look upon her, because from the perspective of his clinging to matter the Active Intellect would
not be able to emanate upon him what it emanates without her assistance.
She responded, *What will ye see in the Shulammite?,* meaning that it is impossible for her to prepare anything for them [120] in these investigations but the
knowledge of the attributes and accidents, it being thought at the beginning
of speculation that it is impossible to understand the essence of the things
themselves. He responded that they already see in her something similar to *a
dance of two companies,* that is, the cycle which takes place in the two companies, they being the heavenly bodies and the physical objects subject to
generation and corruption. This is so because the cycle occurs with respect
to the heavenly bodies such that at one time they come close to it [121] and at
another are distant from it. This cycle is the cause of the cycle which is found
among the things subject to generation and corruption which is the cause of
their permanence. [122] For example, when the sun comes closer to the northern
direction, fire and air become dominant there, whereas when it moves farther
from it, water and earth predominate, and again the matter goes in a cycle.
This is an issue already made clear in physical science. It is as if he were to
say that even though what she prepares for them are attributes and accidents
posterior to the thing itself, and the knowledge of these attributes ab initio is

weak because they are not known through their causes,[123] it can come about
that the matter will become reversed when the attributes of the thing are investigated in the appropriate fashion, leading to understanding of the thing
itself, knowledge of these accidents, and in general the attributes of the thing
then becoming perfect, since one moves to them from their causes, and this
is absolutely wonderful. I mean, that we acquire knowledge of the things
themselves on the basis of the weak knowledge we have of these attributes
and accidents and we then achieve perfect knowledge of these attributes due
to the knowledge we have of the things themselves in themselves.[124] The level
of knowledge thus achieved is so great that it has been thought that this would
be something absurd and impossible; and if there were not another agent
here having a role with respect to this emanation the objection would have
aspects of plausibility. But since there is here another agent—the Active Intellect—our acquisition of perfect knowledge on the basis of the weak knowledge we have from perception is not rendered impossible.

> How beautiful are thy steps in sandals, O prince's daughter
> The roundings of thy thighs are like the links of a chain
> The work of the hands of a skilled craftsman (7:2)

Since with this apprehension he moves from the posterior to the prior, as
we explained, he moves here in the recounting of her praises from her leg to
her head, as opposed to the way in which he praised her earlier with respect
to the other apprehensions. He said that her steps were *beautiful,* that is,
what she prepared for him from the posterior attributes and accidents—even
if they are *in sandals,*[125] which *sandals* restrain her from apprehending them
with a perfect apprehension—was still *beautiful;* this indicates the weakness
of the apprehension and knowledge concerning these accidents *ab initio.* We
have explained *in sandals* after the fashion of *put off thy sandals from off thy
feet* (Exod. 3:5).[126]

He called her *prince's daughter* because of her relation to some extent to
the incorporeal agent, which is the *prince,* since her apprehension is sufficiently spiritual[127] so as to be roughly halfway between an individual perceived entity and that which is intellected from it, since many of the accidents
of sensible things have been abstracted before reaching her.[128]

It is possible that the meaning of this is that these imaginative forms in
her are caused by the intellect, which is the *prince* because he directs her to

determining them and she obeys him by preparing them for him so far as she is able; by this he hinted at the perfection of the preparation [129] which is to be found in what she prepared for him concerning these apprehensions.

He further drew our attention to a wonderful matter, one hidden from some expert philosophers, by calling her *prince's daughter*. They thought that since the imaginative soul is subject to corruption and is so needed by the intellect for the achievement of its perfection that it cannot achieve it without her, and since it is a perfection for her, it must necessarily be the case that the acquired intellect be subject to corruption, for with the corruption of a subject of perfection its perfection will be corrupted. We have already stated the solution to this problem in our commentary to *On the Soul*,[130] and we will therefore state the matter here briefly, in a manner sufficient for this place. We say that if the imaginative form were the cause of the existence of the intelligible form, this objection would be necessitated from every perspective. But the matter is not so. This is so because the imaginative form is in a certain sense a cause of the apprehension of the intelligible form but not of its existence. But the matter is the reverse of this, and this is something the necessity of which has already been made clear in *Metaphysics*,[131] for the intelligible form is a cause of the existence of the sensible form, which in turn is a cause of the existence of the imaginative form, and this is something the necessity of which has been clarified somewhat in *Metaphysics*. All this is so because it is not possible that the enduring order and equilibrium be found in sensible matters, by virtue of which they can be cognized, were they not caused by a rational plan—it being an intellect—just as it is impossible that there be order and equilibrium in artificial things but for the rational plan found in the soul of the craftsman. The matter being so, that is, that the imaginative form is not a cause for the existence of the intelligible form, it is not necessary that the intelligible form be corrupted with the corruption of the imaginative form. This is so because it is not the case that knowledge disappears with the disappearance of one of its causes. For example, a person will be guided toward the knowledge of some mathematical matter when we inscribe for him some particular figure; this will direct him to that representation.[132] It is clear that with the destruction of that figure it is not necessarily the case that the knowledge which was reached through it will be destroyed. This is so very clear that expatiating upon it is unnecessary.

He called her here *prince's daughter* to indicate that her state is caused by the intellect, which is the *prince*. From this it is clear that it is possible for the acquired intellect to be everlasting, notwithstanding the corruption of the imaginative soul.[133] We have already made clear in a fashion which allows no room for doubt in our commentary to *On the Soul*[134] and in *Wars of the Lord*[135] that it is necessary that the acquired intellect be everlasting, and we have solved all the problems which occur with respect to this matter.

His statement *the roundings of thy thighs . . .* hints at the cycle which comes with her apprehension of the posterior first. He said that the roundings of her thighs are absolutely beautiful and well-structured despite the tremendous difficulty in apprehending this cycle.

> Thy navel is like a round goblet
> Wherein no mingled wine is wanting
> Thy belly is like a heap of wheat
> Set about with lilies (7:3)

It is known that the navel is that through which one takes one's nourishment at first, that is, during the time of one's generation. And in that what this female beloved derives[136] from these things at the beginning is characterized by deficiency, as above, he compared this derivation to the taking of nourishment by an unperfected being in the process of its generation. This allegory very wonderfully captures what we are about here. He compared her derivation of these attributes to *a round sahar*[137] in which no *mingled wine is wanting*. It[138] is, according to what I think, a round, concave mirror[139] which is like a stone so polished that it does not lack the appropriate character to record forms in it. With this mirror it happens that when it is approached closely, the form is seen reversed, and when the object mirrored is moved away, the form is seen properly. That this is a property of burning mirrors is clearly shown by sense experience. This is a wonderful allegory of what we are about, as if he said that at the beginning the matter comes from her reversed, and afterwards it is straightened out, combined with what he indicated by allegorically comparing her to a *garden* which is *shut up* (4:12) and the cycle.[140] That the *sahar* is a mirror is clear, since mirrors are called *saharonim*.[141]

By saying *thy belly is like a heap of wheat* he compared what she prepared for him to *a heap of wheat*. This is so because even though the straw in it is not the intended end itself, and it[142] does not contain the wheat potentially, as was the case with the lily, it[143] being the fruit or seed in potential, still, from it, the wheat, the intended end, is taken.[144] The matter is equally so with respect to what she prepared for him from these accidents and attributes, since even though they are not the thing itself of which they are accidents, they are withal a tool [145] for deriving from them knowledge of the thing itself, as above.

His saying *set about with lilies* is to indicate that this straw has been tied up so as to guide one to the subject of research, this because of their being essential and unique to the subject under research.

> Thy two breasts are like two fawns
> That are twins of a gazelle (7:4)

Its explanation has been given above. He did not say *which feed among the lilies* (4:5) [146] since nothing which she might apprehend through the senses from these things is similar to *lilies,* for the thing is not potentially in the accidents and attributes in the way in which the lily is potentially the fruit and seed, as above.

> Thy neck is as a tower of ivory
> Thine eyes are as the pools in Ḥeshbon by the gate of Bat-Rabbim
> Thy nose is like the tower of Lebanon
> Which looketh towards Damascus (7:5)

He said that her neck is *as a tower of ivory*—which is very strong—to indicate that what she emanates upon him is very strong, as strong as is possible here. For this reason he was brief here and did not say *builded with turrets,* and so on (4:4), since this was possible with the mathematical sciences but not with the physical sciences, since its demonstrations are *a posteriori* demonstrations. [147]

His statement *thine eyes are as the pools in Ḥeshbon by the gate of Bat-Rabbim* is wonderful. This is so because *Ḥeshbon* and *Rabbim* were cities, but their names also indicate repetition and mulitiplicity, [148] and thus it says, according to the allegory, that what she encompasses and apprehends are like *pools* of water *in Ḥeshbon* and *by the gate of Bat-Rabbim* which continuously fill themselves. [149] This [would be] the case if there were pools of water of this sort in *Ḥeshbon* and *by the gate of Bat-Rabbim.* If there were no pools of water of this sort there, however, then the whole passage [would] accord with the intended meaning of the allegory. Its meaning according to the intended meaning of the allegory is that she will prepare for him what she will through the repetition[150] and with the stupendous multiplicity which is gathered to her through the intermediation of the faculty of memory, and it is that which he allegorically compared to springs like the *pools* of water from which to water the intellect.

By his statement *thy nose is like the tower of Lebanon* he means that her way of looking and studying is strong and beautiful and aimed at the best possible end, *like the tower of Lebanon,* it being the temple.[151]

He said *which looketh towards Damascus* for in Damascus will be found a choice of exotic fruits, as if to say she is strongly inclined toward that which will bring the intellect to the intended end with respect to these subjects of inquiry.

> Thy head upon thee is like Carmel
> And the hair of thy head like purple
> The king is held captive in the tresses thereof (7:6)

He said that just as the *Carmel*[152] is fit for the growth of plants and fruits, and perfectly prepared for it, so she prepares what is fitting in an absolutely fitting fashion, preparing the "head" toward that which she intends, it being the things which are being researched. This is a consequence of the excellence of her guidance of him in what she prepares from among the attributes and accidents. Just as the *Carmel*[153] has the head upon it for which the immediate potential is intended, it being the fruit, so the "head" which plans her activities is upon her in immediate potential.[154]

His saying *and the hair of thy head is like purple* accords with both the allegory and the intended meaning. According to the allegory, it indicates her beauty. According to the intended meaning of the allegory it says that the attributes of her "head" which she prepared for him to acquire a demonstration from them about the "head" are absolutely beautiful and well-structured.

By his saying *the king is held captive in the tresses thereof* he means that due to the beauty of these attributes which she prepared, *the king*—it being the material intellect—is almost *held captive in the tresses thereof,* to drink from them forever.[155] He allegorically compared this to *troughs* for these *troughs* are the attributes which she prepared, compared in this, his allegory, to *pools* (7:5) of water. It is possible that the meaning of this is that the material intellect is *held captive in* those *troughs* to drink from them always in his research, for he cannot do anything other than what she prepares for him.

Or, it means, allegorically, that the Active Intellect, to the extent that it emanates upon the material intellect, *is held captive in* those *troughs,* for it cannot emanate upon the latter anything of this if the material intellect does not
have sensual apprehension before this, that is, with respect to what the Active Intellect emanates unto the material intellect from among the imaginative forms.[156]

He called the Active Intellect *king*[157] because it rules him.

> How fair and how pleasant art thou
> O love, for delights (7:7)

He said that she is very beautiful and very pleasant, desiring him and lov-
ing him in an absolutely perfect way, in order to guide him toward the apprehension of the truth in these matters, in which there is wonderful delight, as
is well known to those who know the truth: that pleasure is beyond all relation to physical pleasures.[158]

> This thy stature is like to a palm-tree
> And thy breasts to clusters of grapes (7:8)

He said that she ascends properly to perfection as the *palm-tree,* which
is very tall and straight. Her breasts, with which she emanates to him what
she emanates, are compared to *clusters of grapes* due to the excellence of her
steering herself directly toward that which will progress toward the end, it
being the fruit. Moreover, he said this because these specific things which he
is investigating have a rational ordering—in which the posterior is more worthy than the prior—for example, first he ought to research minerals, after
that plants, and after that animals, and this is the way she ascended properly.

> I said, I will climb up into the palm-tree
> I will take hold of the branches thereof
> And let thy breasts be as clusters of the vine
> And the smell of thy countenance like apples (7:9)

The intellect said, "When I [saw] your perfection in preparing for me
what I need, *I said* to myself that *I will* already *climb up into the palm-tree*
until I get as high as possible, this being when I *take hold of the branches*

thereof and *climb up,* limb after limb; and I trust according to what I see of you that *thy breasts,* with which you emanate unto me what you emanate, will be for me *as clusters of the vine, and the smell of thy countenance,* that you look on these matters that you prepare for me assuring that they be *like apples.*" All this indicates that they directly steer themselves absolutely perfectly toward the intended end, which is the "fruit" in this allegory.

> And the roof of thy mouth like the best wine
> That glideth down smoothly for my beloved
> Moving gently the lips of those that are asleep (7:10)

He said that *the roof of thy mouth,* with which you test these attributes which you prepare for me, is like the *best wine,* which *glideth down smoothly,* for this is one of the attributes of *the best wine,* as was mentioned in Proverbs.[159] This is so because what you prepare from this is directly steered to my beloved—it being the Active Intellect—in the best possible fashion so that it emanates unto me and thus stimulates me to investigate it.

By saying *moving gently the lips of those that are asleep* he means that just as the *wine* causes *the lips of those that are asleep* to move gently, and this is known to be a characteristic of *wine,* so *the roof of thy mouth* will cause to speak *those that are asleep,* they being the material intellect and the Active Intellect from the perspective of its emanating upon the material intellect, for this will not be perfected for them without her.[160]

> I am my beloved's
> And his desire is towards me (7:11)

She said, "As you thought, so I will do. I am prepared to be *my beloved's with a strong hand* (Isa. 8:11), and it is incumbent upon me to fulfill what he desires so that what he sought to investigate is perfected for him."

> Come, my beloved, let us go forth into the field
> Let us lodge in the villages (7:12)
> Let us get up early to the vineyards
> Let us see whether the vine hath budded
> Whether the vine-blossom be opened
> And the pomegranates be in flower
> There I will give thee my love (7:13)

She said allegorically that they went forth *into the field* and looked at the plants to see if they had begun to give forth their fruit. The meaning of this is that they went to see if that which she needed from the senses for this investigation had been perfected, for this needs long and difficult research, which is very difficult to accomplish, as noted above. If that which she needed from the senses has been perfected, then after that, *I will give thee my love* and I will emanate upon you what is fitting, so far as it can be done.

> The mandrakes gave forth fragrance
> And at our doors are all manner of precious fruits
> New and old
> Which I have laid up for thee, O my beloved (7:14)

She said that these plants have given forth their fragrance, that is, that what is necessary has already been prepared for them by the senses, so that *all manner of precious fruits* which they will need in these researches have been prepared for them *at their doors.*

The meaning of her statement *new and old, which I have laid up for thee, O my beloved* is that what has been apprehended anew from these things through the senses, with what was apprehended of old, was all stored for him in the faculty of memory by her so that the appropriate sensual repetition of this could be accomplished.[161] This is accomplished either through what she apprehends through the senses or through what she apprehends from another and this indeed is added to her, as is well known.[162] This is so because there exist here many things which cannot in any fashion be fully apprehended by any individual alone, as is the case with the species of animals and what is similar to them, as Aristotle mentioned in *On Animals* 11.[163] Thus, the correct way to proceed is to gather what has been apprehended concerning these matters by those among the ancients who are trustworthy and thus to bring to completion what is needed from the senses.[164]

> Oh that thou wert as my brother
> That sucked the breasts of my mother
> When I should find thee without, I would kiss thee
> Yea, and none would despise me (8:1)
> I would lead thee, and bring thee into my mother's house
> That thou mightest instruct me
> I would cause thee to drink of spiced wine
> Of the juice of my pomegranate (8:2)

That these verses accord with the allegory can be made clear with minimal explanation. Thus, she said, indicating the strength of her longing to approach him so far as is possible for her, that she longs for him to be to her *as a brother* and to *suck the breasts* of her mother so that she should be able to kiss him in a public place without shame, for a maiden is not ashamed to kiss her still-nursing brother in front of any person, and people would not despise her for doing so.[165] Were the matter so,[166] she said, "I would behave thus and bring you *into my mother's house* that *thou mightest instruct me* and lead me, and I would cause you to drink delicious beverages."

According to the intended meaning of the allegory, however, it means that she, because she apprehended from the senses with difficulty what she needed to prepare for the intellect in these investigations—and this for two reasons: first, the difficulty of the matter itself and second, her difficulty in guiding the senses to search for what must be searched[167] with the senses and her consequent fear lest a mistake occur in her apprehension—she therefore said, "*Oh that* you could be *as my brother that sucked the breasts of my mother* so that you could lead the sense faculties to what must be investigated," for without a doubt, if they be not directed in this by the intellect, this apprehension will not be completed; this is self-evidently clear. Then, *when I should find thee without,* that is, when you are not burdened with the care of leading them, and this will be when the necessary sense apprehension of that which must be searched is completed, then I will cleave to you *and kiss thee.* This is the reason for the ease of your apprehension of that which is sought. Further, they subordinate themselves to you when the guidance over them is ordered from you better than they subordinate themselves to me, for they *despise* me, but you *they would not despise* but, rather, long to satisfy your will. In this fashion I will lead and bring you *into my mother's house,* where *thou mightest instruct me*—it[168] being the sentient soul—to cause you to drink from the beverages which I apprehended from the senses and the faculty of memory.

> His left hand should be under my head
> And his right hand should embrace me (8:3)

She said that that which she had longed for was completed, so that that which might have diverted her from the path of truth in this apprehension, despite [its] difficulty, has yielded *under* her head, *with no breach and no going forth* (Ps. 144:14), and that that which directs one toward the correct apprehension desired by her beloved cleaves to her and embraces her. According to the allegory, this also indicates that their joining together has been perfectly completed in this fashion and that they have returned to the custom of lovers in their joining together.

> I adjure you, O daughters of Jerusalem
> Why should ye awaken, or stir up love
> Until it please? (8:4)

She said, *I have* already *adjured you, O daughters of Jerusalem,* that you not, because of the strength of your desire to seek the end, break through by taking the apprehensions out of their order, because if you break through in this and [do] not work at your apprehensions in the appropriate order, nothing will remain in our hands, and our strivings will have been for naught. This is what she meant by saying *why should ye awaken, or stir up love until it please?* that is, that it would do them no good. But now, having taken the apprehensions in correct order, they have reached the measure of perfection already mentioned; what remains is to reach absolute speculative perfection, it being metaphysics, that which was longed for ab initio.

We could say that this adjuration was that they not break through and conduct research in metaphysics before satisfying the necessary conditions, as we will state below.[169] However, she did not say *by the gazelles and by the hinds of the field* (2:7) because, due to the distance of these matters from the senses, perplexity would be increased however they begin with it. For this reason he did not recount in connection with this adjuration that which might stimulate running. She did not say *that ye awaken not . . .* (2:7) but said *why should ye awaken* to indicate that if they begin with this without satisfying the conditions necessary to it, they will not succeed with it at all.

PART SIX

8 : 5 – 8 : 1 4

From the statement *Who is this who cometh up from the wilderness . . .*
to the end of the book, he indicates the attainment of metaphysics.

> Who is this that cometh up from the wilderness
> Leaning upon her beloved?
> Under the apple-tree I awakened thee
> There thy mother was in travail with thee
> There was she in travail and brought thee forth (8 : 5)

He said, beginning to tell about this apprehension, that is, metaphysics, and
about the difficulty in its acquisition, *who is this that cometh up from the wilderness,* as one who wonders whether[1] it is possible that this apprehension
be brought to completion from a wasteland which can be neither worked nor
planted. This is so because in the other sciences the things under investigation
were apprehended through the senses, and through them everything that one
strives to apprehend with respect to these things would be brought to completion from the things themselves.[2] In this matter, however, there is no way
to apprehend it but with remote premises.[3] Therefore he said that she is *leaning upon her beloved,* that is, that her heart is aroused within her[4] for the
sake of her *beloved* because she is not able to satisfy his desire. This word,
leans upon, is a hapax legomenon,[5] and I think that its meaning according to
its context is as I explained. It is also possible to say, and it is more correct,
that *leans upon* is derived from *marpeq,*[6] which is the arm, as Rabbi Moses
explained in his commentary on the Mishnah, saying there that it was thus
in Arabic.[7] Here then it would mean that because of her great love and longing she puts her arms *upon her beloved;* this accords with the allegory.

But according to the intended meaning of the allegory, he means by these arms[8] that she will help him with all her strength to produce for him what she can produce to serve as an entryway into the researches which he wishes to conduct, and she apologizes and says to him *under the apple-tree I awakened thee,* that is, I have already helped you with the apprehension of the sensible things—they being the subject matter of physics—for there she grew up, and they are things close to us, perceived by us through this apprehension which he now investigates,[9] and she cannot figure out how he could derive any assistance from her, but despite all this she is full of longing to fulfill his desire so far as she can.

> Set me as a seal upon they heart, as a seal upon thine arm
> For love is as strong as death
> Jealousy is cruel as the grave
> The flashes thereof are flashes of fire
> A very flame of the Lord (8:6)
> Many waters cannot quench love
> Neither can the floods drown it
> If a man would give all the substance of his house for love
> He would utterly be contemned (8:7)

She said to him because of the strength of her love and the greatness of her desire to fulfill his wish so far as she is able that he should set her *as a seal upon* his heart, that is, with respect to what he needs for the speculative intellect; she also said to him that she would do what was necessary for him with respect to the practical intellect; thus she said, *as a seal upon thine arm,* meaning that just as a man seals with a seal when he wishes, so she will always be ready so far as she is able to "seal" for him those imaginative forms which he needs. She said, giving a reason for this, that her love for him is absolutely strong, no man could deflect it in any fashion, like *death* and the *grave,* both of which are absolutely strong, the manner of their strength being that no man can deflect them in any fashion, and that this love burns in her with a great burning such that it cannot be quenched by *many waters, [neither can the floods] drown it;* they cannot deflect her with their abundance for she contemns everything when compared to her love, and for that reason she works at nothing but what will cause her to progress toward the object of his desire.

> We have a little sister
> And she hath no breasts

> What shall we do for our sister
> In the day when she will be spoken for? (8 : 8)

The Active Intellect and the acquired intellect, that is, the material intellect perfected with those perfections discussed above, together said, *We have a sister,* referring to this female beloved mentioned above.[10] They called her their *sister* because of her perfection, which is so great that she was called *Shulammite* (7 : 1) above, and because of her helping them in their activity, that is, in what the material intellect receives from the emanation of the Active Intellect. They called her *little* because of her small role in the apprehension they need here.[11] He thus said that she has no *breasts* with which to emanate to them what they need for this apprehension.[12] This fits the allegory, for a *little one* does not have breasts ready to nurse. The matter being so, *what shall we do for our sister in the day when she will be spoken for,* so that she may emanate unto us what is necessary for us with respect to this science, and in what way can we direct her to this emanation, for she cannot do this by herself if we do not direct her?

The statement *in the day when she will be spoken for* comes to indicate that the fulfillment of many conditions is necessary for this.[13] Among them are training in the art of rhetoric, as was mentioned in the beginning of the *Rhetoric,*[14] and a settled mind and the quieting of the effervescence of one's nature.[15] For this reason our ancient sages did not permit it to themselves except in their old age.[16] This is so because in this art one uses generally accepted premises,[17] a characteristic of which in most cases is that one may find demonstrations on their basis for both a thing and its opposite, and it is therefore fitting that the mind of the researcher in it be so settled that it takes from these generally accepted premises true premises only. It is also proper that he not delve as deeply into this as he delves into the other sciences which may be delved into, for it is proper that the way of research in each science accord with the level of confirmation achievable in each.[18]

> If she be a wall
> We will build upon her a turret of silver
> And if she be a door
> We will enclose her with boards of cedar (8 : 9)

They said that if she is enclosed[19] with the enclosure fitting for one who wishes to commence the investigation of this science, then *we will build upon her* the building we are trying to build in the most perfect of ways. *And if she be a door,* that is, if she is broken open,[20] without *a wall,* then *we will enclose her with boards of cedar,* that is, we will strengthen her and seal her breach with *boards of cedar.*

> I am a wall
> And my breasts like the towers thereof
> Then was I in his eyes
> As one that found peace (8:10)

She said that she is *a wall,* that is, that she is enclosed, *with no breach, and no going forth* (Ps. 144:14); her breasts, with which she emanates what she emanates, are like the strong *towers* of a city, which add considerably to its security. The meaning of this is that she will prepare from these premises only that which will guide to that which is correct in this science.

The meaning of her statement *then was I in his eyes as one that found peace* is that when her beloved heard this from her she became *in his eyes as one that found peace,* for, were the matter not so, the discord and argument concerning these premises would be great, and thought would turn now to one alternative of the contradiction and now to the second.

> Solomon had a vineyard at Ba'al-Hamon
> He gave over the vineyard unto keepers
> Every one for the fruit thereof brought in
> A thousand pieces of silver (8:11)

He said, recounting the way in which this apprehension is acquired and its substance,[21] that *Solomon*—he being the intellect[22]—*had a vineyard* which was *at Ba'al-Hamon,* that is, at "Ba'al-ha-Ribbui,"[23] it being the sensible existence, for in it there is multiplicity. Intelligible existence, however, of which the sensible existence is an effect,[24] has no multiplicity in it at all. He further said that this *vineyard* was given over *to keepers* to guard the fruit which comes of it, this being the intelligible order potentially found in it, in order to present it to the intellect. These *keepers* are the powers of sensation and the faculties of imagination and memory, for they guard this fruit and work at seeing to it that all of that fruit goes *to Solomon.* This will take place when one moves from the order found in sensible existence to the intelligible order, of which the order in sensible existence is an effect.

The meaning of his statement *every one for the fruit therefore brought in a thousand pieces of silver* is that one who perfectly investigates the sensible existence will completely apprehend from it this fruit which we have mentioned.[25] He expressed this in language indicating both unity in number and multiplicity, that is, *a thousand.*[26] For one who examines the multiplicity of forms in this sensible existence will apprehend from them the one form of which they are effects and which stands to them in the status of form, agent, and end, so that he ascends in this fashion from multiplicity to the one.[27] This is so because some of them stand in the status of form to some of them, and they do not cease from ascending in this fashion until they end with the final form.[28]

> My vineyard which is mine is before me
> Thou, O Solomon, shalt have the thousand
> And these that keep the fruit thereof two hundred (8:12)

She said that this vineyard is in front of her and that she will endeavor [to see to it that] that the *thousand pieces of silver* (8:11) become his—it being the fruit in what came above[29]—and that the *keepers* will endeavor to apprehend the discrete matters, the apprehension of which is related to them, until the intellect move from what was gathered to it by all the *keepers* to the apprehension of this one which was mentioned above, which is the fruit of the intellect and its end.[30] He expressed it with this number, that is, *two hundred,* to indicate that when that which all of the senses—of which there are only five, as has been established in *On the Soul*[31]—apprehend for him is gathered together, there was gathered together from this that which is potentially the fruit,[32] which is *a thousand pieces of silver* (8:11), for five times two hundred is one thousand.

> Thou that dwellest in the gardens
> The companions hearken for thy voice
> Cause me to hear it (8:13)

He called her *that dwellest in the gardens* because of her *dwelling* in this sensible existence from which she prepares for them[33] what they need for their apprehension. And because this indeed is completed from it[34] through different apprehensions which reach her from the senses, they said *in the gardens,* in the plural, and called themselves her *companions,* for she is in their company in a certain fashion, to the extent that she prepares for them by taking from among these premises that upon which this art is built.[35] He said that they incline their ears to her words and for this reason she besought the [36] acquired intellect that he might allow her to emanate unto him what he needs from her in this science, for without this the Active Intellect will not be able to emanate to him [37] the emanation he needs from it in this science, as above.[38]

> Make haste, my beloved
> And be thou like to a gazelle or a young hart
> Upon the mountains of spices (8:14)

She said to him that she had already prepared for him what he needs from this and that he should endeavor to ascend with dispatch and the greatest possible speed *upon the mountains of spices*—it being metaphysics, as above [39]—and that he not be negligent about this.

This is what appears to us as correct in the explanation of this scroll, and it well fits both the language and the meaning.

We think that we have, without a doubt, determined the general conceptions [40] which were intended in this book; behold, the language of the book and its order testify for us. However, concerning the detailed conceptions, it is possible that we have missed some of them, so that there may be significance to some things which we said pertained to the allegory only, but I think that these are few.

This commentary is completed here. Its completion was at the end of Tammuz, 5085.[41]

Praise is due to God alone, who helped us with his mercy and grace. May his name be blessed and exalted above every blessing and praise.

NOTES

ABBREVIATIONS

Works frequently cited have been identified by the following abbreviations:

Aristotle	*The Complete Works of Aristotle*, ed. Jonathan Barnes
Guide; Guide of the Perplexed	Maimonides, *Guide of the Perplexed;* trans. Shlomo Pines
Husik	Isaac Husik, "Studies in Gersonides." References to this source are keyed to item, not page, numbers.
Leipzig	*Milḥamot ha-Shem* (Leipzig, 1866)
Mashbaum	Jesse Stephen Mashbaum, "Chapters 9–12 of Gersonides' Supercommentary on Averroës' *Epitome of the* De Anima"
Touati	Charles Touati, *La pensée philosophique et théologique de Gersonide*
Wars of the Lord	Gersonides, *Wars of the Lord*, trans. Seymour Feldman

PREFACE

1. Gersonides' *Milḥamot ha-Shem* (*Wars of the Lord*) is divided into six treatises. References to *Wars of the Lord* cite treatise number, part number (where applicable), and chapter number, followed by the page number of the 1866 Leipzig edition of the Hebrew text (henceforth Leipzig). The first four treatises have been translated into English by Seymour Feldman in Gersonides, *Wars of the Lord*. Translations from the first four treatises are Feldman's.

2. For a blatant example of this approach, see Pines, "Appendix: Problems in the Teachings of Gersonides"; on 457 Pines opines that Christian philosophy "is the natural historical context of Gersonides' thought."

NOTE ON THE HEBREW TEXT AND THIS TRANSLATION

1. See Rabin, "Hebrew and Arabic in Medieval Jewish Philosophy," 235: "The translations are almost all couched in an awkward, difficult style that carries into

the Hebrew many semantic and syntactical features of the Arabic original, and even the original Hebrew works affect for the most part a similar arabicizing idiom, whether their authors were speakers of Arabic or of European languages. Of one author, who wrote a work in the most obscure arabicized syntax, R. Levi ben Gerson, it is usually assumed that he could not read Arabic at all."

2. *Commentary on the Torah*, 21d/98/183; on citation to the Torah commentary see Note to the Reader, below.

TRANSLATOR'S INTRODUCTION

1. For a very useful chronological table of Gersonides' writings set against the (few) known events of his life and events of contemporary historical significance, see Weil-Guény, "Gersonide en son temps." For an exhaustive descriptive survey of writings by and about Gersonides, see my "Bibliographia Gersonideana."

2. On the Job commentary, see Touati, 64. This text was translated into English by Lassen and analyzed by Bleich in *Providence in the Philosophy of Gersonides* and by Kellner in "Gersonides, Providence, and the Rabbinic Tradition." See also Wirszubski, "Giovanni Pico's Book of Job."

3. See below, at the end of the translation of the text. Gersonides worked on many of his books simultaneously; thus, even though he finished working on *Wars of the Lord* after writing the commentary on Song of Songs, the latter work is occasionally cited in the former.

4. For a recent, extremely valuable study of the terms *peshaṭ* and *derash/midrash*, see Halivni, *Peshaṭ and Derash*. Further, see Gelles, *Peshaṭ and Derash in the Exegesis of Rashi*; Kamin, "Rashi's Exegetical Categorization"; and Kamin, *Rashi*, 35–56.

5. Funkenstein, "Gersonides' Bible Commentary," 309. Further on Gersonides' stance as a Bible commentator, see Feldman's valuable "Appendix: Gersonides and Biblical Exegesis," 211–47 in the second volume of his translation of *Wars of the Lord*. Gersonides seems to have paid no explicit attention to contemporary debates (between Rashi and his grandson Rashbam, for example) over whether Scripture should be interpreted according to its literal or its midrashic meaning. On this debate see Gelles, *Peshaṭ and Derash in the Exegesis of Rashi*. Gersonides was apparently unacquainted with Rashi's commentary on Song of Songs. One indication of this is the fact that had he known Rashi's commentary on Song of Songs 8:5 he would have commented on the Arabic root *r-p-q* differently. See my notes there. On Rashi on Song of Songs, see Marcus, "Song of Songs in German Ḥasidism."

6. In what follows I survey commentaries similar to that of Gersonides. For other medieval Jewish commentaries on Song of Songs, see Walfish's masterful "Annotated Bibliography." Walfish surveys the philosophical commentaries as well, of course, and should be consulted in conjunction with what I write here.

7. See "Laws of the Foundations of the Torah," 2:12, 6:9; "Laws of Torah Study," 5:4; and "Laws of Repentance," 10:3.

8. 3:51 (623, 628); 3:54 (636).

9. This approach, it should be noted, is risky in the sense that although the rabbinical interpretation renders the sting implicit in Song of Songs harmless by reading it exclusively in terms of the love between God and the House of Israel—thus rendering

a carnal interpretation impossible—when the poem is read as referring to individuals (God and those individuals who love God) and not to a corporate entity such as the House of Israel, it is an easier step to move from interpreting the poem as an exaltation of the love of the "God intoxicated" individual for God to interpreting the poem as an exaltation of carnal love between two human individuals.

10. See Halkin, "Ibn Aknin's Commentary on the Song of Songs," 396; Twersky, "Some Non-Halakic Aspects of the *Mishneh Torah*," 103; and Twersky, *Introduction to the Code of Maimonides*, 145.

11. Abraham ibn Ezra, in the introduction to his commentary on Song of Songs, says that "the philosophers [*anshe ha-meḥqar*] have interpreted this book as dealing with universal matter, and the way in which the supernal soul joins with the body." I do not know to whom he is referring, but from his comment we may infer that at least one philosophically oriented commentary on Song of Songs was composed before the first half of the twelfth century, when ibn Ezra flourished. (Ibn Ezra is quoted often by Gersonides in his commentary on the Torah; there are also a number of places in the commentary on Song of Songs where his commentary might have influenced Gersonides.) Rabbi Abraham ben Meir ibn Ezra's *Commentary on Canticles* was edited by H. J. Matthews.

12. The Arabic text of that commentary with Hebrew translation was published by Halkin under the title *Hitgalut ha-Sodot ve-Hofaʿat ha-Meʾorot*. On ibn ʿAknin, a contemporary of Maimonides' but not the Joseph ben Judah to whom he addressed the *Guide,* and on his commentary to Song of Songs, see Halkin, "Ibn Aknin's Commentary on the Song of Songs"; "The Character of R. Yosef ben Yehudah ibn ʿAknin"; and "History of the Forcible Conversion during the Days of the Almohades."

13. Although there is some scholarly debate over whether Gersonides knew Arabic, there is little doubt that had he known that language to any serious extent he would have made efforts to acquire copies of Averroës' commentaries in Arabic instead of relying on translations he knew to be problematic. For this last see Mashbaum, 184. Furthermore, I have found only four texts in which Gersonides demonstrates any familiarity with the Arabic language. Three are in the *Commentary on the Torah* (21d/98/183; 47b/237/494; 203b) and one is in the commentary on Ecclesiastes (at 34c). None of these examples proves any but the slightest familiarity with Arabic. See also below in the commentary to Song of Songs 8:5.

14. Sirat, *History of Jewish Philosophy,* 222.

15. This was published in Lyck in 1874 under the title *Perush ʿal Shir ha-Shirim.*

16. On Immanuel, see the introduction to *Maḥberot Immanuel ha-Romi,* ed. Yarden, 11–19. The nonphilosophical portions of Immanuel's commentary were published by Eschwege under the title *Der Kommentar zum Hohen Liede.* Immanuel's philosophical commentary was published and analyzed, and the subject of philosophic commentaries on Song of Songs summarized, in I. Ravitzky, "R. Immanuel b. Shlomo of Rome." This thesis is an extremely valuable source of information on our topic.

17. Ibn Kaspi's brief comments were published with an English translation by Ginsburg in *The Song of Songs,* 47–49. Last also published the text in his edition of Ibn Kaspi, *ʿAsarah Klei Kesef,* 183–84. Berlin translated a brief excerpt from Kaspi's commentary on Song of Songs in *Biblical Poetry through Medieval Eyes,* 105–7.

18. See my "Communication or Lack Thereof" on this issue and for an extensive

discussion of philosophical commentaries on Song of Songs. In that essay I also discuss Gersonides' unusual (if not unique) claim that Solomon composed Song of Songs in his old age and not in his youth.

19. On *haṣlaḥah* (which I usually translate as "felicity") see Rosenthal, "The Concept *Eudaimonia*." Rosenthal traces the term through the Arabic *saʿada* to the Greek *eudaimonia,* offering "beatitude" as an English translation.

20. Song of Songs contains no commandments, no narrative history, no moral exhortation, no prophecy, no wisdom, no references to God or Israel—in short, nothing that can instruct the simple reader.

21. See Schwartz, "Tension Between Moderate Morality and Ascetic Morality," 204–5.

22. Feldman comments: "Like most philosophers in the Arabic and Hebrew medieval orbit, Gersonides did not write on epistemology as such." "Platonic Themes in Gersonides' Doctrine," 261.

23. See Aristotle, *On the Soul,* 2:5,417b, and *Posterior Analytics* 2:8,75b, 22–25.

24. As he says, knowledge "must itself be stable and be of a stable entity." *Wars of the Lord,* 1:6 (Leipzig, 47; Feldman, 1:162).

25. For a discussion of Gersonides on God's knowledge, see Samuelson, "Gersonides' Account of God's Knowledge of Particulars."

26. For important background to this discussion, see Davidson, *Alfarabi, Avicenna, and Averroës on Intellect.*

27. On this subject, in addition to Touati, 394–442, and Feldman, "Platonic Themes in Gersonides' Doctrine," see Davidson, "Gersonides on the Material and Active Intellects"; Feldman, "Gersonides on the Possibility of Conjunction"; H. T. Goldstein, "*Dator Formarum*"; Ivry, "Gersonides and Averroës on the Intellect"; and Möbuss, *Die Intellektlehre des Levi ben Gerson.*

28. *Wars of the Lord,* 1:5 (Leipzig, 36; Feldman, 1:145). Davidson, "Gersonides on the Material and Active Intellects" (205), summarizes the position thus: "The human material intellect is, then, a disposition that has the body as its ultimate subject, that resides immediately in the imaginative faculty of the soul, and that is not mixed with either the imaginative faculty or the body."

29. *Commentary on the Torah,* 14b/54/88.

30. See Mashbaum, 150.

31. Further on all this, see my "Gersonides on the Role of the Active Intellect."

32. Compare *Wars of the Lord,* introduction (Leipzig, 6; Feldman, 1:98). Gersonides returns to this subject in *Wars of the Lord* 1:14 (Leipzig, 91; Feldman, 226); in both places he maintains that there can be no contradiction in fact between reason and Torah. See also *Wars of the Lord* 6:2.1 (Leipzig, 419). For an analysis of Gersonides' position on the relation between Torah and philosophy, see Staub, *Creation of the World According to Gersonides,* 81, 84–85, 148–53.

33. Gersonides' comments here call to mind *Guide of the Perplexed,* 3:27 (510). For parallels to this passage in Gersonides' thinking, see my "Politics and Perfection."

34. Touati, 75, tells us that in all of Gersonides' many supercommentaries on Averroës he cites the Bible only twice. This may be an indication that the intended audience for his commentaries on Averroës was very different from the audience to which he directed his biblical commentaries. This may also be the place to note that Gersonides cites his commentary on Song of Songs more than a dozen times in his other com-

mentaries. I have found such references in the following places: (a) *Commentary on the Torah*, 14a/51/84, 14b/53/88, 14c/54/90, 14d/56/93, 15a/58/98, 18b/76/136; 105b, 157b, and 215b; (b) commentary on Ecclesiastes, 7:23 (34c), 9:9 (36c—twice); (c) commentary on Proverbs, 1:21; 2:17–3:3, first *to'elet;* 6:20. None of these citations contain any surprises.

35. That does not mean that the philosophical positions in the commentary are presented in a hackneyed fashion. Where Gersonides disagrees with prevailing opinion he presents his own. Thus, in this commentary he diverges from common philosophical opinion concerning the division of the sciences and supplements his unique discussion of human cognition as found in the *Wars of the Lord.* On the first of these issues, see my "Gersonides on the Song and Songs and the Nature of Science" and, on the second, my "Gersonides on the Role of the Active Intellect." But creative or not, Gersonides' accounts presuppose next to no philosophical sophistication on the part of his reader and make modest demands on his or her intelligence. This should be contrasted with his stance in the commentary on the Pentateuch as described by Eisen in *Gersonides on Providence, Covenant, and the Jewish People,* 53–54, 99–113.

36. On Gersonides' division of the sciences and its significance, see my "Gersonides on the Song of Songs and the Nature of Science."

37. Gersonides' commentaries on Genesis and Job contain much the same material as his philosophic accounts in *Wars of the Lord,* 6.2 and 4. The commentaries are no simpler than those accounts.

38. It might be objected that although Gersonides repeatedly "threatens" to reveal secrets of philosophy here in the Song of Songs commentary he does not in fact do so. That is simply incorrect. The secret teaching of Song of Songs is that it is an account of a dialogue between the material intellect and the Active Intellect and that humankind's ultimate felicity lies in intellectual perfection.

39. See, e.g., in Gersonides' introduction to his commentary, text at n. 49 after n. 58, and before n. 102.

40. See also Gersonides' comments on Song of Songs 4:13–14 at the very end of his introduction.

41. Compare Maimonides, *Guide of the Perplexed,* 2:45, who maintains that it is not really prophecy at all. In his commentary to 1 Kings 3:12, it should be noted, Gersonides suggests that even if Solomon was not the wisest man who ever lived or ever will live, he was still certainly the wisest man of his generation and of the generations preceding and succeeding him.

42. See *Wars of the Lord,* introduction (Leipzig, 8; Feldman, 1:100–1) and the first two paragraphs of Gersonides' introduction to Song of Songs.

43. It might be objected that concentrating in this fashion on Gersonides' commentary on Song of Songs is unwarranted and illegitimate. It is, after all, only one of his many Bible commentaries and one of four he wrote on the "Five Scrolls." But Gersonides himself construes Song of Songs as being unique. It is the only book of the Bible the outward meaning of which conveys no advantage. Further, as noted above, the commentary is unique in literary terms. In its form and structure it is simply unlike all of Gersonides' other Bible commentaries, including the Job commentary, which preceded it.

44. For the text of the ban of 1305 (actually three letters), see Solomon ben Abraham, *Teshuvot ha-Rashba,* ed. Dimitrowsky, pt. 1, 2:722–38. On the ban see Sap-

erstein, "Conflict over the Rashba's Ḥerem on Philosophical Study" and the sources cited there. To those sources may be added Yehuda Rosenthal, "Anti-Maimonidean Controversy"; Halkin, "Why Was Levi ben Hayyim Hounded?"; Zinberg, *History of Jewish Literature,* 3 : 5 5 – 77; and Ben-Shalom, "Communication and Propaganda between Provence and Spain."

45. See *Guide of the Perplexed,* introduction, 5–6. On Maimonides as a Bible commentator, see Rosenberg, "Bible Exegesis in the *Guide of the Perplexed,*" and Klein-Braslavy's two studies, *Perush ha-Rambam le-Sippur Bri'at ha-Olam* and *Perush ha-Rambam le-Sippurim al Adam bi-Parashat Bereshit.*

46. *Guide of the Perplexed,* 6.

47. *Guide of the Perplexed,* 12.

48. See A. Ravitzky, "*Mishnato shel R. Zeraḥiah*"; "Samuel ibn Tibbon and the Esoteric Character"; "The Study of Medieval Jewish Philosophy"; and "Secrets of the *Guide of the Perplexed.*"

49. This commentary has not yet been published. See A. Ravitzky, "*Mishnato shel R. Zeraḥiah,*" 14.

50. On this book see Vajda, "Analysis of the *Ma'amar Yiqqawu ha-Mayim.*"

51. See A. Ravitzky, "*Mishnato shel R. Zeraḥiah,*" 46. Further on the Tibbonian school and the question of revealing the secrets of the Torah to the masses, see my "Gersonides' Commentary on Song of Songs: For Whom Was It Written, and Why?"

52. See Halkin, "Yedaiah Bedershi's Apology," 173, 175; Twersky, "Some Non-Halakic Aspects," 205.

53. On this see Freiman, "A Passage from Gersonides' Commentary on the Torah"; Touati, "Le problème du *Kol Nidrey.*"

54. This is the burden of Gersonides' complaint in his commentary on the Torah (16d/67/115) that some of his recent predecessors had over-allegorized the Torah in their commentaries. See also 28b/133/268.

55. This is not to say that Gersonides escaped criticism for making public things better kept under wraps. This is the gist of several criticisms of Gersonides made by Isaac Abravanel in his *Commentary on the Torah.* See, e.g., his commentary on Genesis, 115, 122, 241. For other critiques of Gersonides, see Touati, 541–59, and my "Gersonides and His Cultured Despisers."

56. Husik identified Gersonides as the author whom Judah ben Jeḥiel Messer Leon (fifteenth century) characterized as "the wise in his own eyes." See Husik's *Judah Messer Leon's Commentary,* sec. xii, 93–108.

57. There is considerable evidence to the effect that large numbers of Gersonides' contemporaries in the south of France had at least some philosophical knowledge. If nothing else, the ban of 1305 points to this. For the generation or two before Gersonides, see Saperstein, *Decoding the Rabbis,* ch. 7.

58. On this see my "Gersonides on *Imitatio Dei.*"

INTRODUCTION TO THE COMMENTARY ON SONG OF SONGS COMPOSED BY THE SAGE LEVI BEN GERSHOM

1. Much of what Gersonides wrote appears to have been motivated by the fact that he found earlier treatments of the subjects unsatisfactory. See, e.g., how he opens

his discussion of astronomy in *Wars of the Lord,* 5:1.1 (in the translation of B. R. Goldstein, *Astronomy of Levi Ben Gerson,* 22). Similarly, see the introduction to *Wars of the Lord* (Leipzig, 3; Feldman, 1:93). Further on the passage here, see my "Communication or Lack Thereof."

2. On the midrashic approach to Song of Songs, which sees the text as a description of the love between God and Israel, see Urbach, "Homiletical Interpretations of the Sages." For an up-to-date survey of the subject, see Hirshman, *Ha-Miqra u-Midrasho,* 65–73.

3. Or: "only endeavor to explain them according to their intention."

4. Gersonides takes his own advice in his *Commentary on the Torah,* dividing his commentary into several parts: a *peshat*-oriented "explanation of the words of the passage," a philosophical and halakhic "explanation of the content [*divrei*] of the passage," and a list of lessons to be learned from the passage.

5. Compare the *Commentary on the Torah,* 2c/3/4. Compare also Gersonides' repetition of this point near the end of the next paragraph of our text here.

6. The importance of distinguishing substantial from accidental matters is an issue which seems to have exercised Gersonides a fair amount. He explains why in his *Commentary on the Torah,* there writing that confusing substantial and accidental matters leads one to think that one has apprehended universal matters appertaining to the intellect when in reality all one has apprehended is particulars, something which animals also apprehend. (It is the universals, abstracted from particulars, which are the "intelligibles" [*muskalot*], the true objects of knowledge.) See also *Commentary on the Torah,* 16a/64/110.

7. In seeking to make the true meaning of Song of Songs explicit in his commentary, Gersonides is opposing the position of at least one of the talmudic rabbis. In *Midrash Shir ha-Shirim,* on Song of Songs 1:2, R. Illa, playing on the word *yishaqeni* (Let him kiss me), says, "There are things on which the mouth should be closed [*mashiqim*]." See *Midrash Shir ha-Shirim,* 18.

8. Compare Gersonides' *Commentary on the Torah,* 2c/3/4. He allowed himself considerable latitude in rejecting rabbinical explanations of biblical passages, distinguishing between rabbinical midrash and the *correct* interpretation; see, e.g., 24c/112/217, 27d/131/265, and 37d–38a/185/383. For discussions of Gersonides' Bible commentary relevant to this theme, see Feldman's appendix to vol. 2 of his translation of the *Wars of the Lord,* "Gersonides and Biblical Exegesis," 211–47; W. Z. Harvey, "Quelques réflexions"; Funkenstein, "Gersonides' Bible Commentary."

9. Hebrew: *ḥiqquyim.* This term, deriving from the Hebrew root meaning "to portray" (see Ezek. 8:10) and in medieval and modern Hebrew used in the sense of "imitation," is not easy to translate. Gersonides uses it as a synonym for *mashal* (translated here as "allegory") in *Wars of the Lord,* 2:6 (Leipzig, 109; Feldman, 2:56); he there defines *ḥiqquy* as *ḥiddah* ("riddle" or "enigma") or *mashal.* Feldman translates it as "representation," offering "symbol" as an alternative. I think that this translation is a bit too vague (although it nicely catches the senses of portrayal and imitation from the Hebrew); it does not emphasize sufficiently that we are dealing with a figure of speech. I therefore use "symbolic representation." For an example of the term's use in the sense of "imitation" in medieval Hebrew, see ibn Tibbon's translation of *Maimonides' Treatise on Logic,* ch. 8.

10. The Hebrew *mashal* is here translated as "allegory." In his commentary to Prov.

1:1 Gersonides defines the term as follows: "A *mashal* is something said by way of similarity, sometimes to provide a representation (*ṣiyyur*) of the thing about which one wishes to speak; sometimes to point out some aspect of the thing which is intended because it is unfamiliar (*meruḥaq*) . . . for in describing unfamiliar things a *mashal* to something a little similar to it will make the intended thing clear." Compare Qimḥi's commentary to Ezekiel 17:2. For background, see the discussion on Maimonides' use of the term *mashal* in Klein-Braslavy, *Perush ha-Rambam le-Sippur Bri'at ha-ʿOlam,* 39–46. For Maimonides on *ḥiddah,* see Klein-Braslavy, "Maimonides' Commentaries on Proverbs 1:6," 123 n. 10.

11. Note must be taken of the implication of Gersonides' words here. He is claiming that rabbinical interpretations of Song of Songs will be rendered clearer by his own commentary on the scroll. The implication is that the talmudic rabbis meant through their midrashic exegesis to hint at the philosophic import of Song of Songs. In this, of course, Gersonides is following in the footsteps of Maimonides, who maintained that the rabbis were actually philosophers as well as halakhists. On this, see my *Dogma in Medieval Jewish Thought,* 234 n. 169, and the analysis of Maimonides' "Parable of the Palace" (*Guide of the Perplexed,* 3:51) in my *Maimonides on Human Perfection,* 13–39, esp. 34–35.

12. Gersonides, like Maimonides before him, both promises to devote a separate treatise to the philosophic exposition of rabbinical midrashim and, so far as we know, fails to keep that promise. For Maimonides, see his introduction to the tenth chapter of Mishnah Sanhedrin (*Pereq Ḥeleq*), in *Mishnah im Perush ha-Rambam,* ed. Kafiḥ, 4:140, and his introduction to *Guide of the Perplexed,* 9. Gersonides repeats his promise to write a book explaining rabbinical midrashim near the end of his commentary on Genesis (48d/245/517). There are other books which Gersonides planned to write and which, so far as is known, he never wrote. See, e.g., the introduction to his *Commentary on the Torah,* 3d/11/14. Note his use here of the highly traditionalist phrase "if God wills and decrees that I live," a phrase that he cannot mean literally, since Gersonides' God does not know of Gersonides' specific existence and does not individually determine whether anyone will live or die. In general, Gersonides uses much more traditionalist ways of expression in his Bible commentaries than in the *Wars of the Lord.* Most interpreters tend to ignore this, interpreting the Bible commentaries in light of the *Wars of the Lord* while admitting that the former may be couched in formulations not strictly allowable to Gersonides on his own terms. This might be a case in point. Given that he explicitly distances himself from esoteric writing (in the introduction to the *Wars of the Lord* [Leipzig, 8; Feldman, 1:100]) and given that he cites the *Wars of the Lord* again and again in the Bible commentaries, there is little point in surmising that he sought in the Bible commentaries to hide his true views.

13. Hebrew: *ha-haṣlaḥah ha takhliti'it.* Compare *Wars of the Lord,* 1:13 (Leipzig, 90; Feldman, 1:225). On the term *haṣlaḥah,* see my translator's introduction, n. 19.

14. One of Gersonides' best-known disputes with Maimonides concerns the question of whether and to what extent we can know God. Maimonides made the claim that God is unknowable in *Guide,* 1.52. Gersonides takes issue with this claim throughout *Wars of the Lord,* vol. 3, most especially in chapter 2. For details of their debate, see Samuelson, "On Knowing God"; Wolfson, "Maimonides and Gersonides on Divine Attributes."

15. Hebrew: *yoshram. Yosher* has been translated in a variety of ways. Different scholars have chosen "organization," "arrangement," "regularity," and "rightness." My own choice reflects that of Wolfson, *Crescas' Critique of Aristotle*, 349. On this term see the important comments of Freudenthal, "Cosmogonie et physique chez Gersonide," 305.

16. Hebrew: ʿ*al mah she-hem* ʿ*alav;* on this expression see Husik, no. 34. Gersonides' position here can be made clearer by taking note of another important debate between him and Maimonides. For the latter, to the extent that any knowledge can bring us to perfection, it must be knowledge of metaphysical matters. For Gersonides, learning truths about the physical universe also perfects us and brings us to immortality. For details of this debate, see my "Gersonides on the Song of Songs and the Nature of Science." As Gersonides will make clearer as he proceeds, knowledge of the physical universe is valuable not only in and of itself but also for bringing us to knowledge of God (the point being made here briefly). Compare further his *Commentary on the Torah,* 170d, 172d, where the temple, its implements and cult, and the Sukkot festivals' four species are all explained in terms of the lessons concerning physics we learn from them, lessons that in turn lead us to knowledge of God.

17. Hebrew: *muskalot,* sing. *muskal.* This term could easily be translated as "concept." *Muskal* means "that which is apprehended by the intellect," that is, things known intellectually as opposed to things apprehended by the senses; in simple terms, concepts. The use of "intelligible," however, preserves the medieval flavor of the text and is used in this unique sense here, whereas the English term *concept* can be used in a variety of senses. There is a considerable amount of literature on Gersonides' use of the term; for a recent and valuable study, see Manekin, "Logic and Its Applications."

18. We know God, that is, not as the effect of better-known causes but as the cause of empirically known phenomena. It was a staple of medieval philosophy that the examination of nature (= the natural sciences) yields a measure of knowledge concerning God. See, e.g., S. Harvey, *Falaquera's "Epistle of the Debate,"* 88. Gersonides makes the point in many places. See, e.g., *Wars of the Lord,* 5:1.2: "The prophets and those who spoke by virtue of the Holy Spirit made us aware that it is appropriate to expand this investigation [of astronomy] because from it we are led to understand God, as will become evident in this study." I quote from B. R. Goldstein, *Astronomy of Levi Ben Gerson,* 24.

19. That is, our apprehension of God, not God's apprehension; the translation here reflects the ambiguity of the Hebrew.

20. See *Wars of the Lord,* 3.1 (Leipzig, 121; Feldman, 2:90 and nn. ad loc.); *Wars of the Lord* 5:3.3 (Leipzig, 241); Touati, *Les Guerres du Seigneur, III–IV,* 42; Samuelson (trans.), *Gersonides' On God's Knowledge,* 98.

21. Aristotle, *Physics,* 2:4-6. Aristotle, of course, made no reference to Epicurus. Gersonides, it should be noted, knew Aristotle primarily, if not exclusively, through Averroës. Gersonides' references to Aristotle are usually actually references to Averroës' commentaries on or epitomes of Aristotle (compare Mashbaum, xv). Wherever possible, however, I have sought to find sources in Aristotle for the positions attributed to him by Gersonides.

22. Aristotle, *On the Soul,* 3:5. For Gersonides on Averroës on this, see Mashbaum, 126. For a further text in which Gersonides refers to this passage in *On the Soul,*

see S. Harvey, "Did Gersonides Believe in the Absolute Generation of Prime Matter?"

23. See Aristotle, *Posterior Analytics,* 1:1–3 generally and the opening of the book (71a1) in particular. There Aristotle says, "All teaching and all intellectual learning come about from already existing knowledge." Compare *Wars of the Lord* 1.9 (Leipzig, 55; Feldman, 1:174).

24. In *Wars of the Lord,* Feldman, 1:95, translates these terms as "primary cognition" or "undemonstrable or intuited principle" and "derived cognition" or "derived, or demonstrable, principle." In his *Treatise on Logic,* Efros, trans., 47–48, Maimonides presents as examples of a primary concept "when we know that the whole is greater than the part, that two is an even number, and that things equal to the same thing equal each other." Examples of secondary concepts are "geometric theorems and astronomic calculations, which are all true, because they may all be demonstrated by premises, most of which come close to first ideas." See further Gersonides' commentary on verses 3:5 and 4:5.

25. Compare *Wars of the Lord,* 1:6 (Leipzig, 46; Feldman, 1:161) and *Wars of the Lord,* 1:10 (Leipzig, 68; Feldman, 1:195). We find the same idea in Gersonides' supercommentary on Averroës' *Epitome of De Anima* (Mashbaum, 37). Feldman and Mashbaum both refer the reader further to *Posterior Analytics,* 2:19, 99b. For a helpful commentary on this chapter see Barnes, *Aristotle's* Posterior Analytics, 248–60.

26. Compare Mashbaum, 19.

27. Compare Aristotle, *Posterior Analytics,* 1:18, 81b1. See further Aristotle, *Topics,* 1.18, 108b10. Compare the parallel passage in Mashbaum, 37. By *gezerah kolelet* (translated here as "universal statement") Gersonides means a general sentence of the form "Every woman is living" or "Everything living is body." See Gersonides, *Sefer ha-Heqqesh ha-Yashar,* treatise 1, par. 7, Manekin, trans., 55; see also 322, s.v. "universal."

28. Aristotle, *On the Soul,* 3:5.

29. *Mishpaṭ bilti baʿal takhlit;* that is, a sentence that is unlimited in its application.

30. Compare *Wars of the Lord,* 1:6 (Leipzig, 46–47; Feldman, 1:162) and Gersonides' discussion in his supercommentary on Averroës' *Epitome of De Anima,* Mashbaum, 159 ff. Gersonides' point here is to explain how we can arrive at universals without positing the existence of Platonic forms. The coming paragraphs explain how this comes about. I am very grateful to Professor Charles Manekin for helping me to understand this paragraph. Many of the issues in the last two paragraphs are taken up again in the commentary to 3:5.

31. Gersonides' sources here are not in Aristotle's writings themselves but in Averroës' commentaries on them. With respect to the first, see Mashbaum, 30–31. With respect to the second, see Averroës' *Epitome of Parva Naturalia,* 26. Compare *Wars of the Lord,* 1:3 (Leipzig, 21; Feldman, 1:122). See further Mashbaum, liv. In his discussion here Gersonides explains how our sense perceptions are rendered more and more abstract (= "spiritual") as they are transmitted from one internal sense of the soul to the next. On this theory of abstraction, see Feldman, "Platonic Themes in Gersonides' Doctrine," 262, and the sources he cites.

32. Hebrew: *roshem;* my translation here is supported by Feldman, "Platonic Themes in Gersonides' Doctrine," 262, who points out that "the sense organ is a material thing and the sense object is a material object. . . . Gersonides' term . . . expresses the idea of a physical impact."

33. Literally, "as if you were to say." This is an expression Gersonides uses frequently in this text and one which I have not seen in other writers.

34. Davidson, in "Gersonides on the Material and Active Intellects," 244, translates this expression (*shavah ha-ṣurah ha-hi be-ʿaṣmah kolelet*) as "that very form becomes universal."

35. Aristotle, *Metaphysics*, 1.6, 1.9, 13.4–5 (esp. 1078b). Compare *Wars of the Lord*, 1.6 (Leipzig, 46–47; Feldman, 1:162). It is Gersonides' point here that his account of knowledge (as summarized in the preceding paragraphs) solves the problems that led the skeptics to claim that knowledge as such was impossible and that led Plato, rejecting the claim of the skeptics, to the theory of forms. Compare Mashbaum, 164–65.

36. In dealing with these impediments at this point, Gersonides is acting in accord with advice he will give later in his *Commentary on the Torah* (56c, *toʿelet* 10), namely, that one should always seek to determine the impediments that might arise in any project one undertakes before beginning the project itself.

37. Compare Maimonides, *Guide of the Perplexed*, 1.34 (76–77), 3.51 (627). Gersonides refers to this matter again in his *Commentary on the Torah*, 171b, 171d, maintaining there, in effect, that "intellect improves with age." The weakening of physical powers allows for strengthening of the intellect; the screen of matter is diminished in old age. The issue comes up again below, in the commentary to 8:8.

38. It would seem that Gersonides is confusing two distinct issues here: (a) that true knowledge of the physical world depends on our grasp of the commonalities exemplified through particular beings and (b) the need to study these things in an orderly fashion. With respect to the latter, compare his commentary on Prov. 1:2 and 28:26.

39. Literally, "does not disappear."

40. Gersonides' use of this term (root: *h-r-s*) probably follows Samuel ibn Tibbon's translation of Maimonides' *Guide*, 1.5 (Pines, 30), following Exod. 19:21, *lest they break through unto the Lord to gaze, and many of them perish*. Ibn Tibbon discusses the term in his *Perush ha-Millot ha-Zarot,* explaining it as referring to the act of entering into a place one has no right to enter in order to see that which one ought not to see. In this explanation ibn Tibbon is followed by ben Yehudah, who also brings the more customary meaning of the term ("destroy"), citing Lam. 2:2. Pines translates "overhasty" and Kafiḥ uses the root *p-r-ṣ*. See further 3:5 below and Gersonides' commentary on Ecclesiastes, 31c, 32d, for the need to study the sciences in their proper order. Gersonides uses the term in his commentary to Proverbs 11:2 in the sense proposed here. See Husik, no. 3.

41. Compare *Guide of the Perplexed*, 1.34, 73–74.

42. Literally, "it."

43. The importance of studying each science with the method appropriate to it is a subject to which Gersonides returns several times in this commentary (e.g., at 2:15 below). For background and explanation, see Funkenstein, *Theology and the Scientific Imagination,* 36.

44. That is, the difficulties involved in empirical observation. Gersonides was acutely aware of such difficulties; they moved him to propose the idea of the microscope, and he may have been the first scientist to propose the instrument. See Freudenthal, "Human Felicity and Astronomy," 62, citing Gersonides' supercommentary on Averroës' *Epitome of the Book of Animals*, Ms. Vat. Urb. 42 (JNUL 681), at 9b–10a. Further

on Gersonides' involvement in physical experimentation, see *Wars of the Lord*, 5.1, in B. R. Goldstein, trans., *Astronomy of Levi Ben Gerson*, 55. See further Goldstein, "Levi ben Gerson: On Astronomy and Physical Experiments."

45. Or: "tinyness."

46. That is, the subject under study.

47. In *Guide*, 1.34 Maimonides lists five "causes that prevent the commencement of instruction with divine science [metaphysics], the indication of things that ought to be indicated, and the presentation of this to the multitude" (72). They are (a) "the difficulty, subtlety, and obscurity of the matter itself" (72); (b) "the insufficiency of the minds of all men at their beginnings" (73); (c) "the length of the preliminaries" (73); (d) "the natural aptitudes" (76–77); and (e) "that men are occupied with the necessities of the bodies" (79). Under the fourth heading Maimonides explains that the attainment of the moral virtues is a necessary prerequisite for the attainment of the rational virtues.

48. Compare Maimonides' discussion in *Guide*, 3:27.

49. Note should be taken of the different attitudes of Maimonides and Gersonides toward "the masses" (*he-hamon*). They both were interested in the welfare of the masses (as is proved in Maimonides' case by the details of his biography and in Gersonides' case, for example, by his rejection of obscurantist writing, "unless it was the intention of the author to conceal [his ideas] from the masses so that only a few would understand [his words], because such ideas, would, if understood, cause harm to the masses" [*Wars of the Lord*, Leipzig, 8; Feldman, 1:100–1]), but Gersonides seems to have less disdain for them than did Maimonides. Maimonides' concern for the well-being of the masses seems to have been motivated by a sort of noblesse oblige and the religious obligation to keep them from making certain types of gross theological errors (on which, see my *Dogma in Medieval Jewish Thought*, 34–49). Maimonides saw as fully human only those individuals who had achieved a level of metaphysical insight apparently well beyond the abilities of most of his contemporaries; only these few would enjoy immortality. Opposed to this, Gersonides maintained that insight into physics was sufficient to actualize one's human potential and make entry into the world to come possible. See my "Gersonides on the Song of Songs and the Nature of Science." On the differences between Gersonides and Maimonides on esotericism, which is obviously relevant here as well, see my "Gersonides on *Imitatio Dei*."

50. In his commentary to Prov. 2:7 Gersonides explains that even small mistakes concerning metaphysical matters "distance a man from his perfection." Compare below, commentary to 4:8.

51. Gersonides' point in the last two paragraphs would appear to be as follows: the purpose of the commandments is to bring us to moral perfection; moral perfection is a prerequisite for intellectual perfection, a point often reiterated in this commentary (see, e.g., the "first impediment" just above, concerning the "effervescence of our natures" and 1:9, 1:12, 1:17, and 2:10) and in *Wars of the Lord* (see, e.g., 4:6 [Leipzig, 177; Feldman, 2:193]) and emphasized by Maimonides (on this see my *Maimonides on Human Perfection*, 26–28). The Torah, however, is not interested in advertising this point to the masses. Nevertheless, the ultimate end ought to guide all of the means adopted to achieve that end. The Torah, therefore, cunningly intermixes exoteric moral teaching with esoteric philosophical teaching.

52. See Gersonides' *Commentary on the Torah,* 104a–5b.

53. Gersonides appears to be saying not that the rewards promised by the Torah do not actually devolve upon those who earn them but that such benefits are not truly felicities (*haslahot*). In his *Commentary on the Torah,* 215d, Gersonides explicitly states that obedience to the Torah leads not only to spiritual benefits but to "wondrous physical benefits" as well. He emphasizes the point again in the Torah commentary on 240d and 241d. In his commentary to Ecclesiastes, 27d, he dismisses physical pleasures, when compared to delights of wisdom, as vain and worthless.

54. Grammatically, this sentence leaves a bit to be desired, although the intent is clear enough: since most people do not understand the point of the Torah they would not perform the commandments were not the promise of reward and the threat of punishment held out before them.

55. This is a difficult passage since the Hebrew seems to imply that a prophet need not be a savant (Hebrew: *hakham*), contradicting Gersonides' expressly stated position in *Wars of the Lord,* introduction (Leipzig, 4; Feldman, 1:94), 2:6 (Leipzig, 111; Feldman, 2:59), and 6:2.11 (Leipzig, 453–54) and in the *Commentary on the Torah,* 248b (seventh lesson). See further Kreisel, "Philosopher and Prophet"; Eisen, *Gersonides on Providence,* 74–76, 215. A more literal translation of the passage here would be "because this is not the [objective] of a prophet qua prophet but [of a prophet] qua savant, to the extent that he is one." For a similar expression, but one which does not appear to contradict the claim that prophets must be savants, see *Wars of the Lord,* Leipzig, 4; Feldman, 95: "It is possible that there are things that a wise man who is not a prophet cannot apprehend, but which can be known by a wise man who is a prophet insofar as he is wise." A possible solution to our conundrum lies in the fact, noted by Touati, 59–65, that for Gersonides, prophets can err in scientific matters. See the *Commentary on the Torah,* 24d/115/222 and the commentary on Job 39:30. The point of our text would then appear to be that although the Torah does teach scientific truth, it does not teach it in the way in which it is taught in other ("scientific") contexts.

56. That is, the authors of the *Ketuvim* ("sacred writings"), which, of course, include Song of Songs.

57. Literally, "perfection of the intelligibles." Gersonides makes a similar distinction in his commentary on Deut. 6:4 (211d). *Hear, O Israel,* he says, refers to hearing, believing, *and* understanding. (Perfected) individuals *understand,* the multitude *believes.*

58. In his commentary to Prov. 4:22, Gersonides says that the point of the book is to guide its readers to intellectual and moral perfection.

59. Hebrew: *derikhah.* This term, which Gersonides may have coined (he uses it frequently, other writers almost not at all, as may be seen from the references in the dictionaries of Klatzkin and ben Yehudah), derives from the Hebrew root *d-r-kh,* "to step or stamp down, as in squeezing grapes; to bend or draw a bow." It connotes readiness, preparation, process, transition, tendency, passage, passing through, moving in the direction of.

60. On this division of the sciences, see my "Gersonides on the Song of Songs and the Nature of Science." Compare Aristotle, *Metaphysics,* 6:1.

61. Compare Aristotle, *Metaphysics,* 1061a 29 ff.: "The mathematician investigates

abstractions (for in his investigation he eliminates all the sensible qualities, e.g., weight and lightness, hardness and its contrary, and leaves only the quantitative and continuous . . . and the attributes of things qua quantitative and continuous)."

62. In other words, physics deals with a more specialized aspect of the subject matter of mathematics and thus follows it in the order of study and in the order of nature. Compare *Wars of the Lord,* introduction (Leipzig, 7, as emended and translated by Feldman, 1:99): "Knowledge of mathematical matters precedes by nature knowledge of matters in the natural sciences . . . for the mathematician investigates body in the abstract, whereas the natural scientist investigates body not only in the abstract but also insofar as it is in motion." Gersonides implies in this paragraph that one might have thought otherwise, since mathematics is more general than physics, and that in terms of generality, then, the proper order of the sciences is physics, mathematics, metaphysics. The clause I skipped in the ellipsis in the quoted passage reads as follows: "Although the one subject [mathematics] is more general than the other [natural sciences]." Note that where I translate *ḥokhmat ha-ṭeva'* as "physics," Feldman uses "natural sciences."

63. Aristotle, *Physics,* 1:1, 1:5, esp. 189a. Gersonides' comments on mathematics and physics here seem to mean that whereas the mathematical sciences deal with concepts such as weight in the abstract, physics deals with the actual weight of specific bodies. Compare Aristotle, *Metaphysics,* 4:2, 1004b. The confusing way in which Gersonides formulates his discussion here seems to be a consequence of the fact that medieval Hebrew apparently had no term for the abstract concept "weight." Compare, e.g., Maimonides' "Laws of the Foundations of the Torah," 3:3: "All of the spheres are neither light nor heavy," echoed in Gershom ben Shlomoh's *Sha'ar ha-Shamayim* 13:2, 82a. Gershom wants to say that the spheres are weightless and expresses himself thus: "the spheres are neither light nor heavy." Gershom ben Shlomoh, it might be noted, is popularly considered to be the father of Gersonides and is identified as such on the title page of *Sha'ar ha-Shamayim.* For the known facts of the situation see Touati, 34–36. For important background to the issues raised here see Glasner, "Gersonides' Theory."

64. Which entanglement complicates matters; knowledge derived from material matters, as we have seen, must undergo many stages of abstraction before it becomes knowledge.

65. Note here Gersonides' implied claim that mathematics also actualizes our intellects, a position Maimonides, as we have noted, would have rejected altogether.

66. Hebrew: *mofet;* in modern logical parlance the preferred translation would probably be "proof." "Demonstration," however, not only reflects the Latin *demonstratio* (and thus helps preserve some of the medieval flavor of our text) but also better reflects the Hebrew, which in the Bible means "miraculous sign" or "demonstration." It also draws attention to the fact that the purpose of a *mofet* is to *convince* one of the truth of some proposition or other, just as for Gersonides the purpose of a miracle is to *convince* its witnesses of the reliability of the prophet with whom it is associated. On this, see my "Gersonides on Miracles."

67. Absolute demonstrations proceed from causes to effects, from prior to posterior, where what is prior to us in knowledge is also prior in existence. See S. Harvey, "The Hebrew Translation," 81. Mathematical proofs are classically deductive. H. T. Goldstein translates Narboni's commentary to *Guide,* 1:71, in which he explains this

term: "He means by 'decisive demonstration' what Aristotle called 'absolute demonstration,' namely, *demonstratio causae et essendi.* And this is true, for this kind of
demonstration, whose existence is very rare, does not often exist with respect to physical things." See H. T. Goldstein, *Averroës' Questions in Physics,* 119. Isaac Husik is
typically very clear on the issue. An "absolute demonstration" is "a syllogism in
which the middle term is by nature prior to the last term and the cause of it. . . . An
example would be the following: All men are mortal, A is a man, therefore A is mortal. The middle term, 'man,' is prior to 'mortal' and the cause of it." See Husik, no. 1.

68. Ptolemy, *Almagest,* 1:1, ed. Toomer, 36. Gersonides repeats this point below in
his commentary to 3:6. The *Almagest* was translated into Hebrew by Jacob Anatoli
between 1231 and 1235.

69. Hebrew: *takhlit;* also translated here as "goal" or "end," depending on the needs
of English style. The final clause of this sentence reads as follows: "*lefi she-ḥokhmat
mah she-aḥar ha-ṭevaʿ holekhet mimmenah mahalakh ha-shelemut ve-ha-takhlit.*" It
may be that we are dealing here with an Arabism, *yelekh mimmenu mi-madregah,* in
which case the sentence should be translated as follows: "Physics necessarily precedes
the divine science which is metaphysics since metaphysics stands to it in the relation
of [its] perfection and purpose." On the phrase in question, see Husik, no. 21. On the
notion of priority raised here, see Feldman's note in *Wars of the Lord,* 1:99–100 and
the lengthy discussion in Staub, *The Creation of the World,* 173–78.

70. That is, metaphysics assumes the existence of incorporeal causes, something
that is proved in physics.

71. Hebrew: *moftei re'ayah;* in Latin, *demonstratio per signum* or *demonstratio
quia.* See H. T. Goldstein, *Averroës' Questions in Physics,* 59. In this kind of nonde-
monstrative proof, Goldstein points out, "the middle term is a cause only for our
knowledge of the conclusion, and not for the existence of the conclusion." She quotes
Narboni on this (see above, n. 67): "The existence of God is also proved by *demonstratio per signum,* namely, from the posterior, not from the prior; for He is prior to
all things, and there is nothing prior to Him, and how could His existence be proved
by a *demonstratio causae* when He is the cause of everything?" See further S. Harvey,
"The Hebrew Translation," 81. Husik, no. 1, explains this as a proof in which a cause
is inferred from a consequence and cites the following example: "All wetness is the
result of a liquid, this spot is wet, therefore there was liquid here."

72. Since having a "settled mind" (*yishuv ha-daʿat*) comes only after one overcomes
the "effervescence of youth," Gersonides is implying here that the different sciences
are best studied at different ages. See above, n. 37.

73. That is, those who seek absolute, apodictic verities in physics are in for a dis-
appointment. The point is made clearer in the coming paragraph. With respect to the
ordering of the verifiability of the sciences found in this paragraph, compare Maimonides' comment in *Guide,* 1:31, 66: "The things about which there is this perplexity are very numerous in divine matters, few in matters pertaining to natural
science, and nonexistent in matters pertaining to mathematics." On this statement see
Altmann, "Maimonides on the Intellect," 113. Further on this subject, see the extensive treatment in S. Harvey, *Falaquera's "Epistle of the Debate,"* 43.

74. The point is that the premises of metaphysics are based on commonly accepted
"reputable" opinions "which are accepted by everyone or by the majority or by the
wise—i.e., by all, or by the majority, or by the most notable and reputable of them"

(Aristotle, *Topics*, 1:1, 100b). Compare *Wars of the Lord,* introduction: "Our knowledge of the essence of the First Cause is very slight" (Leipzig, 2; Feldman, 1: 92). Because of the limitations of our knowledge, metaphysics cannot be based on apodictic proofs. See further *Wars of the Lord,* 6:1.5 (Leipzig, 307). Compare below the commentaries to 8:5 and 8:8.

75. With respect to Gersonides' use of the term *fruit* here, compare Pines, "What Was Original in Arabic Science?" 181 (original), 329 (reprint): "We find accordingly that these three sciences [medicine, astrology, alchemy] were sometimes considered as 'the fruit,' that is, the goal of knowledge." In a number of places in his Torah commentary Gersonides calls knowledge *peri kol ha-'adam,* a phrase that may be rendered liberally as "the ultimate fruit of human endeavor." See 115d and 134c for examples of this usage.

76. That is, metaphysics.

77. For the story of Elisha ben Abuyah, the notorious apostate Tanna, see Mishnah Ḥagigah 15a. The phrase translated here as "with what he sees fit" is *lifi mah she-ya'ut lo.* A possible alternative is "in accordance with what pleases him." The point is that Elisha, led astray by his lusts, allowed his desires to determine his metaphysical conclusions instead of basing them on objective reality. Compare Maimonides, *Guide of the Perplexed,* 1:32. In *Wars of the Lord,* 5:3.13 (Leipzig, 289) Gersonides explains that Elisha's mistake was theological dualism: thinking that the God who rules the sublunary world is not the same as the God who rules the superlunary world. This mistake was based on his supposition that the principle (*hathalah*) of corruptible entities must be distinct from the principle of incorruptible entities; this view led him to deny immortality to human beings as well.

78. As has been noted several times already, the study of physics, therefore, and not only of metaphysics, brings one to "utmost human felicity."

79. The Hebrew text of the Bible is divided into *parashot,* or paragraphs; it is to these that Gersonides refers here.

80. Compare Averroës' approach to the writing of introductions; see S. Harvey, "The Hebrew Translation." In a personal communication to me Prof. Harvey was kind enough to make a number of comments on this sentence. He suggests translating it as "and its rank, its method" and emending the last word from "its purpose" (*takhlito*) to "its utility" (*to'alto*). My own preference is to leave texts untouched unless absolutely compelled to emend them.

81. That is, the author of Song of Songs. An alternative translation for the phrase rendered here and below as "he indicates" would be "the book makes reference to."

82. Literally, "from the perspective of."

83. The difficulty in understanding Song of Songs resides in the fact that it deals with difficult matters and is couched in symbolic language. Having explained in broad outlines the content of the book, Gersonides now turns to give an explanation of the symbolic language in which it is written.

84. Or: "matters contained in this book."

85. That is, entities compounded of matter and form, as opposed to the separate intellects, which are pure form.

86. That is, a sign of human perfection is that humans contain in themselves, as it were, the entire universe. On the notion of human beings as a microcosm, see *Guide,* 1:72, 190–92. Further on the subject, see the article "microcosm" in the *Ency-*

clopaedia Judaica and the sources in Sherwin, "The Human Body and the Image of God," 80.

87. In his commentary on Ecclesiastes (at 37c) Gersonides says that man's material intellect ought to be his king.

88. See also Gittin, 56b. Gersonides repeats this idea in his *Commentary on the Torah,* 208c (with reference to Deut. 3:25). Compare Vermes, "The Symbolical Interpretation of 'Lebanon' in the *Targums.*"

89. The Hebrew here is unclear; this is the best sense I could give it.

90. Here we have Gersonides, the master of the ambiguous antecedent, at his indeterminate best. His point is that the author of Song of Songs repeated this allegory as frequently as he did in order to stimulate the reader of the book to understand the author's intention to the best of the reader's ability.

91. Gersonides makes use here of words drawn from 2:17 and 4:6 without exactly quoting those verses.

92. Literally, "perfection in wisdom." My translation may be anachronistic, carrying with it the modern connotations of the term *science.* But since the "wisdom" Gersonides is referring to is first physics and then metaphysics I think that the translation offered here best captures Gersonides' sense for the modern reader.

93. Achieving perfection in the sciences is the "fruit" of human endeavor. In fruit-bearing plants, seeds grow in the fruit, and the fruit grows out of the flowers. The seed is thus the ultimate end of the process, the fruit a means toward achieving that end, and the flower a means toward achieving the fruit. That which one needs in order achieve perfection in the sciences, then, is likened to flowers, that which one needs in order to make fruit and seed possible. Furthermore, botanically and temporally, flowers precede fruit, as the work of the imagination precedes perfection in the sciences. Although he quotes 2:16 here, Gersonides' actual discussion of this issue is mainly found in his commentary to 2:1.

94. Two things, then, may be said to "feed among the lilies": the intellect vis-à-vis the imagination and the imagination vis-à-vis the impressions conveyed to it by the senses.

95. That is, for the human (material) intellect to be perfected and achieve actualization, it needs two things: the presence of the Active Intellect emanating towards it and the activity of the faculty of the imagination, which involves the presentation to the human intellect of imaginative forms, abstracted from the senses, to be rendered yet more abstract and thus turned into concepts.

96. That is, the intellect.

97. That is, the imagination.

98. For the Aristotelian source of the doctrine that the male contributes the form, the female the matter, see *Generation of Animals,* pt. 1, bk. 2, ch. 3, at 732a. Compare also *Guide,* 1:17, 43, where Maimonides traces the idea to "Plato and his predecessors."

99. To rephrase this paragraph in a less ambiguous fashion, Gersonides says that the human material intellect is perfected through the emanations down to it, so to speak, from the Active Intellect and up to it, so to speak, from the imagination. This only occurs, however, when the faculty of imagination is disciplined and remains subservient to the material intellect, placing itself entirely at the disposal of the material intellect. This being so, Gersonides says, the author of Song of Songs likened

the attraction between material intellect and faculty of imagination to the sexual attraction between male and female, where the intellect corresponds to the male and the imagination to the female.

100. That is, the imaginative forms stand to the intelligible forms as milk stands to the nourishment needed by the body. As milk nourishes the body, so the imaginative forms nourish the intelligible forms. The material intellect, then, nurses from the breasts of the faculty of imagination. On this passage, compare Davidson, "Gersonides on the Material and Active Intellects," 236. In the preceding two paragraphs, "emanate" and "influence" are used to translate variants of the Hebrew *shefaʿ*.

101. Gersonides reverses the word order in the verse.

102. Literally, "[male] object of desire." The two figures in Song of Songs are called by Gersonides *ḥashuq,* "[male] object of desire," and *ḥashuqah,* "[female] object of desire." It does not sound as bizarre in Hebrew as it does in English.

103. The root *t-q-n* in Mishnaic Hebrew can mean "edit," "systematize," "arrange," or "bring to order." See Lieberman, *Hellenism in Jewish Palestine,* 90. Further on the expression, see Havlin, "On *Ḥatimah Sifrutit,*" 154–55. In this context it is likely that Gersonides is echoing Eccles. 12:9 (*And besides that Kohelleth was wise, he also taught the people knowledge; yea, he pondered, and sought out, and set in order [t-q-n] many proverbs*), a verse he quotes in his commentary to 1:1.

104. In his commentary to 3:9 Gersonides explains that the intellect is called "king" because the faculties of the soul all subordinate themselves to its service. The claim is repeated in Gersonides' commentary to Prov. 20:2 and 20:5. One way of expressing the point of this paragraph is that individuals who actualize their intellects become, in effect, kings, as happened literally with Solomon.

105. This verse is cited out of order (appearing here between 2:10 and 2:14).

106. Gersonides explains in his commentary to 7:2 that at the end of the process of intellection the acquired intellect is eternal. The different verses cited here refer to different stages on the way to that perfection. Thus, by 2:10 the soul has achieved moral perfection, by 4:8, perfection in the physical sciences, and so on.

107. Gersonides explains this in his commentary to 8:4 with reference to the greater level of care that must be taken when dealing with metaphysics than with physics.

108. 4:1–5.

109. 6:4–8.

110. 7:2–6.

111. Gersonides explains this significance in his commentary to 7:2, clarifying there that the different descriptions of the beloved refer to the difference between inductive and deductive approaches in the sciences.

112. And indeed Gersonides explains this significance in his commentary to 2:17, there noting that the plural usage in 2:17 refers to the mathematical sciences, which are numerous, the singular usage in 4:6 refers to physics, a science with one specific subject matter, and the plural usage in 8:14 refers to metaphysics, a science with many subjects of research. Specific spices are designated in the second description (4:6) because physics investigates specific existents, whereas the text refers to spices generally in 8:14 because, even though metaphysics does concern itself with many subjects, in the final analysis it investigates absolute existence as such.

113. That is, the author of Song of Songs.

114. In his commentary to 5:1 Gersonides explains that the study of physics in-

volves "intermingling and generality" because of the general nature of the apprehensions involved in that science.

115. That is, the division of the text into sections, each one dealing with another aspect of the problem of achieving intellectual perfection. See above, text following n. 78.

PART ONE: 1 : 1 – 1 : 8

Note to epigraph: This is the way in which Gersonides summarizes the first part of Song of Songs in his introduction; see there the paragraph ending with note 80.

1. The text actually says "Solomon, peace upon him." Throughout the translation I drop such honorifics.

2. Ordinarily I translate the word *mashal* as "allegory" but given the immediate context, and the fact that Solomon was identified as the author of the book of Proverbs, I think that "proverbs" is preferable here. Compare above, Gersonides' introduction, note 103.

3. On the basis of the discussion in Gersonides' introduction (at n. 49) and in conformity with Maimonides, *Guide,* 3:27, I assume that Gersonides is referring here to ethical perfection and to intellectual perfection. Compare further Gersonides' comments to verses 1:9, 1:12, and 1:17, his commentary to Prov. 1:2, and *Wars of the Lord,* 4:6 (Leipzig, 177; Feldman, 2:193).

4. In *Guide,* 2:45, Maimonides distinguishes eleven degrees of prophecy. The second of these is "speaking through the holy spirit." According to Maimonides, all of the Hagiographa, including explicitly Song of Songs, was composed in this manner. It is likely that this is Gersonides' immediate source for saying that Song of Songs was written by one speaking by virtue of the holy spirit. For a discussion of Maimonides' views on speaking through the holy spirit, see Klein-Braslavi, "Solomon's 'Prophecy' in Maimonides' Writings."

5. Literally, "to speak."

6. Mishnah Yadayim, 3:5, and *Midrash Shir ha-Shirim,* 1:11, both attribute the following to R. Akiva: "All the writings are holy, but the Song of Songs is the holy of holies." For the expression "all the *poems* are holy," see the comments of Lieberman in his "Appendix" (to Scholem, *Jewish Gnosticism*), 118, and the references there.

7. That is, 1 Kings 5:12 says that Solomon composed 1,005 poems ("songs"), all of which were holy; Song of Songs was the holiest of them. Note the subtle but important shift in emphasis here. The texts in Yadayim and in *Midrash Ḥazita* say that Song of Songs is the holiest of all the sacred writings (*Ketuvim,* Hagiographa); the text quoted by Gersonides and explained here simply says that it is the holiest of all of Solomon's poems, a much less emphatic claim. If R. Akiva's comment meant that Song of Songs is the locus classicus of Jewish mystical speculation, one can understand why he attaches so much importance to it (he introduces his comment about it by saying that the day on which Song of Songs was "given" was more important than the day on which the world was created); if my interpretation of Gersonides' understanding of Song of Songs is correct (see my introduction) he could hardly attach the same importance to it. In general, Gersonides ignores (or was unfamiliar with) Kabbalah altogether.

8. That is, the intention to emphasize the holy character of this text.

9. That is, the author of Song of Songs.

10. A reference, it is likely, to the opening verses of Proverbs and Ecclesiastes.

11. That is, the book is about the intellect; the "benefit" of the book is that it teaches how to perfect the intellect. With respect to this, compare the comments in my introduction about why Gersonides wrote his commentary.

12. The letter lamed serves as a preposition meaning, among other things, both "to" (in the sense of possession) and "for." Song of Songs is the intellect's both in the sense that it is about the intellect and in the sense that it is "for" the intellect, since it is meant to bring about its improvement.

13. On this expression see *Guide of the Perplexed*, 1:72; Altmann, "Maimonides on the Intellect," 80; Jospe, *Torah and Sophia*, 247–48; and, with specific reference to Gersonides' use of it here, Davidson, "Gersonides on the Material and Active Intellects," 243. As Altmann points out, *ha-sekhel ha-nikneh ha-ne'eṣal* is ibn Tibbon's translation of *al-ʿaql al-mustafād*, "acquired intellect." The acquired intellect is not emanated upon us by the Active Intellect in the sense that it is a "gift" or "intrusion" into our minds; rather, without the emanative activity of the Active Intellect, we cannot perfect our intellects. It is in that sense, and in that sense only, that the acquired intellect is "emanated." On the role of the Active Intellect in human intellection, see my "Gersonides on the Role of the Active Intellect in Human Cognition."

14. There are two contrasts implied here: poetry vs. prose and allegory vs. clear speech.

15. Compare S. Harvey, "The Hebrew Translation of Averroës' Prooemium." Gersonides seems to be following Averroës here in his concern for proper introductions to books.

16. This term (*ṣiyyur*) is not used here in its epistemological sense ("conception" as contrasted to *immut*, "verification"), nor to denote the faculty of imagination. Feldman, in *Wars of the Lord*, 2:215, translates it (in the sense used here) as "allegory." For discussions of the term in its various senses, see Husik, no. 109; Touati, 411–31; Altmann, "Gersonides' Commentary," 12, n. 29; W. Z. Harvey, "Albo's Discussion of Time," 217, n. 27; Hyman, "Aristotle's Theory of the Intellect," 182; Wolfson, "The Terms *Taṣawwur* and *Taṣdiq*"; and, very important, Manekin, "Logic and Its Applications."

17. That is, according to Gersonides, Song of Songs is both expository, describing ultimate human felicity, and persuasive, seeking to encourage its readers to strive for their felicity.

18. Hebrew: *derishah*, from the root *d-r-sh*. The biblical root means "to research" or "to investigate" (Deut. 13:15, 17:4); in post-biblical Hebrew it came to mean "to search out a Scriptural passage or expound it" (Strack, *Introduction to the Talmud and Midrash*, 6; cf. the more extensive discussion in the new edition by Strack and Stemberger, 255–56) and thus *midrash*. See Manekin, "Gersonides: Logic, Sciences, and Philosophy," 297; Manekin, *Logic of Gersonides*, 24, 122, 320.

19. *Be-teḥilat ha-ʿinyan* that is, at the beginning. Gersonides uses this term (and variants of it) quite a bit, and I could find no better way to translate it than to use the Latin expression.

20. Since wine does not ordinarily pursue anyone, Gersonides offers an alternative interpretation of Isa. 5:11.

21. See Shabbat 105b. Gersonides' version differs slightly from that in the printed

editions of the Talmud. The point here is that the evil inclination seduces one into ever more serious transgressions.

22. The Hebrew here is in the passive voice.

23. Here again we see that it is knowledge of physics, not only metaphysics, that is the essence of human felicity. This accords with the way in which Gersonides led his life, devoting, it would seem, the lion's share of his time to scientific investigations. See Freudenthal, "Human Felicity and Astronomy," 64.

24. That is, the route to perfection.

25. See Freudenthal, "Human Felicity and Astronomy," 62, where the author shows how Gersonides suggested using a magnifying glass to observe tiny life forms. Freudenthal notes that Gersonides is the first known scientist to conceive of the principle of the microscope. Compare Gersonides' introduction, n. 44.

26. That is, drawing conclusions from an investigation based on a too small sample can lead to mistakes.

27. We may summarize Gersonides' arguments here as follows: The achievement of human perfection appears to be impossible because (1) we cannot accomplish an end unless we can both picture it before we set out to achieve it and have an antecedent desire to accomplish it. Since ab initio we cannot picture our perfection, we can have therefore no desire to achieve it; this being the case, we cannot achieve our end because we cannot even begin to accomplish it; (2) in our youth, we desire nothing other than the satisfaction of our physical cravings; the more we satisfy them, the more they demand to be satisfied; freeing ourselves of this bondage is so difficult as to be well-nigh impossible, and thus the achievement of human perfection is nearly impossible; (3) even if one could picture one's perfection to oneself, the way of achieving it (which, Gersonides remarks parenthetically, is the disciplined, detailed, step-by-step study of the natural sciences) would still be unknown and thus its actual achievement next to impossible; (4) making scientific observations is very difficult, so it is unlikely that one will ever be able to arrive at a comprehensive description and understanding of any natural phenomenon; that being the case, the principles one derives from one's observations will be flawed; (5) comprehensive investigation of many phenomena can only be accomplished over such a long period that few live long enough to accomplish it.

28. Literally, "man's achievement of his perfection falls under the definition of the impossible."

29. Gersonides talks about the instruments prepared for human beings to bring them to their perfection in his discussions of providence in Wars of the Lord, 4:5 (Leipzig, 165 f.; Feldman, 2:176 f.) and in his commentary on Job (Lassen, trans., 251–52, 264). These "instruments" are our well-designed limbs and our intellects.

30. Gersonides refers back to this point in his commentary on Eccles. 7:23 (34c).

31. This "new translation" is mentioned by Touati, 40, and Klein-Braslavy, "Gersonides on Determinism," 34. In the textual tradition known to Gersonides, what we call book 1 of the Metaphysics was known as book 2 and vice versa. See Pines, "Truth and Falsehood Versus Good and Evil," 103, 114. Perhaps Gersonides' reference to a "new translation" is to an edition of the Metaphysics following the order known to us today as standard. Gersonides himself wrote a supercommentary on Averroës' commentary on the Metaphysics, a supercommentary now unfortunately lost. See Steinschneider, Die hebraeischen Übersetzungen, 167–68; see also Wars of the Lord

(Feldman, 1:29). It is remotely possible, I suppose, that Gersonides could be referring to Michael Scot's "new" Latin translation of the *Metaphysics,* which appeared c. 1220–30. On this latter see Dod, "Aristoteles latinus," and Diem, "Les traductions gréco-latines de la *Métaphysique.*" In any event, getting back to the passage cited here from Aristotle, the reference is to the famous first line of the *Metaphysics:* "All men by nature desire to know." With respect to the issue of the inborn human desire to learn, compare Gersonides' comments in *Wars of the Lord,* 6:1.15, 356 and 358. Gersonides refers back to his comment here twice in his commentary to Proverbs (to 1:21 and in the first *to'elet* to the passage stretching from 2:17 to 3:3) and once in his commentary to Ecclesiastes (34c). Gersonides gives a graphic account of his own great desire to learn and know in an autobiographical aside in his commentary to the Torah, 114b.

32. See Gersonides' introduction, text at n. 16.

33. In this sentence I have used "explanation" as a translation for *sibbah,* ordinarily translated as "cause." By "explanations which account for existence," I surmise that Gersonides is referring to Aristotle's oft-made claim that full understanding demands understanding of a thing with its causes. See, e.g., *Physics,* 2:3, 194b, 16 ff.

34. See Aristotle, *De Sensu et Sensibili* (the first part of *Parva Naturalia* and the part from which the whole collection took its Hebrew name, *Ha-Ḥush vi-ha-Muḥash*), 1, 436b, 18 ff. Compare further Gersonides' commentary on the Torah, 104d, 227b (on Deut. 19:21), and his commentary on Proverbs 20:12.

35. Compare the argument in Scotus (c. 1265–c. 1307) from the prologue to John Duns Scotus' *Ordinatio* as found in Shapiro, ed., *Medieval Philosophy,* 446. My thanks to Seymour Feldman for drawing my attention to this passage. The question of Gersonides' relation to his contemporaries among the Latin philosophers is a matter of continued scholarly interest and debate. As noted above in the preface, Shlomo Pines went so far as to state that Christian philosophy is "the natural historical context of Gersonides' thought." See p. 457 in his "Problems in the Teachings of Gersonides." The emphasis I place in these notes on Gersonides' relation to Maimonides may be seen as a corrective to Pines' position. The issue has recently been taken up at length by Möbuss, *Die Intellektlehre des Levi ben Gerson.* Möbuss argues that Gersonides' theory of the intellect reveals Ockhamist influences that contrast with its overall Averroist thrust.

36. Literally, "knowledge of the truths" (both here and in the next sentence). Here again we see reference to Gersonides' position that knowledge of all conceptual truth, not just metaphysical truth, can constitute our perfection.

37. Literally, "than these physical perfections." We are immediately aware of perfections of the body and cannot deny the possibility of achieving them; there is no like immediate awareness of perfection of the spirit.

38. That is, even if we know from the very first that there are perfections beyond the physical, that does not mean that we know what those perfections are; and even if we know from the very first what they are, that does not mean that we seek to achieve them.

39. That is, human beings by nature desire their perfection but few of us are willing to make the necessary effort actually to achieve it; at best, we give up after having taken only the preliminary steps on the road to our perfection. We are thus left with the desire only. It *killeth* us because we thus deny ourselves life after death.

40. Aristotle's dictum "Nature never makes anything that is superfluous" (*Parts of Animals,* 691b4, 694a15, 695b19; *Generation of Animals,* 739b20, 744a37) "was often invoked by the Arabs," Shlomo Pines tells us, "especially when some biological problem was being discussed. But it generally served as a heuristic principle which did not necessarily have anthropomorphic or theological overtones. In other words, it did not by any means imply that a hypostasized nature pursues certain ends and avoids everything that is not conducive to them." See Pines, "What Was Original in Arabic Science?" 189 (original), 337 (reprint). Compare below, n. 45.

41. Compare *Wars of the Lord,* 4:2 (Leipzig, 158; Feldman, 2:164). See further Gershom ben Shlomoh, *Sha'ar ha-Shamayim* 1:9, 66b and 68b (in Bodenheimer's English translation, 293 and 300).

42. In the medieval Arabic tradition, three of Aristotle's biological works were grouped together under the name *Book of Animals.* This included *History of Animals* in ten parts, *Parts of Animals* in four parts, and *Generation of Animals* in five parts. Gersonides apparently received this as one book containing nineteen parts and cited it as such (in his commentary to Song of Songs 7:14, e.g.). On this, see Aristotle, *Generation of Animals: The Arabic Translation,* 1. I have not found the specific reference cited here.

43. My supposition that the Hebrew here (*melekhet ha-refu'ah*) refers to the practice of medicine generally and not to a specific book called *The Art of Medicine* is strengthened by the way in which Gersonides uses the term in his *Commentary on the Torah* (38b/187/386).

44. This formulation would appear to come from ibn Tibbon's translation of the *Guide,* 3:54, at 635. Gersonides quotes Maimonides' formulation but gives it a different twist: it is not just knowledge of metaphysical concepts ("the divine things") that constitutes true human perfection, but all true conceptual knowledge.

45. Note how Gersonides slides between "nature" and "God" in this passage. In his mind there seems to be very little difference between the two, calling to mind Spinoza's famous formulation, "Deus sive natura." The use of the Hebrew word *teva'* for "nature" raises interesting problems concerning the transition from discussions of the natures of particular things to nature in general. For comments on the history of the term in medieval Hebrew, see Malter, "Medieval Hebrew Terms for Nature." Compare below, in the commentary to 1:8.

46. The Hebrew, *be-ka'n,* often refers to the sublunary world but can also mean the existence of some thing or another in general. See Husik, no. 57.

47. This is an extremely important passage, one in which the difference between Maimonides and Gersonides on the question of human perfection is made forcefully clear. See the discussion on this in my "Gersonides on the Song of Songs and the Nature of Science."

48. That is, our teachers will either tell us explicitly what it is or they will set us on the right path so that we can discover it ourselves.

49. That is, the teacher need not explain to the student the purpose of the action in question in order for the student to carry it out.

50. See *Wars of the Lord,* 1:6 (Leipzig, 37; Feldman, 1:147). Compare *Wars of the Lord,* 1:7 (Leipzig, 49; Feldman, 166). Erwin Rosenthal notes that the motif of master and subordinate sciences goes back to the opening of the *Nicomachean Ethics* and that it had a long and important history in medieval Islamic political thought. See his

Political Thought in Medieval Islam, 127. See also E. Rosenthal, *Averroës' Commentary on Plato's* Republic, 119, 257 f.

51. That is, Solomon.

52. The myth that the ancient Israelites had achieved a high level of perfection in the sciences known to the medieval world was widespread throughout that world. My friend and colleague Dr. Abraham Melamed has collected hundreds of references to this belief and plans to write a comprehensive study of the entire issue. In the meantime, see Roth, "The 'Theft of Philosophy' by the Greeks from the Jews." This notion played an important role in Maimonides' thought, on which see see my *Dogma in Medieval Jewish Thought,* 234, and my *Maimonides on Human Perfection,* 34, 80.

53. More literally, "emanation"; the Hebrew is *hashpaʿah.*

54. We see here the high value that Gersonides placed on the cooperative nature of the scientific venture. See the discussion of this issue in my "Gersonides on *Imitatio Dei.*"

55. For the rabbinical source of the claim that Moses, Aaron, and Miriam "died by a kiss" see Bava Batra, 17a, and parallels. In Maimonides (who also cites Song of Songs 1:2), see *Guide,* 3:51 (627–28); for a discussion of other uses of the expression, see Idel, *Mystical Experience in Abraham Abulafia,* Albany: SUNY Press, 1988, (180–84). My translation here smoothes out some of the choppiness of the Hebrew text.

56. God is active in the human quest for knowledge in the sense that without the unceasing intellectual emanations from God through the Active Intellect humans could not actualize their intellects, thereby achieving self-realization. Samuelson has proposed a helpful metaphor to illustrate this: God functions like a high-powered radio transmitter. The transmissions themselves are not enough, since one must also tune into them. Human perfection depends on God's universal unceasing intellectual emanations, aimed at no one individual in particular, and the action of individuals doing their utmost to "tune into" those emanations. See his "The Problem of Free Will." We see Gersonides here continuing to emphasize the role of the Active Intellect in human cognition.

57. There appears to be a play on words here: *ruah* as breath and as spirit.

58. That is, as an *example* of the physical pleasures.

59. Gersonides seems to offer two different explanations for our desire to know God as much as possible: (a) it is a natural, inborn human trait and (b) the wisdom evident (even to the beginning observer) in the order of the natural universe causes us to seek to understand what we can about its creator.

60. Gersonides here defines the Hebrew term *ʿalmah* as "virgin," using the language of Lev. 21:3 to define the expression in technical terms as a woman who has never had sexual relations with a man. Given the use made by medieval Christian polemicists of the term *ʿalmah* in Isa. 7:14 (to emphasize the virgin birth of Jesus), it appears strange that Gersonides would play into their hands here, especially since the explanation of *ʿalmah* as "virgin" is not necessary for his interpretation of the text. By contrast, the *Nizzahon Vetus* explicitly denies that *ʿalmah* means "virgin," citing Song of Songs 6:8 as proof. See Berger, *The Jewish-Christian Debate,* 100, 104, 275–76, 278. Gersonides' behavior here is all the more unusual in light of the following comment by Berger (10): "When a Jewish exegete reached a passage that was a crux of a Christian polemic, he would frequently make an effort, whether implicitly or explicitly, to undermine the christological interpretation." Gersonides certainly made no

such effort here! On this, see further E. Rosenthal, "Anti-Christian Polemic." Gersonides' behavior here is perhaps explicable in light of the commentaries of ibn Ezra and Rashi. Ibn Ezra says that *'alamot* means "young girls," whereas Rashi renders the word "virgins" (*betulot*); Gersonides combines both commentaries in his explanation of the verse. With respect to Rashi, Kamin, "Rashi's Commentary on Song of Songs," shows that Rashi's commentary betrays clear acquaintance with Christian interpretations of the scroll and was written with clear polemical intent. Thus, if Rashi translates *'almah* as "virgin" it is either because he was unaware of the Christian polemic on the issue or because the issue was not important to him. But he clearly was not writing without intent to contravene Christianity. In short, Rashi's and Ralbag's interpretation of *'almah* as "virgin" would appear to have no special significance.

61. See, e.g., Baba Batra 22a and Midrash Kohelet 3:13.

62. *Guide,* 1:30 (at 63–64); of Gersonides' three prooftexts from the previous paragraph, Maimonides cites only the verse from Isaiah, but he cites it twice.

63. Gersonides' wording here is probably influenced by Prov. 31:29.

64. Let not the reader suspect that the antecedents are clearer in the Hebrew than in the translation! Gersonides is saying that the order and equilibrium of natural entities brings one to examine those entities with an eye toward understanding that order and equilibrium.

65. It is not clear to me how this verse from Psalms proves Gersonides' point that *goodly oils* are necessarily "processed oils"; nor is it evident to me why he thought the point important.

66. Gersonides refers back to this commentary in his discussion of Eccles. 9:9 (at 36b) and in his commentary to Prov. 1:21 with respect to the natural human desire to achieve wisdom.

67. Gersonides uses teleological arguments to prove the creation of the world, if not God's existence, in *Wars of the Lord,* 6:1.7, 9. See Feldman, "Gersonides' Proofs."

68. Gersonides is playing on the ambivalence of the Hebrew *yada'*: "knowledge" vs. "carnal knowledge."

69. That is, the intellect. The root here for "direct" (*y-sh-r*) is also the root of the word translated as "sincerely" at the end of the verse.

70. Perhaps "subordinate themselves."

71. *'Avodah* can mean "work," "worship," or "sacrificial cult." The Hebrew expression here, *'avodat ha-sekhel,* carries with it connotations the translation cannot hope to capture.

72. Compare Maimonides' comment on this verse at *Guide,* 3:33 (532): "Similarly to the totality of intentions of the Law there belong gentleness and docility; man should not be hard and rough, but responsive, obedient, acquiescent, and docile.... By way of a parable it is said about this, *Draw me, we will run after thee.*" As Pines indicates, this interpretation seems to follow that of the Midrash, which has the verse referring to Israel's acceptance of the Torah at Sinai.

73. That is, it is not the intellect, in the company of other faculties of the soul, that runs after God, but the intellectual person, in the company of like-minded individuals. This is consistent with the stress that Gersonides repeatedly lays on the cooperative nature of scientific inquiry. Note that Gersonides' comment here shows how seriously he takes his allegorical interpretation of Song of Songs: he is sincerely convinced that he is reading his interpretation *out* of the text, and not *into* it.

74. Possibly "in order to draw that emanation to him." That is, Gersonides is saying either that one cannot approach God without God's assistance or that one needs divine help in order to draw down God's emanation upon oneself.

75. Literally, "have no relation to it."

76. See, e.g., Aristotle, *Parts of Animals*, 1 : 5 (644b23). Gersonides himself makes a similar point in *Wars of the Lord*, 5 : 1.2 (in the translation of Goldstein, *The Astronomy of Levi ben Gerson*, 26).

77. One of the seven marriage blessings.

78. That is, knowledge of things of God's degree (which is, of course, only God) gives us the greatest happiness.

79. If I may say so, Gersonides does not express himself well here. Human perfection does not consist in simply desiring to acquire knowledge of God to the greatest extent possible but in the actual acquisition of that knowledge. It is the longing to achieve that end that aids us in accomplishing it. The reference here is to the text at note 32 above.

80. As Gersonides noted above (commentary to 1 : 4), we naturally desire to satisfy our intellectual longings. Abner of Burgos, the fourteenth-century convert to Christianity who became Alfonso de Valladolid, gives piquant expression to this idea: "Since my youth and until my old age, I begged of God . . . one single thing, namely to know whether it is possible to find a rectilinear surface equal to the surface of the circle, according to the truth and not approximately." The text is found in Gluskina, *Alfonso, Meyasher ʿAqov*, 139. This text was drawn to my attention by Gad Freudenthal.

81. The Hebrew for "sincerely" is *meysharim,* which actually means "sincere [straightforward] individuals."

82. The root of *yosher* is *y-sh-r,* also the root of *meysharim,* translated here in the verse as "sincerely." In the Hebrew, then, Gersonides' connecting between those who sincerely love God and those who "arouse themselves" to study the physical universe is much clearer.

83. Gersonides translates the Hebrew root *z-kh-r* here as "sniff" ("inhale," "savor") and not as "remember," "mention," or "praise." In his commentary on this verse Gordis writes: "*nazkirah,* not 'we shall praise' but 'we shall inhale'; on this meaning of the root, cf. Lev. 24 : 7; Isa. 66 : 3 . . . as Ibn Janah recognized long ago." See Gordis, *Song of Songs*, 78. Pope expands on this: "This unusual rendering of *zkr,* 'remember,' reflects the difficulty the translator sensed with regard to the usual meaning of the causative conjugation of this verb, mention, recite, extol, celebrate, or the like. Gordis, following Ibn Janah, rendered 'We shall inhale thy love rather than wine.'" Pope goes on, preferring "savor" over Gordis' "inhale" since it "combines the sense of smell and taste involved in the appreciation of fine wine." I am content with the more prosaic "sniff." See Pope's Anchor Bible edition of *Song of Songs*, 304 – 5. Gordis and Pope help us understand Gersonides here with respect to his rendering of the verse. His citation of Lev. 2 : 2 and Exod. 20 : 21 is still obscure, however, since in those places the verb *z-kh-r* most definitely does *not* mean "sniff," and in his commentaries to those verses Gersonides passes in silence over the whole issue. Perhaps the text here is corrupt and Gersonides meant to contrast the meaning *z-kh-r* here with its use in Lev. 2 : 2 and Exod. 20 : 21.

84. Although the term for "material intellect" in Hebrew (*ha-sekhel ha-hiyulani*) is

masculine, Gersonides uses the feminine in this context because the speaker here, who represents the material intellect, is female.

85. Literally, "separate."

86. I usually translate variants of 'iyyun with variants of "speculation" but there seemed no elegant way of doing it here, and I offer, without enthusiasm, "philosophically studied" instead.

87. That is, the author of Song of Songs.

88. That is, in Kedar.

89. Plural of the name of the eleventh letter of the Hebrew alphabet, kaf, rendered in the translation of Song of Songs used here by the word "as."

90. Compare Gersonides' further discussion of this verse at the end of his commentary to 1:12.

91. From the same root as the word translated as "black" in the previous verse.

92. That is, the other faculties of the soul.

93. See Eccles. 1:3.

94. The activity of the sun is known to us through its impact on natural entities in the sublunary world.

95. In his commentary to this verse Gersonides makes it refer to acquisition of material possessions, which are subject to generation and corruption.

96. That is, the other faculties of the soul; instead of aiding her in achieving intellectual perfection, they seduced her into serving their narrow, "selfish" needs.

97. This calls to mind the opening sentences in the first of Maimonides' "Eight Chapters": "Know that the soul of man is a single soul. It has many different actions, some of which are sometimes called souls. One might therefore think, as the physicians do, that man has many souls." See *Ethical Writings of Maimonides*, ed. Weiss and Butterworth, 61.

98. Gersonides identifies activity with masculinity, passivity with femininity.

99. It appears that Gersonides here is distinguishing between the five external senses, which are seen as passive (compare *Guide*, 1:47), and the "internal senses," or faculties of the soul, which do not depend on external stimuli in order to function (memory and imagination, for example, can function without the presence of external stimuli). For an illuminating discussion, see Jospe, *Torah and Sophia*, 201–10, 233–34. I found no reference to our subject in Wolfson's classic "The Internal Senses."

100. The Hebrew for "swarthy" here is created from the root for "black" (sh-ḥ-r), with the last two letters repeated.

101. *Yafyafita*, created from *yafeh* by the same sort of doubling.

102. That is, the Active Intellect perfects and actualizes the material intellect.

103. Not surprisingly, in his commentary to Job 1:7 Gersonides presents that verse (and the entire opening story) as an allegory.

104. That is, the impediments symbolized by swarthiness.

105. That is, the material intellect does not know the nature of its perfection and certainly, therefore, does not know how to achieve it.

106. In this sentence "he" refers to the Active Intellect, "she" to the material intellect.

107. Or: "in order to achieve."

108. The fate of the material intellect (i.e., its perfection) is allegorically compared to the bright light of noon. The connection of light with intellectual perfection is a

standard medieval idea, probably deriving from Plato's parable of the cave. For its use in Maimonides, see, e.g., *Guide,* 2:12 (280), 3:52 (629). For comments on Gersonides' use of the light allegory in connection with intellection, see Davidson, "Gersonides on the Material and Active Intellects," 242.

109. By "these things" it is likely that Gersonides means those physical things subject to generation and corruption that were said in the commentary to the previous verse to be "under the sun," the sensual apprehension of which is the first step on the way toward the apprehension of the intelligibles.

110. Of the last two sentences, the first makes some sense, the second none. The text appears to be hopelessly garbled. Rather than attempting an imaginative and creative reconstruction of what Gersonides may have written here, I prefer to leave it as is. The second sentence can be somewhat improved by emending *hasagah* to *hashgahah* (a correction supported by none of the six mss. I examined), thus reading, "For example, metaphysics and the way of protecting it from doubt and perplexity."

111. Or: "how this will be."

112. On this interpretation, the verse is no longer spoken by the material intellect addressing the Active Intellect; rather, it is the material intellect itself that is being addressed.

113. This expression, *be-shoresh ha-beri'ah,* is not one I have seen elsewhere.

114. Gersonides here reverts to the interpretation of the material intellect addressing the Active Intellect.

115. *Golah* is here understood as deriving from the root *g-l,* from which are derived the Hebrew words for scroll, small sphere, wave, rounded sickle, and other items whose basic shape is curved. The more ordinary understanding of *golah,* "exile," makes no sense here.

116. The verse as a whole reads: *Behold, the Lord will hurl thee up and down with a man's throw; yea, he will wind thee round and round.*

117. Leviticus 13:45: *And the leper in whom the plague is, his clothes shall be rent, and the hair of his head shall go loose, and he shall cover his upper lip, and shall cry: "Unclean!" "Unclean!"* In his commentary on this verse Gersonides explains that the intention is that the leper cover himself (or herself) more than is normally done and cover the upper lip, as mourners do. On covering the upper lip as a sign of mourning, see Ezek. 24:17; Maimonides, "Laws of Mourning," 4:19.

118. That is, of the soul.

119. That is, to the intellect.

120. That is, the relation of active to passive. Near the end of his commentary to the previous verse (1:6) Gersonides distinguishes between active (masculine) and passive (feminine) faculties of the soul, calling the latter "daughters of Jerusalem."

121. We are confronted here with a hierarchy of activity and passivity. The Active Intellect is active vis-à-vis the material intellect; the material intellect is active vis-à-vis the internal faculties of the soul (imagination, memory, and so on), which are themselves active vis-à-vis the external senses (the *daughters of Jerusalem*). Since the internal faculties are in one sense active, they may be fittingly called companions of the material intellect.

122. An individual cannot achieve perfection if the material intellect and the faculties of the soul do not act in concert.

123. Literally, "related to me."

124. Literally, "and impede my activities which are related to me."

125. Gersonides' almost interchangeable use of 'God' and 'nature,' to which attention has been drawn above (n. 45), finds expression here.

126. See above, the commentary to 1:2, paragraph following note 47.

127. Moses and David are prominent examples of this. See, e.g., Exodus Rabbah 2:2–3.

128. The passive faculty referred to here is the material intellect, passive vis-à-vis the Active Intellect, active vis-à-vis the other faculties of the soul.

PART TWO: 1:9–2:7

Note to epigraph: Gersonides thus describes this section of his commentary in his introduction, in the text following note 80.

1. Gersonides notes that Pharaoh is king in Egypt not because he thought that his readers would not know this but to emphasize that Pharaoh's horses would be the best in Egypt. Alternatively, perhaps his comment should be understood in the light of a claim he makes in his *Commentary on the Torah* (46b/232/480) to the effect that no one in Egypt was allowed to ride a horse without the king's permission.

2. "They" refers to beautiful horses.

3. That is, the Egyptians.

4. That is, the person whose material intellect is under discussion here.

5. See Zech. 3:3. Compare Gersonides' commentary on Eccles. 9:7–11:9 (36c), where he says that despicable moral qualities are compared to filthy garments. He makes a similar comment in the same work (on 4:17–7:1) at 31d.

6. Gersonides, like Maimonides, makes moral perfection a necessary (but not sufficient!) condition for achieving intellectual perfection. On Maimonides, see my *Maimonides on Human Perfection*, 26–28. For Gersonides, compare the commentary to 2:8; *Wars of the Lord*, 4:6 (Leipzig, 174; Feldman, 2:193); and the commentary to Prov. 1:7, 1:1–19 (second *to'elet*), 12:1, 15:32.

7. The reference is to al-Ghazzali's *Maqasid al-Falasifah*, known in Hebrew as *Kavvanot ha-Pilosophim* (*Intentions of the Philosophers*).

8. For the source of this parable in the writings of al-Ghazzali, texts in Arabic and in English translation, and extensive discussion, see Lazarus-Yafeh, *Studies in Al-Ghazzali*, 312–20.

9. The antecedent of this pronoun is not clear; it could be Solomon or al-Ghazzali.

10. That is, the material intellect.

11. Midrash *Shoher Tov* to Ps. 18.

12. Compare Maimonides, *Guide of the Perplexed*, 3:51 (623); my *Maimonides on Human Perfection*, 32; and Idel, "*Sitre 'Arayot* in Maimonides' Thought": "It was thus possible, according to Maimonides, to maintain the state of contemplation probably even during sexual intercourse" (81).

13. The antecedent of this pronoun is typically unclear. But since the pronoun is masculine, not feminine, it is likely that the referent is the individual seeking perfection, as opposed to the material intellect, represented by the female in Song of Songs. Of course, Gersonides could be referring to the material intellect in and of itself and not its representation in the allegory of Song of Songs, in which case the masculinity of the pronoun is no longer decisive.

14. See the commentary to 1:2, in the paragraph ending with n. 47.

15. As opposed to "decoration" understood as moral perfection, as in the commentary to 1:9.

16. Gersonides is referring to the distinction drawn between mares and stallions in his commentary to 1:9.

17. That is, she is disposed to achieve intellectual perfection, not that she has already achieved moral perfection. There is an important point to be made here, I think. The fact that Gersonides goes to so much trouble to offer alternative readings of the verses, each consistent with his overall interpretation of Song of Songs, is an indication that Gersonides is convinced that he is actually *interpreting* Song of Songs, not merely using a convenient biblical text as a hook on which to hang his philosophical ruminations.

18. That is, apprehension of the intelligibles as in the previous paragraph.

19. Alternatively: "the Active Intellect cannot convey the primary intelligibles . . ."

20. See Gersonides' introduction, in the paragraph ending with n. 30.

21. I translate *parashah* here as "passage" and not as "paragraph" (see Gersonides' introduction, n. 79) since the verses referred to here are divided into two paragraphs (1:9–1:14 and 1:15–2:7) in the biblical text.

22. Hebrew: *ve-sam ha-koaḥ ha-nafshi asher yelekh be-madregat ha-hiyuli*. On the expression *asher yelekh be-madregat . . .* , see Husik, no. 21.

23. In the hierarchical system of Aristotelianism, form and matter can be relative terms: a block of marble, itself consisting of form and matter, stands in the relation of matter to the form of the statue made out of it. In our case, there is a faculty of the soul inferior to the material intellect and on which the material intellect operates; this faculty (which turns out to be the imagination; see below in this verse) stands to the material intellect in the relation of matter to form.

24. That is, female = passive = matter; male = active = form. Gersonides adopts these equations even though according to his commentary the female here is active (the lover) and the male passive (the beloved). My English translation here is awkward; the Hebrew in this case is much more supple. "Female lover" translates *ḥosheqet* and "male beloved" *ḥashuq*.

25. That is, there is a shift here; hitherto, the female stood for the material intellect. Thus, for example, Gersonides says in his commentary to 1:9, "The Active Intellect said to the material intellect, the female in this passage. . . ." Here, however, the female is made to stand for the imagination.

26. See Gersonides' supercommentary on Averroës' *Epitome of* De Anima, Ms. Bodleian Opp. Add. 4° 38, 198b. Jesse Stephen Mashbaum has prepared a critical edition of this text, due to be published by the Israel Academy of Sciences. I record here my profound gratitude to him for his kindness in providing me with a copy of his critical edition. Portions of his text were published in Mashbaum; see also Mashbaum, 17.

27. That is, the imagination.

28. That is, the material intellect.

29. See Gersonides' introduction, the paragraph ending with n. 29, and my annotation there.

30. Gersonides' comment here depends on a play on words based on the similarity of the Hebrew for "at his table" and "rotates."

31. Compare n. 23 above.

32. A reference, I assume, to the formless matter that preexists the universe. See Touati, 243–67. In *Wars of the Lord,* 6:2.4 (Leipzig, 421), Gersonides refers to this as *ḥomer raḥoq,* whereas here he calls it *ha-hiyuli ha-raḥoq.* For an English translation of the text from *Wars of the Lord* and extensive commentary, see Staub, *The Creation of the World,* 183–84. For further discussion, see S. Harvey, "Did Gersonides Believe in the Absolute Generation of Prime Matter?"; Freudenthal, "Cosmogonie et physique chez Gersonide."

33. Gersonides' precise position on the question of God and the universe is not easily stated. On one hand, he adopts immanentist language, using "God" and "nature" in effect interchangeably (see above, commentary to 1:2, nn. 40, 45). In many places in his *Commentary on the Torah* he affirms that God is the tenth intellect (when we start counting from "below," of course; beginning from God, the Active Intellect is the tenth intellect); see 158a, 171b, 174d, 201b. Compare further 194a and 210b, where God is described as a type of form. On the other hand, Gersonides is careful to distinguish God from the separate intellects (Torah commentary, 208a, 209d, 211d, 215b, 246b) and explicitly takes issue with those philosophers who affirm that God is the intellect that moves the sphere of the fixed stars (175a). This last issue is taken up explicitly in *Wars of the Lord,* 5:3.11 (Leipzig, 276–78). See Davidson's discussion of this last text in "Gersonides on the Material and Active Intellects," 211.

34. From God, the Creator, I take Gersonides to mean, we return to the world.

35. That is, we move from observation to principles, and from principles thus established we can make determinations concerning observable entities.

36. I understand this to mean that the material intellect should do that which is appropriate for to it to do, considering its "place"—that is, the cognition of intelligibles.

37. This, as noted above, is the interpretation that Gersonides gives to the text to this point. He goes on immediately to say that from this point in Song of Songs the meaning of the allegory changes and the male beloved, instead of referring to the Active Intellect, refers to the material intellect, and the female lover, instead of referring to the material intellect, refers to the faculties of the soul that serve it, particularly the faculty of imagination.

38. That is, the faculty of imagination.

39. That is, that the same term in an allegory should have two separate meanings.

40. That is, the author of Song of Songs.

41. From this point on in the commentary to this verse Gersonides offers an alternative explanation, according to which there is no change in the allegorical meaning of the key terms in Song of Songs, since we can understand the text as if all along "the male beloved" referred to the material intellect (and not the Active Intellect) and "the female lover" referred to the imagination (and not the material intellect). Once again we see Gersonides taking very seriously his attempt to interpret Song of Songs in accordance with his allegorical view of the text. He sincerely believes that the author of Song of Songs intended the allegory Gersonides finds in it; he is not simply using the text as an *asmakhta,* a convenient hook on which to hang his theories.

42. Here and in the rest of the paragraph, the intellect.

43. That is, these impediments function as a screen or curtain keeping the material intellect from perfecting itself and becoming like King Solomon (an allegory, as Gersonides claims toward the end of his introduction [text at n. 87], for the intellect *in actu*).

44. That is, the imagination.

45. As I understand Gersonides here, he says that the other faculties of the soul rebelled against the attempt by the imagination to act in loco parentis, as it were, forcing them to act in their own ultimate best interest, which is abandonment of the pursuit of pleasure for a career of subservience to the quest of the material intellect to achieve intellectual perfection.

46. Literally, "straightened."

47. A play on words. In the imperfect tense, the second person masculine singular and third person feminine singular are identical.

48. An apparent play on the words of the last verse of Daniel (12:13): *Ve-atta, lekh la-qeṣ ve-tanuaḥ ve-taʿamod le-goralkha le-qeṣ ha-yamin.* ("But go thou thy way till the end be and thou shalt rest, and shalt stand up to thy destiny at the end of days.")

49. That is, the second explanation, according to which all along "the male beloved" refers to the material intellect and "the female lover" to the imagination.

50. That is, in the first twelve verses of the book the male beloved is the Active Intellect and the female lover the material intellect.

51. See *Problems*, 12:1, 906a25. The talmudic rabbis make the same claim about myrrh in *Song of Songs Rabbah (Midrash Ḥazita)*, 1:58 (ed. Dunsky, 46). It is interesting that Gersonides cites the Aristotelian source when he presumably knew the rabbinical one as well. It is certain, at least, that at one point in his life he owned a copy of the text. See Weil, *Bibliothèque de Gersonide*, 78.

52. Given that myrrh is a resinous gum it would appear that Aristotle and Gersonides are, not surprisingly, correct here.

53. Presumably the bag is the impediment.

54. *Havayah.* Perhaps, "generated thing."

55. Joshua 15:48–62.

56. See Song of Songs 2:1.

57. In other words, we are given our other faculties in perfected form; one might think, therefore, that they are superior to the material intellect, which begins its career, so to speak, as an imperfect potential only. When actualized, however, the material intellect is of a higher degree than the faculties that are perfected ab initio.

58. One wonders whether Gersonides was familiar with the canons of courtly love and troubador poetry prevalent in his time.

59. That is, the faculty of imagination.

60. Literally, "emanate."

61. Maimonides cites this verse in *Guide*, 2:47 (407) to prove that ʿeres means "bed." The word here translated as "fresh" is *raʿanan*, which JPS renders as "leafy" and which can also be translated as "green" or "luxuriant."

62. Here, the author of Song of Songs.

63. Literally, "physical apprehensions."

64. Probably aloe; compare Maimonides' *Pirqe Mosheh (Medical Aphorisms)*, 13:13.

65. That is, the perfection of the imagination is facilitated by the other faculties of the soul, whereas the perfection of the material intellect is facilitated by its acquisition of the imaginative forms from the imagination.

66. That is, the author of Song of Songs.

67. See Gersonides' introduction, the paragraph ending with n. 94.

68. That is, flowers exist only so that fruit or seeds may be produced.

69. On individuation in Gersonides, see Rudavsky, "Individuals and Individuation" and "Individuals and the Doctrine of Individuation."

70. For the source in *On the Soul* see Mashbaum, 139; I have not found the source in the *Metaphysics*.

71. Gersonides here tells us that the speaker in the verse is the material intellect, describing its "beloved," the faculties of the soul, preeminently the faculty of imagination. This accords with his analysis of the allegory in Song of Songs presented in his commentary on 1:12.

72. That is, the imagination, when turned toward the intellect, is like a lily among the baser and thus thornier faculties of the soul, turned as they are toward the satisfaction of physical desire.

73. I am not sure to what faculties other than the intellect Gersonides is referring.

74. That is, immortality depends on perfection of the intellect and on that perfection alone.

75. The term here translated as "sublunary" is *shafel,* which literally means "low" (as in Ezek. 17:6, 17:24) and, by extension, "contemptible" or "base" (as in Mal. 2: 9). When figures such as Gersonides use the term, they surely have the primary meaning in mind (the sublunary world is physically lower than the heavens) and probably the secondary meaning as well, since they held that the sublunary world is of much lower value than the superlunary realm. For a discussion of this issue, see my "Gersonides and His Cultured Despisers."

76. That is, the point of the very creation of the world is the intellectual perfection and consequent immortality of individual human beings. The question of what exactly "first [or prime] matter" is in Gersonides is a source of considerable and very technical debate. See Staub, *Creation of the World,* 188–211; Freudenthal, "Cosmogonie et physique chez Gersonide." In his *Commentary on the Torah* (115d) Gersonides calls knowledge *peri kol ha-'adam,* "the entire fruit of man" or "the fruit of all men."

77. That is, the first matter can be perfected in other ways, but these are all intermediate stages between unperfected first matter and perfected intellect, and all these intermediate stages exist in order to bring about the perfection here discussed.

78. That is, were it possible to eat this "fruit."

79. This reading of the allegory is the opposite of that presented in the previous paragraph: there her longing for him convinced her that his fruit must be sweet; here the sweetness of his fruit brings about her longing for him. Once again we see Gersonides taking seriously the idea that Song of Songs was actually written as an intellectualist allegory. Henceforth I will leave this particular dead horse to lie in peace and will refrain from beating it further. It is possible that the last two words of this sentence (*tov me'od,* "very good") hint at Gen. 1:31 and God's satisfaction with creation.

80. That is, that which the intellect "drinks" is what God emanates on it.

81. As it stands in the Hebrew, this sentence is difficult, and I have been forced to rearrange the word order a bit in order to arrive at the meaning given it here.

82. That is, to the intellect, and not directly to God.

83. *Po'el,* "actor" or "agent," and not *po'al,* "verb."

84. That is, the verb *hevi'ani* should be understood as "I have been brought" and not as "he hath brought me."

85. Literally, "the nature according to which I was formed."

86. That is, the innate nature and will.

87. That is, the encouragement of the material intellect to abandon the physical desires and cooperate in the pursuit of perfection is a sign of its great love. The expression "great love" (*ahavah rabbah*) is drawn from the blessing said just before the recitation of the *Shema'* in the morning prayer according to the Ashkenazi rite. The expression in the Sephardi rite is "eternal love" (*ahavat 'olam*). The difference can be traced back to the Babylonian Talmud (Berakhot 11b). The Ashkenazi rite follows the decision of the Tosafot, ad loc. (s.v. "Ve-Rabbanan"). For further details, see Jacobson, *The Weekday Siddur*, 135 f. Given that it is unlikely that Gersonides chose this expression at random, this detail may be of interest to historians of Jewish liturgy.

88. Gersonides' comment here is similar to that of Rashi.

89. Possibly a reference to Song of Songs Rabbah (*Midrash Ḥazita*), 1:45 (to Song of Songs 1:9); ed. Dunsky, 37. There it says that the accusers stand to God's left, as it were. See further Numbers Rabbah 22, where the evil inclination is associated with the left (compare the Yalkut on Deuteronomy, 263). *Zohar* Genesis 255 preserves a tradition that may be Gersonides' source; there the evil inclination is called Satan. It is interesting to note in this connection once again that so far as I can determine, Gersonides makes no reference anywhere in his writings to Kabbalah or kabbalistic doctrines.

90. Satan.

91. Literally, "straight intellect."

92. That is, from the perspective of the intellect the female is, so to speak, to its right, or so Gersonides seems to mean here.

93. Literally, "until it reaches the end."

PART THREE: 2:8-2:17

Note to epigraph: Gersonides thus describes this section of the commentary in his introduction, in the paragraph in which n. 82 is found.

1. For this translation of *maḥshavah*, see Mashbaum, 204-7.

2. These words reoccur in 8:5; it is not likely that Gersonides meant that the third section of the text might have extended to that point.

3. Hebrew: *enam mekuvanim le-'aṣman ḥoshqam;* my translation reflects the best sense that I could give the phrase.

4. A reference, I surmise, to the moral perfections that were the subject of the previous section.

5. The text here is problematic, and my translation reflects that fact.

6. That is, "stammer."

7. Hebrew: *ḥelke ha-soter.* Compare Husik, no. 33 ("contradictory alternatives") and *Wars of the Lord* (Feldman, 2:157) ("possible alternatives"). On *soter* as "contradictory" see Manekin, *The Logic of Gersonides,* 316. Gersonides uses this expression as well in his commentary to Prov. 24:24.

8. Gersonides here begins to explain the matter raised in his introduction (in the paragraph following n. 104) concerning the different names used for the female beloved. Whereas in the previous section the female beloved was only in the process of becoming morally perfected, and was thus only called *my love,* in this section she has already attained moral perfection and is thus called *my love, my fair one.*

9. See Aristotle, *Meteorology,* 2:3, 360a2–5. Compare *Meteorology,* 1:9, 346b.

10. This addition is necessary to make sense of the passage, but there is no basis for it in the text.

11. See Gersonides' introduction, the paragraph ending with n. 30.

12. See Gersonides' commentary to 1:2, at n. 34.

13. That is, lacks the natural dispositions necessary for achieving perfection. The word translated here as "prepared" comes from the same root as the word translated as "disposed" in the next sentence.

14. As has been seen above, and will be seen below, Gersonides is very sensitive to the fact that different sciences have different methodologies; using an incorrect methodology is a sure recipe for disaster.

15. This sentence, unclear as it appears to be, seems to mean that it will be easy for the impediments (the *little foxes*) to interfere with the work of the imagination since it is still only at the first stages of its work. The continuation of the paragraph seems to support this reading.

16. That is, the vineyard was at the first stages of producing its fruit, which, being immature, was easily damaged.

17. See Gersonides' introduction to the commentary (in the paragraph ending with n. 94).

18. Hebrew: *Ḥaluqah.*

19. Hebrew: *Hafshatah.*

20. That is, in mathematics one abstracts the numerical properties of entities from their concrete existence. Compare Aristotle, *Metaphysics,* 11:3, 1061a29.

21. That is, physics deals with sublunary nature, constantly subject to the process of generation and corruption (and thus "changeable"). This may be contrasted with the unchangeable nature of the superlunary realm. Compare Maimonides, "Laws of the Foundations of the Torah," 2:3.

22. I add the bracketed words in order to make sense of the passage; they are not at all supported by the Hebrew text.

23. On this term see Gersonides' introduction, the paragraph ending with n. 73.

24. How this part of the nature of physics connects it to spices is not clear to me.

25. See Aristotle, *Metaphysics,* 4:2–3 (1005a–b), 6:1 (1026a).

26. The inconsistency in number here ("science," "are many," and "its subjects") reflects the Hebrew. It may be that the Hebrew should be read *ḥokhmot ha-'elohut* and not *ḥokhmat ha-'elohut* ("metaphysical sciences" as opposed to "metaphysics"), but that does not help much in making the sentence parse better and is inconsistent with the usage in the rest of the paragraph.

27. Given the summary nature of the previous sentence, it appears to me that this sentence was an afterthought added by Gersonides.

PART FOUR: 3:1–4:7

Note to epigraph: This is the way Gersonides summarizes the fourth part of Song of Songs in his introduction (see p. 11).

1. That is, the imagination cannot achieve its final perfection at this stage of its development, but if the project is undertaken in the proper way and in the proper order,

its final end will indeed be achieved. A similar interpretation to this verse is given by Jacob Anatoli (thirteenth century) in his *Malmad ha-Talmidim,* 41b.

2. Literally, "with its resting."

3. The external senses report their sensory impressions to the common sense, which processes them; when the processing is completed (and the common sense "rests"), the results are reported on to the imagination. In an important sense, then, the imagination plays a passive role in this process; thus the senses, which are the "watchmen," must *find* the imagination.

4. The common sense cannot process the information reaching it, and pass it on to the imagination, while it is being bombarded, as it were, with sensory information being conveyed by the senses; it can do this job only when the senses are basically quiescent. This explains why abstract concepts (intelligibles) arise in the intellect only some time after the sensory impressions on which they are based have been received.

5. That is, the material intellect.

6. In this sense the faculty of memory is the "mother" of the imagination.

7. Possibly, "It is the name of . . ."

8. This interpretation is, admittedly, rather forced: the memory is the "mother" of the imagination in that it stores the sensibilia on which the imagination works; the imagination, in turn, is the "mother" of the material intellect in that without the enthusiastic cooperation and support of the imagination, the material intellect cannot achieve its perfection.

9. Borrowed from Exod. 19:21: *And the Lord said unto Moses: "Go down, charge the people, lest they break through unto the Lord to gaze, and many of them perish."* Ordinarily the root *h-r-s* means "destruction"; it is more likely than not that Gersonides had that meaning in mind here as well as the biblical usage. Compare Gersonides' introduction, n. 40.

10. Here, and throughout part 4, *parashah.* In his use of the term here, Gersonides seems to have Song of Songs part 4 (according to his division) in mind.

11. Note the commentary to 2:8.

12. Hebrew: *Derushim;* compare Gersonides' commentary to Song of Songs 1:2, n. 18.

13. That is, Gersonides rejects the Platonic conception that we have innate knowledge of mathematical principles.

14. Literally, "they are with us."

15. Aristotle, *On the Soul,* 3:5. Compare Mashbaum, 126, and Gersonides' introduction, at n. 22.

16. That is, that we are born with mathematical ideas; Gersonides' penchant for ambiguous antecedents reaches new heights here.

17. As noted in Gersonides' introduction (n. 23), the reference is to the very beginning of the *Posterior Analytics.*

18. For an explication of the issues raised in this paragraph, see my nn. 23 through 30 to Gersonides' introduction.

19. See 3:2.

20. See 3:3.

21. Translated there as *Scarce had . . .*

22. See 3:4.

23. Literally, "the strength of forgetfulness concerning these sense impressions from which are derived these first principles."

24. That is, the strength of this longing is so great that she had to adjure them not to run headlong into scientific investigation.

25. Hebrew: *derishah;* compare above in the commentary to this verse, n. 12.

26. Hebrew: *petiḥah;* the term usually denotes a poem or preamble in which a text is joined to a verse. See Strack, *Introduction to the Talmud and Midrash,* 204 (266 in the new edition of Strack and Stemberger). Here Gersonides means either his commentary on the previous verse or the third section into which he divided Song of Songs (2:8–2:17), which includes the commentary on 2:8, in which he introduced the two alternative explanations. It is more likely that he meant the commentary on the previous verse since in the continuation of this sentence he uses a different term, *parashah,* to refer back to the third section of Song of Songs. For that reason I translate *petiḥah* here as "comment."

27. That is, according to Gersonides' division, the third part of Song of Songs (2:8–2:17) deals with moral perfection, whereas the fourth and present part (3:1–4:7) deals with perfection in the mathematical sciences.

28. Gersonides' point here appears to be something like the following: ordinarily, deserts cannot be traversed; in the present case the female beloved comes directly out of the desert, with apparent ease, going straight up like a pillar of smoke. All this indicates how easily and straightforwardly one can learn the mathematical sciences.

29. Hebrew: *Yosher;* I usually translate this as "equilibrium" (as in the continuation of this sentence); other possibilities in this context include "correctly" and "honestly." The point appears to be that smoke rises straight up; were "straightly" acceptable English I would use it in the place of "directly."

30. The point here, simply stated, is that mathematics is a deductive science. On "absolute demonstrations" see Gersonides' introduction, n. 67.

31. In his commentary to 2:17 above Gersonides says that *myrrh* in 4:6 refers to physics. The question then arises, why is it mentioned here? Gersonides' answer is that there is much in the mathematical sciences that is close to physics.

32. Gersonides alludes to the importance of mathematics for the other sciences in the introduction to *Wars of the Lord* (Leipzig, 3; Feldman, 1:92). He makes the point clearly, and with explicit reference to the *Almagest,* in *Wars of the Lord,* 5:1.2 (in B. R. Goldstein's translation, *The Astronomy of Levi ben Gerson,* 24).

33. The reference seems to be to *Almagest,* 1:1 (Toomer, trans., *Ptolemy's Almagest,* 36–37).

34. Literally, "sought-after matter of study." On the term *mevuqqash* see the sources cited from Manekin at the commentary to Song of Songs 1:2, n. 18.

35. Literally, "they."

36. Gersonides refers to ancient systems of arithmetic having a base of 60 instead of a base of 100; this system was preserved in medieval astronomy (as it is in modern astronomy)—360 degrees (6 × 60) in a circle, 60 minutes in an hour, 12 hours (12 = 1/5 of 60) in a day, and so on—and it is no surprise that Gersonides was familiar with it.

37. Hebrew: *Be-ka'n;* this term usually denotes the sublunary world, but not always;

compare Husik, no. 57. In the present context Gersonides may indeed mean the sub-lunary world (in which or, rather, from which, astronomical observations are made with difficulty), but this is not clear, and my translation reflects that lack of clarity.

38. For similar uses of the term "fruit" see below, the commentary to 8:12, and Gersonides' introduction to his commentary on Ecclesiastes, 25d.

39. Literally, "hidden from."

40. The reference appears to be to *Almagest,* 9:2 (Toomer, 420–21); compare Gersonides' critique of the astronomical observations available in his day in *Wars of the Lord,* 5:1.3 (Goldstein, *The Astronomy of Levi ben Gerson,* 27–30).

41. Literally, "thing."

42. Literally, "art" or "craft."

43. Hebrew: *mah she-koho koah zeh ha-'inyan;* the expression *koho koah* is tal-mudic (see, e.g., Baba Qamma 19a) and means "indirect action."

44. Possibly a reference to *Metaphysics,* 2:3.3, 995a12–14. On the ordering of books 1 and 2 of the *Metaphysics* see above, commentary to 1:2, n. 31.

45. In the commentary to 4:6 Gersonides explains that darkness is an allegory for ignorance. Compare *Guide of the Perplexed,* 3:10.

46. See Gersonides' introduction, after n. 88.

47. It is interesting that Gersonides knew that in ancient times purple dye (*arga-man*) was more valuable than gold; Menahot 39a might have been his source. On this subject see Spanier, *The Royal Purple.*

48. See Gersonides' introduction, just before n. 87.

49. As opposed to any specific faculty of the soul.

50. That is, the soul raises the intellect over its other faculties.

51. See Gersonides' introduction, after n. 99.

52. See 4:2.

53. That is, progress in astronomy depends on repeated observations, symbolized by the way in which the hair of goats trailing down from Mount Gilead is pleated or matted.

54. The imagination has prepared for the intellect a series of consistent observa-tions, which cohere without contradiction, thus strengthening one another.

55. In the commentary to 6:6.

56. Hebrew: *Rehelim;* here the text of Song of Songs has *'eder.* One of three things seems to have happened here: either Gersonides' text of Song of Songs was corrupt, or he confused 6:6 for 4:2, or the copyists of the mss. confused the two.

57. In 1:12 Gersonides says that "fruit" means moral perfection; in the introduc-tion (at n. 92) he says it denotes perfection in the sciences; the latter sense seems to be preferable one here.

58. See Gersonides' introduction, the paragraph ending with n. 94.

59. This sentence makes absolutely no sense as it stands. According to the interpre-tation given it here, and according to Gersonides' reference to his introduction (see the previous note), this verse must clearly refer to *both* the allegory and its intended meaning.

60. That is, this rule (that one proceeds from the prior to the posterior when one judges the existence of one thing from something else) has very few exceptions.

61. Hebrew: *temunot;* alternatively, "forms" *or,* in other contexts, "models."

62. That is, astronomy seems to present a case of going from the posterior to the prior.

63. Literally, "action" (and so for the rest of this paragraph).

64. Hebrew: *temunat ha-'ayin* (I emended the text from *temunat ha-'iyyun*). This is the third time that Gersonides has used the term *temunah* in this paragraph; in each place I have had to translate it differently.

65. We seem to have an expression of Gersonides' realist approach to science here: astronomical models must really accord with the phenomena they are meant to describe, explain, and predict. On this issue, see my "Gersonides on the Song of Songs and the Nature of Science."

66. The astronomical discussion here concerns the derivation of the spherical shape of the moon from the boundary between the light and dark parts throughout the month, whereas Aristotle derives the spherical shape of the moon from the boundary seen during eclipses. On the latter, see *On the Heavens,* 2:5, 291b19. The effects "in this sublunary world" referred to here may be astrological. What we "strive to attain" here is not clear to me.

67. I have given this difficult sentence the best meaning I could. Literally, the last clause says, "because it is necessary that we acquire from the senses which we determine through sense all the axioms which we acquire." On the relation of sensation to the formation of axioms, see Gersonides' introduction, the paragraph between nn. 23 and 30.

68. This verse, then, serves as a transition from part 4 of Song of Songs (mathematics) to part 5 (physics).

69. See the commentary to 2:17.

PART FIVE: 4:8 – 8:4

Note to epigraph: This is the way Gersonides summarizes the fifth part of Song of Songs in his introduction (see p. 11).

1. See Gersonides' introduction, after n. 88.

2. Hebrew: *ḥippus;* the term can also mean "induction," on which see Husik, no. 108.

3. That is, even though the study of the physical sciences involves the examination of physical phenomena, this study is so difficult that it must be guided from the very beginning by the intellect. The problem that Gersonides must avoid is that of circularity: we, in effect, "construct" our intellects through what we learn from the senses, but to use the senses correctly, we must be instructed and guided by the intellect. The commentary here gives expression to Gersonides' realist conception of the nature of science. See further my "Gersonides on the Song of Songs and the Nature of Science."

4. See Mashbaum, 37 ff.

5. *Wars of the Lord,* 1:10.

6. See Deut. 3:9.

7. Gersonides mentions this "danger" in his introduction at n. 50.

8. See Neh. 10:1, 11:23 for usages that may be Gersonides' source for this observation.

9. On the connection between "existence" and "truth" see Maimonides, "Laws of

the Foundations of the Torah," 1:3–4 and the discussion of Isaac Abravanel on this passage in *Rosh Amanah*, ch. 20. See Abravanel, *Principles of Faith*, 173–86. In my edition of the original Hebrew text the passage is on pp. 131–40. See further Fox, *Interpreting Maimonides*, 243.

10. See *Metaphysics*, 2:993b30: "As each thing is in respect of being, so is it in respect of truth." As I have had occasion to note above (commentary to 1:2, n. 31), Gersonides considered what we take to be the second book of the *Metaphysics* as the first book.

11. That is, the "first mover" and "remote matter."

12. I have not found the sources for these references.

13. Perhaps a play on the root *ḥ-r-m*, which can mean "destruction," as in Josh. 1:26.

14. The Hebrew reads, *me-rosh Amanah, me-rosh Snir ve-Hermon,* "from the top of Amanah, from the top of Senir, and Hermon," as Gersonides reads it here; the Hebrew word *rosh* ("head," "top," or "beginning") is applied to Amanah and Senir but not to Hermon. The author of Song of Songs was hinting thereby, according to Gersonides, that we should not mistakenly associate "firstness" (as in first matter) with privation.

15. Gersonides is arguing against the identification of matter with privation; if these two principles are identified, then generation would be from absolute privation (i.e., ex nihilo), a possibility that Gersonides (following Aristotle) denies. Gersonides seems to be referring to a passage in Aristotle's *Physics* (1:8, 191a25 ff.) in which Parmenides appears to be the thinker criticized. For discussions of Gersonides on these and related issues, see Feldman, "Gersonides' Proofs for the Creation of the Universe" and "Platonic Themes in Gersonides' Cosmology."

16. The Hebrew in this sentence contains an apparent play on the similarity between the words *'ayin,* "eye," and *'iyyun,* "speculation," "intellectual examination."

17. That is, the neck has a front and back, or a left and a right side.

18. The point here seems to be a comparison of the absolute demonstrations available in mathematics to the a posteriori proofs available in physics. On this, compare Gersonides' introduction, at nn. 67 and 71 and the sources cited there. Compare also the commentary to 6:7.

19. Hebrew: *tiqqun*; perhaps, "well structured."

20. Compare the first paragraph of the commentary to 4:7.

21. In his commentary on this verse (14d/56/93) Gersonides makes it refer to the emanation of the material intellect on the other faculties of the soul.

22. Gersonides here refers to a discussion in Sanhedrin 99a. The Talmud there makes use of Isa. 64:3—*And whereof from of old men have not heard, nor perceived by the ear, neither hath the eye seen a God beside Thee, Who worketh for him that waiteth for Him*—in connection with a discussion of phenomena the true measure of which has not yet been seen. At the end of the pericope Resh Laqish says that *neither hath the eye seen* refers to Eden. The text goes on to use Gen. 2:10 to distinguish Eden from the garden in which Adam and Eve lived: the verse, after all, tells us that the river *went out of Eden* in order to water the garden; Eden and the garden cannot, therefore, be the same. Gersonides makes use of this talmudic discussion in his commentary on Gen. 2:10. There he tells us that Eden symbolizes the Active Intellect (14c/54/89). Interestingly, in the talmudic text the verse from Isaiah is quoted verbatim; in his two discussions, Gersonides paraphrases the verse: here in Song of Songs

he says *she-lo ra'ahu 'ayin me-'olam*, whereas in his Genesis commentary he says *she-lo shaltah bo 'ayin me-'olam*. The verse itself reads *'ayin lo ra'atah*.

23. See Mashbaum, 146.

24. See *Wars of the Lord*, 2:4.

25. See Averroës' *Epitome*, bk. 2, ch. 3; in Blumberg's translation, 39–53, esp. 42, 47.

26. See Altmann, "Gersonides' Commentary," 10–11, 24.

27. Gersonides' meaning here is not transparent to me. On the one hand, the text seems to support the following interpretation: the first type of emanation is the impact of the Active Intellect on "normal" intellection; the second refers to dreams, divination, and prophecy. The problem with that interpretation is that it runs counter to Gersonides' position in *Wars of the Lord*, 2:6 (Leipzig, 111; Feldman, 2:59) that prophecy—unlike dreams and divination—depends on wisdom, which is surely a matter of "choice and striving." Interpreting the text here in light of the discussion in the *Wars of the Lord*, the first type of emanation would be dreams and divination, the second prophecy. This second interpretation is superior, I think, since it better coheres with Gersonides' thought generally, even if it is not explicitly supported by the wording of this paragraph.

28. Literally, "the speech in these two verses comes to indicate."

29. Literally, "things mentioned for the sense." The point would appear to be that the apprehension of general things (universals) begins with sensory impressions.

30. See Aristotle, *Meteorology*, 1:13, 350a1–14.

31. The fact that Gersonides cites no source for this meteorological-agricultural claim would seem to indicate that it is the product of his own observation; his catholic interest in natural science would seem to have extended to matters as mundane as this.

32. When facing east, of course. The fact that the Hebrew words for "south," *teyman*, and for "right," *yamin*, share the same root (*y-m-n*) indicates that ancient Jewish cartographic custom placed east (not north, as is our custom) at the top of maps, with north to the left and south to the right. Gersonides' comment reflects such an orientation (which very word—*orient*ation—shows that maps used to be made "oriented" to the east, not the north), one that was not uncommon in the Middle Ages. See, e.g., Harley and Woodward, *History of Cartography*, 276, 243, 475. Note further Gersonides' reference to this issue in his *Commentary on the Torah* (42b/210/ 427): "for south [*ha-darom*] is called *yamin* in our language." Compare further Maimonides' usage in *Pirqe Mosheh be-Refu'ah*, 361–62, where *yamin* is used for "South." Maimonides and Gersonides are both following biblical usage in this; see, e.g., Ps. 89:13.

33. That is, the reference to "north" and "south" was an indication that we should orient ourselves correctly in our search for intellectual perfection.

34. See 4:12.

35. Compare the commentary to 4:13–14.

36. This sentence is an important key to understanding Gersonides' overall vision of the universe and the place of the scientist in it. In this text, and in medieval Hebrew generally, the term "emanate" is usually restricted to the activity of God and the separate intellects (= angels). Indeed, Maimonides defines emanation (Arabic: *fayḍ*; Hebrew: *shefa'*, or, as here, *hashpa'ah*) in *Guide of the Perplexed*, 2:12, 279, as "the action of one who is not a body." Gersonides, it is true, is using the term in a bor-

rowed sense here, and he basically means by it "the incorporeal influence of one intellect on another," but he did not *have* to use the term to express the idea. That he did use it is an indication of his position, discussed in my "Gersonides on *Imitatio Dei*," that the sharing of knowledge about the universe is a (perhaps the highest?) form of *imitatio Dei*. See there also for comments on my anachronistic use of the term *scientist* in this note.

37. Aristotle surveys the work of his predecessors, citing their errors, in *Physics* 1 and *Metaphysics* 1; see n. 31 to the commentary to 1:2 for an explanation of Gersonides' citation here.

38. Anyone who has followed this sentence this far will agree that it is not well-constructed grammatically; the fault lies with Gersonides (assuming the text is not corrupt) and not with me. The sentence and those following it in this paragraph contain a catalogue of the problems plaguing research in the physical sciences.

39. Gersonides' use of this verb (ṣ-y-ṣ) might have been suggested to him by Song of Songs 2:9 or by the story in Mishnah Ḥagigah 14b ("Ben Zoma peeked and was injured").

40. Apparently a reference to Mishnah Ḥagigah 2:1, especially as interpreted by Maimonides in his commentary ad loc. For a discussion of Maimonides' identification of *Ma'aseh Bereshit* with physics, which Gersonides seems to be following here, see my *Maimonides on Judaism*, 65–70.

41. That is, the impediments occur with respect to the female lover (the imagination and other faculties of the soul) by nature and with respect to the male lover (the material intellect) only incidentally.

42. Literally, "desire and heart."

43. That is, she is *undefiled*—perfect and complete—because the cooperation between them must be perfect and complete.

44. In his *Commentary on the Torah*, 243b, Gersonides defines *revivim* (Deut. 32:2) as *resise laylah* (*drops of the night*), which he in turn defines as dew. Here he seems to distinguish between dew and *drops of the night*.

45. Gersonides has outdone himself here in convoluted phrasing. He seems to want to say that the imagination puts off doing its job of collecting information from the senses because of the difficulty in so doing. To do the job properly the imagination must be guided by the intellect, which indicates to the imagination the information it needs in each science under investigation. Collecting this information from the senses and processing it for use by the intellect is the imagination's perfection.

46. In this Gersonides follows Maimonides, *Guide*, 1:46, 101.

47. Literally, "and."

48. Hebrew: *teva'im*.

49. The point here appears to be that a certain amount of backsliding takes place; progress in science is not a smooth, steady, upward sweep.

50. In the commentary to 3:3.

51. I have not found the source for this observation.

52. It is not clear whether Gersonides means sensation and imagination together or imagination and intellection together.

53. Another translation, better supported by the Hebrew (*le-ha'ir*) perhaps, but not by the context, is: "she said this to draw attention to the fact that."

54. The whole verse accords with allegory; part of the verse, as we shall see, also accords with the intended meaning of the allegory.

55. That is, the verse says "above ten thousand," meaning "more than ten thousand," with no limit stated.

56. This does not appear to be precisely what Aristotle actually said. See *On the Generation of Animals*, 5:1, 780b33–781a5: "Animals with prominent eyes do not see well at a distance, whereas those which have their eyes lying deep in the head can see things at a distance because the movement is not dispersed in space but comes straight to the eye."

57. For the connection between sight and intellection, compare *Guide of the Perplexed*, 1:4, 1:44.

58. See Gersonides' introduction (the paragraph ending with n. 94) and his commentary to 1:12.

59. See Mashbaum, 52.

60. The distinction between the speculative (or theoretical) intellect (*sekhel ʿiyyuni*) and the practical intellect (*sekhel maʿasi*) can be traced back to Aristotle, specifically to texts in *On the Soul* (3:7, 431b) and in the *Nicomachean Ethics* (6:2, 1139b). The speculative intellect concerns itself with the objects of thought (*muskalot*, "intelligibles"), whereas the practical intellect governs choices that result in activity. "According to Greek Aristotelians," as Shlomo Pines puts it, "the practical intellect has . . . the good as its *telos*; it differs in this respect from the theoretical intellect, whose *telos* is the *truth*." See Pines' exhaustive discussion of this issue in "Truth and Falsehood versus Good and Evil," 127. In the same article (132–36) Pines translates passages from Gersonides' *Commentary on the Torah* (16d ff./62 ff./109 ff.). On 137 Pines comments that Gersonides uses the term "practical intellect" in this context to mean "arts, crafts (and other kinds of work) ordered in such a way that they render the continued preservation of life possible," which certainly fits the context here as well.

61. That is, his hands.

62. The word translated here as "his body" is *meʿav;* a more common translation would be "his internal organs," making Gersonides' comment more intelligible.

63. "Corrupted" in the technical sense of generation and corruption.

64. See the commentary on the next verse.

65. A play on the word translated as "sockets" in the verse.

66. Human immortality depends in an important sense on the action of the Active Intellect. For details, see my "Gersonides on the Role of the Active Intellect in Human Cognition."

67. That is, in the science of physics, which is largely inductive, not deductive.

68. Hebrew: *nimshal*. The three mss. I examined and the editio princeps all say *mashal*. I have emended the text here to make it accord with the rest of the sentence.

69. It is possible to translate this such that the spices are in the garden, but such a translation fits the context less well.

70. That is, the *lilies*.

71. In the commentary to verses 4:8, 5:2, and esp. 5:6.

72. That is, concentration.

73. That is, the reason for their conjunction's being impeded.

74. In the commentary to the previous verse.

75. Or: "all of the faculties of the soul."

76. See, e.g., 1 Kings 15:33.

77. That is, causes him to apprehend.

78. That is, individuated by matter.

79. I have no idea how the expression *terrible as an army with banners* indicates this.

80. Hebrew: *ha-kibbuṣ ha-bilti baʿal takhlit*.

81. See Averroës, *Epitome of* Parva Naturalia, 26–27.

82. Hebrew: *hasagah;* heretofore also translated as "apprehension" but in the sense of intellectual apprehension; in this sentence the meaning appears to be sensory perception.

83. Literally, "that is."

84. Not only is this sentence difficult to understand, but Gersonides seems to have forgotten the claim he made in the previous sentence that this verse accords with the allegory alone; he is here clearly dealing with the intended meaning of the allegory.

85. *Kolelim* usually means "universals," but the Hebrew here is *ha-devarim ha-kolelim* and thus my translation.

86. Aristotle discusses different senses of priority in *Metaphysics,* 5:11 (1018b8–1019a14); see also *Categories,* ch. 12. Compare above, commentary to 4:9.

87. Hebrew: *tiviʿiyim;* the objects of natural science.

88. That is, the second kind prepares items for use by the primary kind.

89. Hebrew: *koaḥ,* also translated here as "faculty."

90. Literally, "defect in formation."

91. From this it seems reasonable to infer that Gersonides himself studied anatomy.

92. See Genesis Rabbah 50, 2. Compare Maimonides' use of "angel" as "force [of nature]." See *Guide,* 2:6, 263: "For all forces are angels." For a discussion of Maimonides' views on this subject, see Goodman, "Maimonidean Naturalism."

93. That is, were it possible for one faculty to order more than one type of activity.

94. That is, arteries, nerves, and muscles.

95. See *On the Parts of Animals,* 3:4, 665b.

96. Literally, "moves more toward."

97. I suspect that Gersonides meant to say *daughters*.

98. That is, we must study the attributes and accidents of physical phenomena in order to understand the phenomena themselves. These attributes and accidents are "posterior" to the phenomena themselves.

99. Chapter 8, 384b24–385b6.

100. See Averroës' *Epitome,* bk. 1, on sense and sense objects (5–21), esp. 12–13.

101. Literally, "move."

102. A possible source for this may be found in Gersonides' supercommentary on Averroës' *Epitome of* De Anima, Bodleian Ms. Opp. Add. 4° 38, at 199b.

103. A prerequisite for understanding any physical phenomenon, in other words, is determining which of its attributes is essential and which accidental. Compare Gersonides' introduction, at n. 6.

104. Most recently in the commentaries to 5:1–2 and 6:3.

105. That is, what she had acquired for him.

106. That is, the light of the dawn is weaker than that of the moon, which in turn is weaker than that of the sun.

107. See the commentary to 6:4.

108. The Hebrew word here, *egoz*, is a *hapax legomenon* but is usually taken in rabbinic literature to mean "walnut"; why Gersonides connects it to a species of perfume is unclear.

109. As explained in Gersonides' introduction (in the paragraph between nn. 23 and 30), one of the fundamental epistemological problems underlying scientific inquiry is how we derive knowledge of universals (the only true knowledge) from our experience of particulars.

110. Translated here in Song of Songs as *my princely people*.

111. Three figures in the Bible are named ʿAminadav (not ʿAminadiv), the best known of whom is the father of Naḥshon (Num. 1:7, etc.).

112. That is, "a princely people" as opposed to "my princely people."

113. In this Gersonides agrees with the commentaries of Rashi and ibn Ezra. Although there is no doubt that he knew the commentary of ibn Ezra, there is no reason to suspect that he was familiar with that of Rashi (as we have noted above).

114. I do not know to what specific text Gersonides is referring here, but in connecting the persistence of universals to the activity of the Active Intellect (as I understand him to be doing), he is, unwittingly, speaking of Aristotle as presented by Averroës, not of Aristotle as he apparently understood himself.

115. That is, matter defeats form. I suspect that the preceding text is not grammatically a sentence; but did Gersonides suspect it as well?

116. Hebrew: *bat nadiv*.

117. See Mashbaum, 146 ff., esp. 154. Compare *Wars of the Lord,* 1:6 (Leipzig, 42–43; Feldman, 156–57).

118. See Mashbaum, 145.

119. That is, both "Shulammite" and the Hebrew word for perfection are derived from the root *sh-l-m.*

120. That is, for the human intellect and the Active Intellect.

121. That is, the world of "physical objects subject to generation and corruption."

122. That is, the process of generation and corruption is governed by astral influences (the cycle of the heavenly bodies) and is necessary for the continued existence of physical things as such; it is not, of course, the cause of the permanence of this or that physical thing.

123. Or, "with their causes"; either way, the point refers back to a central Aristotelian thesis, namely, that knowing a thing involves knowing the "why" of it: "for we aim at understanding, and since we never reckon that we understand a thing till we can give an account of its 'how and why'" (*Physics,* 2:3, 194b16–24).

124. More formally, the most convincing form of argument is deductive; from an approximate knowledge of a thing's attributes we can sometimes arrive at a precise determination concerning the thing itself; having arrived at that determination we may then move deductively to the attributes, which are now known with their cause, and are thus known better than they were before.

125. Gersonides appears to be playing on the similarity between the Hebrew words for "shoe" or "sandal" and for "lock"; the material prepared for the intellect by his beloved is "locked" and thus inaccessible to perfect apprehension.

126. As noted above, the root *n-ʿ-l* denotes either "lock" or "sandal, shoe" in the Bible. It appears that Gersonides is explaining that in the present context the reference

is to footwear and not to locks. Given the use of the root above in 4:12, Gersonides' comment here is perhaps not entirely otiose. In his comments on Exod. 3:5 he makes nothing special of the word *na'al*. A possible alternative explanation, suggested to me by my friend Nisan Ararat, is that just as the sandals that Moses wore in his encounter with the burning bush had to be removed (because of the holiness of the place) and thus in effect impeded his apprehension of God, so here *sandals* impede apprehension.

127. That is, "abstract"; see Gersonides' introduction, the paragraph following n. 30.

128. The process of intellection begins with sensory perception and moves by a series of stages, each more abstract ("spiritual") than the preceding, until an intelligible is acquired; the imagination stands roughly halfway along this continuum.

129. Hebrew: *tiqqun,* carrying the connotation of improvement, correction, repair; the imagination prepares raw material for the intellect, and in so doing improves what is given it.

130. See Mashbaum, 150 ff., esp. 157.

131. I have not located the source for this reference.

132. That is, we learn about the nature of all triangles, e.g., by studying pictures of specific triangles. As Gersonides will point out immediately, erasing those pictures does not destroy our concept of triangles.

133. Gersonides reverts to the issue of the previous paragraph; since the imagination is caused by intellect, the existence of the latter could not be dependent on the existence of the former.

134. See Mashbaum, 150 ff.

135. *Wars of the Lord,* 1:11.

136. Literally, "this taking which this [female] beloved takes."

137. Translated by the JPS as "goblet."

138. The *aggan ha-sahar,* translated by JPS as "round goblet."

139. Hebrew: *mar'ah.* As the continuation of the text shows, Gersonides had in mind either the sort of "burning mirror" that made Archimedes famous or a magnifying glass. In Gersonides' commentary on Averroës' *Epitome of* De Anima, Ms. Vat. Urb. 42 (JNUL 681), 9b–10a, the word clearly means "magnifying glass." The text is quoted by Freudenthal in "Human Felicity and Astronomy," 62.

140. A reference, I presume, to the cycles of the astronomical bodies, mentioned above in the commentary to 7:1.

141. For the apparent source of this unusual claim, see Radaq (R. David Qimḥi), *Sefer ha-Shorashim,* s.v. "sahar."

142. That is, the straw.

143. That is, the lily blossom.

144. That is, even though straw does not stand to wheat in the exact relation in which blossoms stand to the fruit or seed derived from them, the relation is still similar.

145. Literally, "hand."

146. See the commentary to 4:5.

147. See Gersonides' introduction, n. 71. That is, the tower built in the mathematical sciences was strong enough to be *builded with turrets,* whereas the tower built in physics is only *a tower of ivory,* strong, but not as strong as a tower *builded with turrets.*

148. *Heshbon* means "computation," *Rabbim* "many."

149. The root *n-g-r* usually means "to be spilled" or "to be poured down" (e.g., 2 Sam. 14:14), but the substantive *neger* can mean "a small pool" or "irrigation channel" (see BT Beṣah 24b). Either way, my translation of Gersonides' *hagarah* is not precisely literal. My suspicion is that he actually had the root *a-g-r* ("to collect") in mind here and meant to write (or actually did, and was poorly served by his scribes) *agirah*.

150. Here, *heshbon*.

151. See Gersonides' introduction, n. 88.

152. In the Bible, Carmel, in addition to being the name of a place—indeed, the very place in which I am located while typing these words—means either "fresh ears [of corn]" (Lev. 23:14) or any very fruitful place (Jer. 4:26). In the present passage Gersonides uses both of these senses.

153. Here, the ear of corn.

154. The flower produces the fruit without many intermediate steps; so, too, there are not many intermediate steps between what she presents to the intellect and its perfection.

155. Gersonides understands the term here translated as "tresses" to mean "troughs," as above in 1:17 and in Exod. 2:16.

156. Literally, with respect to what it emanates unto him from among the imaginative forms. Gersonides loves ambiguous antecedents.

157. That is, according to the second interpretation just presented.

158. That is, the pleasure of intellectual perfection is far greater than the pleasure derived from the satisfaction of physical desires.

159. Proverbs 23:31: *Look not upon the wine when it is red, when it giveth its color in the cup, when it glideth down smoothly.* Gersonides' commentary on that verse indicates his familiarity with some of the finer points of wine appreciation.

160. That is, without the input of the imagination the material intellect will clearly be "asleep," but so will the Active Intellect with respect to its perfecting this specific material intellect.

161. That is, the memory must store the impressions of previous sensory experiences if their repetition is to be of any use.

162. Or, "because it has become well known"—that is, the scientific accomplishments of others have become available to researchers.

163. As noted above in n. 42 to the commentary on 1:2, *On Animals* 11 is actually *Parts of Animals*, 1.

164. Two points in this sentence are noteworthy: (a) the further reference to Gersonides' conception of the cooperative and cumulative nature of the scientific enterprise and (b) his unwillingness to rely on the authority of the ancients as such. On the latter, compare the following comment by Maimonides: "The great sickness and the *grievous evil* (Eccles. 5:12) consists in this: that all the things that man finds written in books, he presumes to think of as true—and all the more so if the books are old." I cite this passage from Maimonides' "Letter on Astrology," 229. Compare my "Gersonides on *Imitatio Dei.*"

165. Compare ibn Ezra's comment on this verse, which appears to be Gersonides' source for this idea. Note should be taken of what this commentary teaches us concerning the social mores of Gersonides' community.

166. That is, were he as a brother to her.

167. I translate the root *ḥ-p-s* in this sentence twice in the nontechnical sense of "search"; it can also mean "induction."

168. I do not know to what antecedent this refers.

169. Perhaps a reference to the commentary to Song of Songs 8:8.

PART SIX: 8:5 – 8:14

Note to epigraph: This is the way Gersonides summarizes the sixth part of Song of Songs in his introduction (see p. 11).

1. Literally, "how."

2. That is, knowledge in physics is ultimately based on experience.

3. Hebrew: *haqdamot reḥoqot.*

4. That is, she is upset.

5. *En ḥaver le-zot ha-millah* as opposed to the more common *en lo aḥ va-re'ah.*

6. "Elbow" in modern Hebrew.

7. See Mishnah Shabbat 10.3; the comment is found in the standard editions of the commentary, not in R. Joseph Kafiḥ's. Rabbi Kafiḥ cites it in a note. Gersonides' comment here would seem to indicate that he did not know Arabic himself. See above, my introduction, n. 13.

8. That is, those that are leaned on.

9. This makes no sense to me: we are now investigating metaphysics, not physics.

10. For Gersonides' doctrine of the acquired intellect, see my "Gersonides on the Role of the Active Intellect in Human Cognition."

11. That is, the imagination is a "sister" to the Active and acquired intellects because of her important role in achieving the perfection of the latter, and thus she is termed *Shulammite* ("perfect one"). On the other hand, she is a only a "little" sister because of the relatively small role she plays in the achievement of metaphysical (as opposed to physical) knowledge.

12. Compare Gersonides' introduction, the paragraph ending with n. 100.

13. That is, for the apprehension of metaphysics.

14. Perhaps a reference to Aristotle, *Rhetoric,* 1355a22 ff.

15. On this issue, see Gersonides' introduction, n. 37.

16. This observation appears to be based on Mishnah Ḥagigah 13a. Compare Ḥagigah 14a, where Isa. 3:3 is used to suggest that a fit age for such matters is fifty.

17. See Gersonides' introduction, n. 74. As noted there, the premises of metaphysics are based on commonly accepted, "reputable" opinions.

18. This is a fascinating sentence: Gersonides tells his reader to devote more time to the physical sciences than to metaphysics. Within the context of his commentary to Song of Songs, devoted to the attempt to restrain the enthusiasm of insufficiently trained would-be metaphysicians, this might be seen as a "political" claim as opposed to a reflection of Gersonides' true views. Given Gersonides' realist view of science, and his own biography, I am confident that he really held the view advanced here.

19. That is, prepared; Gersonides is simply continuing the symbolism of the verse. There may be a play on the word *g-d-r* here, the root of both "enclosure" and "definition."

20. That is, not properly enclosed.

21. Here, *'inyanah,* from Gersonides' all-purpose word, *'inyan.*

22. See Gersonides' introduction, n. 87.

23. *Hamon* means "multitude"; *ribbui* means "multiplicity."

24. Gersonides' comment depends on a position defended in *Wars of the Lord,* 1:10 (Leipzig, 73; Feldman, 1:201), where he maintains that sensible objects exist in consequence of the logically antecedent existence of the intelligible order of nature in the Active Intellect. We, however, learn of this intelligible order from our examination of sensible objects.

25. See Gersonides' introduction at n. 92.

26. Grammatically, the word *elef* ("a thousand") is singular; it refers, however, to great multiplicity.

27. That is, all the way back to God, the ultimate cause of all existence.

28. For Gersonides on God as final form, see the *Commentary on the Torah,* 194a, 210b. Gersonides' systematic treatment of God vis-à-vis the separate intellects is in the *Wars of the Lord,* 5:3.11–12 (Leipzig, 276–85).

29. That is, in 8:11.

30. That is, knowledge of God is the ultimate end. Despite his apparent preference for physics over metaphysics (on which see my "Gersonides on the Song of Songs and the Nature of Science" and n. 18 above), Gersonides cannot deny that, given the sublimity of its object, metaphysics is "the fruit of the [human] intellect and its end."

31. See *On the Soul,* 3:1, 424b21 ff.

32. Since, in the final analysis, everything we know derives in one way or another from sensory experience.

33. That is, the Active Intellect and the acquired intellect, as in the commentary to 8:8.

34. That is, sensible existence.

35. As when they called her their "sister" in 8:8.

36. Based on 2 Chron. 33:12. The biblical text is *hillah et pene;* Gersonides has *hillah pene.*

37. That is, to the acquired intellect.

38. That is, without the perfection of the material intellect made possible by the service rendered to it by the imagination (the presentation to it of factual knowledge derived from experience), the activity of the Active Intellect (emanating knowledge of universals) would be for naught.

39. See Gersonides' introduction, the paragraph following n. 94, and his commentary to 2:17.

40. Here, *derushim;* in the rest of the book I have translated this word as "subjects of research."

41. The twenty-ninth of Tammuz, A.M. 5085, corresponds to July 11, 1325 C.E.

WORKS CITED

ABBREVIATIONS

AJSReview	Association for Jewish Studies Review
HUCA	Hebrew Union College Annual
JQR	Jewish Quarterly Review
PAAJR	Proceedings of the American Academy for Jewish Research
REJ	Revue des études juives

Abraham ibn Ezra. *Abraham ibn Ezra's Commentary on the Canticles after the First Recension.* Edited by H. J. Mathews. London: Truebner, 1874.

Abravanel, Isaac. *Commentary on the Torah.* Jerusalem: Bnai Arbel, 1964.

———. *Principles of Faith (Rosh Amanah).* Translated by Menachem Kellner. London: Associated University Press (Littman Library of Jewish Civilization), 1982.

———. *Rosh Amanah.* Edited by Menachem Kellner. Ramat Gan: Bar Ilan University Press, 1993.

Adret, Solomon ben Abraham. *Responsa.* Edited by H. Dimitrowski. Jerusalem: Mossad ha-Rav Kook, 1990.

Altmann, Alexander. "Maimonides on the Intellect and the Scope of Metaphysics." In Altmann, *Von der mittelalterlichen zur modernen Aufklärung.* Tübingen: Mohr, 1986: 60–129.

Altmann, Alexander, ed. "Gersonides' Commentary on Averroës' Epitome of *Parva Naturalia,* II.3: Annotated Critical Edition," *PAAJR Jubilee Volume,* Part 1 (1980): 1–31.

Anatoli, Ya'akov. *Malmad ha-Talmidim.* Lyck, 1866; photoreproduction, Israel, 1968.

Aristotle. *The Complete Works of Aristotle.* Edited by Jonathan Barnes. Princeton: Princeton University Press, 1984.

———. *Generation of Animals: The Arabic Translation Commonly Ascribed to Yaḥya ibn al-Bitriq.* Leiden: Brill, 1971.

Astell, Ann W. *The Song of Songs in the Middle Ages.* Ithaca: Cornell University Press, 1990.

Averroës. *Averroës on Plato's* Republic. Translated by Ralph Lerner. Ithaca: Cornell University Press, 1974.

———. *Epitome of* Parva Naturalia. Translated by Harry Blumberg. Cambridge: Medieval Academy of America, 1961.

Barnes, Jonathan. *Aristotle's* Posterior Analytics. Oxford: Oxford University Press, 1975.

Ben-Shalom, Ram. "Communication and Propaganda between Provence and Spain: The Controversy over Extreme Allegorization." In *Communication in Jewish Society in the Pre-Modern Period,* edited by Sophia Menache, 171–226. Leiden: Brill, 1996.

Berger, David. *The Jewish-Christian Debate in the High Middle Ages.* Philadelphia: Jewish Publication Society, 1979.

Berlin, Adele. *Biblical Poetry through Medieval Eyes.* Bloomington: Indiana University Press, 1991.

Berman, Lawrence V. "Greek into Hebrew: Samuel ben Judah of Marseilles, Fourteenth-Century Philosopher and Translator." In *Jewish Medieval and Renaissance Studies,* edited by Alexander Altmann, 289–320. Cambridge: Harvard University Press, 1967.

Bleich, J. David. *Providence in the Philosophy of Gersonides.* New York: Yeshiva University Press, 1973.

Blidstein, Ya'akov Gerald. *'Ekronot Mediniyim be-Mishnat ha-Rambam.* Ramat Gan: Bar Ilan University Press, 1983.

Davidson, Herbert A. *Alfarabi, Avicenna, and Averroës on Intellect.* New York: Oxford University Press, 1992.

———. "Gersonides on the Material and Active Intellects." In *Studies on Gersonides: A Fourteenth-Century Jewish Philosopher-Scientist,* edited by Gad Freudenthal, 195–265. Leiden: Brill, 1992.

D'Entreves, A. P., ed. *Selected Political Writings [of Aquinas].* Oxford: Oxford University Press, 1951.

Diem, G. "Les traductions gréco-latines de la *Métaphysique* au moyen âge: Le problème de la *Metaphysica Vetus.*" *Archiv für Geschichte der Philosophie* 49 (1967): 7–71.

Diesendruck, Zvi. "Samuel and Moses ibn Tibbon on Maimonides' Theory of Providence." *HUCA* 11 (1936): 341–66.

Dod, Bernard G. "Aristoteles latinus." In *The Cambridge History of Later Medieval Philosophy: From the Rediscovery of Aristotle to the Disintegration of Scholasticism, 1100–1600,* edited by Norman Kretzmann, Anthony Kenny, and Jan Pinborg, 45–79. Cambridge: Cambridge University Press, 1982.

Eisen, Robert. *Gersonides on Providence, Covenant, and the Jewish People.* Albany: SUNY Press, 1995.

———. "Reason, Revelation, and the Fundamental Principles of the Torah in Gersonides' Thought." *PAAJR* 57 (1991): 11–34.

Feldman, Seymour. "Gersonides on the Possibility of Conjunction with the Agent Intellect." *AJSReview* 3 (1978): 99–120.

———. "Gersonides' Proofs for the Creation of the Universe." *PAAJR* 35 (1967): 113–37; reprinted in *Essays in Medieval Jewish and Islamic Philosophy,* edited by A. Hyman, 219–54. New York: Ktav, 1977.

———. "'In the Beginning God Created': A Philosophical Midrash." In *God and Creation: An Ecumenical Symposium*, edited by David Burrell and Bernard McGinn, 3–26. Notre Dame: University of Notre Dame Press, 1990.

———. "Platonic Themes in Gersonides' Cosmology." In *Salo Wittmayer Baron Jubilee Volume*, 383–405. Jerusalem: American Academy for Jewish Research, 1975.

———. "Platonic Themes in Gersonides' Doctrine of the Active Intellect." In *Neoplatonism and Jewish Thought*, edited by Lenn E. Goodman, 255–77. Albany: SUNY Press, 1992.

———. "The Wisdom of Solomon: A Gersonidean Interpretation." In *Gersonide en son temps*, edited by Gilbert Dahan, 61–80. Louvain: Peeters, 1991.

Fox, Marvin. *Interpreting Maimonides*. Chicago: University of Chicago Press, 1990.

Freiman, Eli. "A Passage from Gersonides' Commentary on the Torah." In *Me-ʿAlei ʿAsor*, edited by B. Branner, O. Kafih, and Z. Shimshoni, 162–89. Maʾaleh Adumin: Maʾaliyot, 1988 (Hebrew).

Freudenthal, Gad. "Cosmogonie et physique chez Gersonide." *REJ* 145 (1986): 295–314.

———. "Human Felicity and Astronomy: Gersonides' Revolt against Ptolemy." *Daʿat* 22 (1989): 55–72 (Hebrew).

———. "Les sciences dans les communautés juives médiévales de Provence: Leur appropriation, leur rôle." *REJ* 153 (1993): 29–136.

Funkenstein, Amos. "Gersonides' Bible Commentary: Science, History, and Providence." In *Studies on Gersonides: A Fourteenth-Century Jewish Philosopher-Scientist*, edited by Gad Freudenthal, 305–15. Leiden: Brill, 1992.

———. *Theology and the Scientific Imagination*. Princeton: Princeton University Press, 1986.

Gelles, Benjamin J. *Peshaṭ and Derash in the Exegesis of Rashi*. Leiden: Brill, 1981.

Gershom ben Shlomoh d'Arles. *Shaʿar ha-Shamayim (The Gate of Heaven)*. Warsaw, 1875. Reprint, translated and edited by F. S. Bodenheimer, Jerusalem: Kiryat Sepher, 1953.

Gersonides. *The Commentary of Levi ben Gerson (Gersonides) on the Book of Job*. Translated by Abraham Lassen. New York: Bloch, 1946.

———. "Commentary on Averroës' Epitome of *Parva Naturalia* II.3: Annotated Critical Edition," trans. Alexander Altmann, 1–31. In *PAAJR Jubilee Volume*, pt. 1. Jerusalem: American Academy for Jewish Research, 1980.

———. *Ḥamishah Ḥumshei Torah ʿim Beʾur ha-Ralbag, Bereshit*. Edited by Baruch Braner and Eli Freiman. Jerusalem: Maaliyot, 1993.

———. *The Logic of Gersonides (Sefer ha-Heqqesh ha-Yashar)*. Translated by Charles H. Manekin. Dordrecht: Kluwer, 1992.

———. *On God's Knowledge*. Translation and commentary by Norbert Max Samuelson. Toronto: Pontifical Institute of Mediaeval Studies, 1977.

———. *Milḥamot Ha-Shem*. Leipzig, 1866.

———. *Perush ʿal ha-Torah ʿal Derekh ha-Beʾur*. Venice, 1547. Reprints, New York, 1958 (first half of the commentary only); Israel, 2 vols. (n.p., n.d.).

———. *Perushe ha-Torah le-Rabbenu Levi ben Gershom, Sefer Bereshit*. Edited by Yaʿakov Leib Levy. Jerusalem: Mossad ha-Rav Kook, 1992.

———. *The Wars of the Lord*. Translated by Seymour Feldman. Vol. 1. Philadelphia: Jewish Publication Society, 1984; Vol. 2, 1987.

Ginsburg, Christian David. *The Song of Songs*. London, 1857. Reprint, New York: Ktav, 1970.

Glasner, Ruth. "Gersonides' Theory of Natural Motion." *Early Science and Medicine* 1 (1996): 151–203.

Gluskina, G. M., ed. and trans. *Alfonso, Meyasher ʿAqov*. Moscow: n.p., 1983.

Goldstein, Bernard R. *The Astronomy of Levi Ben Gerson 1288–1344: A Critical Edition of Chapters 1–20 with Translation and Commentary*. New York: Springer-Verlag, 1985.

———. "Levi ben Gerson: On Astronomy and Physical Experiments." In *Physics, Cosmology, and Astronomy, 1300–1700,* edited by S. Unguru, 75–82. Dordrecht: Kluwer, 1991.

———. "Levi ben Gerson's Astrology in Historical Perspective." In *Gersonide en son temps,* edited by Gilbert Dahan, 287–300. Louvain: Peeters, 1991.

Goldstein, Helen Tunik. *Averroës' Questions in Physics*. The New Synthese Historical Library: Texts and Studies in the History of Philosophy, no. 39. Dordrecht: Kluwer, 1991.

———. "*Dator Formarum:* Ibn Rushd, Levi ben Gerson, and Moses ben Joshua of Narbonne." In *Essays in Islamic and Comparative Studies,* edited by I. Faruqi and A. O. Nasseff, 107–21. Washington: International Institute of Islamic Thought, 1982.

Goodman, Lenn Evan. "Maimonidean Naturalism." In *Neoplatonism and Jewish Thought,* edited by L. E. Goodman, 157–94. Albany: SUNY Press, 1992.

Gordis, Robert. *The Song of Songs and Lamentations*. New York: Ktav, 1974.

Halivni, David Weiss. *Peshaṭ and Derash: Plain and Applied Meaning in Rabbinic Exegesis*. New York: Oxford University Press, 1991.

Halkin, Abraham S. "The Ban on the Study of Philosophy." *Perakim* 1 (1967/8): 35–55 (Hebrew).

———. "The Character of R. Yosef ben Yehudah ibn ʿAknin." In *Sefer ha-Yovel Likhvod Zvi Wolfson,* 93–111. Jerusalem: American Academy for Jewish Research, 1965 (Hebrew).

———. "Classical and Arabic Material in ibn Aknin's 'Hygiene of the Soul.'" *PAAJR* 14 (1944): 25–147.

———. "The History of the Forcible Conversion During the Days of the Almohades." In *Joshua Starr Memorial Volume,* 101–110. New York: Conference on Jewish Relations, 1953 (Hebrew).

———. "Ibn Aknin's Commentary on the Song of Songs." In *Alexander Marx Jubilee Volume,* 389–424. New York: Jewish Theological Seminary, 1950.

———. "Why Was Levi ben Hayyim Hounded?" *PAAJR* 34 (1966): 65–76.

———. "Yedaiah Bedershi's Apology." In *Jewish Medieval and Renaissance Studies,* edited by A. Altmann, 165–84. Cambridge: Harvard University Press, 1967.

Harley, J. B., and David Woodward, eds., *The History of Cartography*. Vol. 1. Chicago: University of Chicago Press, 1987.

Harvey, Steven. "Did Gersonides Believe in the Absolute Generation of Prime Matter?" In *Shlomo Pines Jubilee Volume,* pt. 1, at 307–18. *Jerusalem Studies in Jewish Thought* no. 7. 1988 (Hebrew).

———. *Falaquera's "Epistle of the Debate."* Cambridge: Harvard University Press, 1987.

———. "The Hebrew Translation of Averroës' Prooemium to His Long Commentary on Aristotle's Physics." *PAAJR* 52 (1985): 55–84.

Harvey, Warren Ze'ev. "Albo's Discussion of Time." *JQR* 70 (1979–80): 210–38.

———. "Quelques réflexions sur l'attitude de Gersonide vis-à-vis du *Midrash*." In *Gersonide en son temps,* edited by Gilbert Dahan, 109–16. Louvain: Peeters, 1991.

———. "R. Ḥasdai Crescas and His Critique of Philosophic Happiness." In *Proceedings of the Sixth World Congress of Jewish Studies* 3:143–49. Jerusalem: World Congress of Jewish Studies, 1977 (Hebrew).

Havlin, Shlomo Z. "On *Ḥatimah Sifrutit* as a Basis for Periodization in Halakhah." In *Meḥqarim be-Sifrut ha-Talmudit: Yom 'Iyyun le-Regel Mele'at Shemonim Shanah le-Shaul Lieberman,* 148–92. Jerusalem: Israel Academy of Sciences, 1983 (Hebrew).

Hirshman, Menachem. *Ha-Miqra u-Midrasho.* Tel Aviv: Ha-Kibbutz ha-Me'uhad, 1992.

Hourani, George F. *Averroës on the Harmony of Religion and Philosophy.* London: Luzac, 1961.

Husik, Isaac. *Judah Messer Leon's Commentary on the "Vetus Logica."* Leiden: Brill, 1906.

———. "Studies in Gersonides." *JQR* n.s. 7 (1916–17): 553–94; 8 (1917–18): 113–56, 231–68. Partial reprint in Isaac Husik, *Philosophical Essays,* edited by Leo Strauss and Milton Nahm, 186–254. Oxford: Oxford University Press, 1952.

Hyman, Arthur. "Aristotle's Theory of the Intellect and Its Interpretation by Averroës." In *Studies in Aristotle,* edited by Dominic J. O'Meara, 161–91. *Studies in Philosophy and the History of Philosophy* 9. Washington: Catholic University of America Press, 1981.

Ibn 'Aqnin, Yehudah. *Hitgalut ha-Sodot ve-Hofa'at ha-Me'orot.* Jerusalem: Meqise Nirdamim, 1964.

Ibn Kaspi, Joseph. *'Asarah Klei Kesef.* Edited by I. Last. Pressburg: n.p., 1905.

Ibn Tibbon, Samuel ben Judah. *Perush ha-Millot ha-Zarot* (printed in many editions of Maimonides' *Guide of the Perplexed*).

Idel, Moshe. "*Hitbodedut* as Concentration in Jewish Philosophy." In *Shlomo Pines Jubilee Volume,* pt. 1, at 39–60. *Jerusalem Studies in Jewish Thought* no. 7. 1988 (Hebrew).

———. "*Sitre 'Arayot* in Maimonides' Thought." In *Maimonides and Philosophy,* edited by Shlomo Pines and Y. Yovel, 79–91. Dordrecht: Martinus Nijhoff, 1986.

Immanuel ben Solomon of Rome. *Der Kommentar zum Hohen Liede.* Edited by S. B. Eschwege. Frankfurt am Main: Louis Golde, 1908.

———. *Maḥbarot Immanuel ha-Romi.* Edited by D. Yarden. Jerusalem: Mossad Bialik, 1957.

Ivry, Alfred. "Gersonides and Averroës on the Intellect: The Evidence of the Supercommentary on the *De anima*." In *Gersonide en son temps,* edited by Gilbert Dahan, 235–51. Louvain: Peeters, 1991.

Jacobson, B. S. *The Weekday Siddur.* Tel Aviv: Sinai, 1973.

Jospe, Raphael. "Rejecting Moral Virtue as the Ultimate Human End." In *Studies in Islamic and Jewish Traditions,* edited by W. Brinner and S. Ricks, 185–205. Atlanta: Scholars Press, 1986.

————. *Torah and Sophia: The Life and Thought of Shem Tov Ibn Falaquera.* Cincinnati: Hebrew Union College Press, 1988.

Kamin, Sara. *Rashi: Peshuto shel Miqra u-Midrasho shel Miqra.* Jerusalem: Magnes, 1986.

————. "Rashi's Commentary on Song of Songs and the Jewish-Christian Dispute." In *Shenaton li-Miqra u-le-Ḥeqer ha-Mizraḥ ha-Qadum* 7–8, edited by Moshe Weinfeld, 218–48. 1984 (Hebrew).

————. "Rashi's Exegetical Categorization with Respect to the Distinction between Peshat and Derash." *Immanuel* 11 (1980): 16–32.

Kellner, Menachem. "Bibliographia Gersonideana: An Annotated List of Writings by and About R. Levi ben Gershom." In *Studies on Gersonides: A Fourteenth-Century Jewish Philosopher-Scientist,* edited by Gad Freudenthal, 367–414. Leiden: Brill, 1992.

————. "Communication or Lack Thereof Among 13–14th Century Provençal Jewish Philosophers: Moses ibn Tibbon and Gersonides on Song of Songs." In *Communication in Jewish Society in the Pre-Modern Period,* edited by Sophia Menache, 227–56. Leiden: Brill, 1996.

————. *Dogma in Medieval Jewish Thought.* Oxford: Oxford University Press, 1986.

————. "Gersonides and His Cultured Despisers: Arama and Abravanel." *Journal of Medieval and Renaissance Studies* 6 (1976): 269–96.

————. "Gersonides' Commentary on Song of Songs: For Whom Was It Written, and Why?" In *Gersonide en son temps,* edited by Gilbert Dahan, 81–107. Louvain: Peeters, 1991.

————. "Gersonides on *Imitatio Dei* and the Dissemination of Scientific Knowledge." *JQR* 85 (1995): 275–96.

————. "Gersonides on Miracles, the Messiah, and Resurrection." *Daʿat* 4 (1980): 5–34.

————. "Gersonides on the Role of the Active Intellect in Human Cognition." *HUCA* 65 (1994): 233–59.

————. "Gersonides on the Song of Songs and the Nature of Science." *Journal of Jewish Thought and Philosophy* 4 (1994): 1–21.

————. "Gersonides, Providence, and the Rabbinic Tradition." *Journal of the American Academy of Religion* 42 (1974): 673–85.

————. "Maimonides and Gersonides on Astronomy and Metaphysics." In *Maimonides on Medicine, Science, and Philosophy,* edited by S. Kottek and F. Rosner, 249–51. Northvale, N.J.: Jason Aronson, 1993.

————. "Maimonides and Gersonides on Mosaic Prophecy." *Speculum* 52 (1977): 62–79.

————. *Maimonides on Human Perfection.* Atlanta: Scholars Press, 1990.

————. *Maimonides on Judaism and the Jewish People.* Albany: SUNY Press, 1991.

————. "Politics and Perfection: Gersonides vs. Maimonides." *Jewish Political Studies Review* 6 (1994): 49–82.

————. "Reading Rambam: Approaches to the Interpretation of Maimonides." *Jewish History* 5 (1993): 71–91.

Klein-Braslavy, Sara. "Gersonides on Determinism, Possibility, Choice, and Foreknowledge." *Daʿat* 22 (1989): 5–53 (Hebrew).

————. "Maimonides' Commentaries on Proverbs 1:6." In *ʿAlei Shefer: Studies in*

Literature and Jewish Thought Presented to Rabbi Dr. Alexandre Safran, edited by Moshe Ḥallamish, 121–32. Ramat Gan: Bar Ilan University Press, 1990 (Hebrew).

———. *Perush ha-Rambam le-Sippur Bri'at ha-ʿOlam.* Jerusalem: Israel Bible Society, 1978.

———. "Solomon's 'Prophecy' in Maimonides' Writings." In *Minḥah le-Sarah,* edited by Moshe Idel, 57–81. Jerusalem: Magnes, 1994 (Hebrew).

Kreisel, Howard Ḥaim. "Philosopher and Prophet in the Teaching of Maimonides and His School." *Eshel Beersheva* 3 (1986): 149–69 (Hebrew).

Lazarus-Yafeh, Hava. *Studies in Al-Ghazzali.* Jerusalem: Magnes, 1975.

Lieberman, Saul. "Appendix: *Mishnat Shir ha-Shirim.*" In Gershom Scholem, *Jewish Gnosticism, Merkabah Mysticism, and Talmudic Tradition.* 2d ed. New York: Jewish Theological Seminary, 1965 (Hebrew).

———. *Hellenism in Jewish Palestine.* New York: Jewish Theological Seminary, 1950.

Maimonides, Moses. *Ethical Writings of Maimonides.* Edited and translated by Raymond L. Weiss and Charles Butterworth. New York: Dover, 1983.

———. *Guide of the Perplexed.* Translated by Shlomo Pines. Chicago: University of Chicago Press, 1963.

———. "Letter on Astrology." Translated by Ralph Lerner in *Medieval Political Philosophy,* edited by Ralph Lerner and Muhsin Mahdi, 227–36. Ithaca: Cornell University Press, 1972.

———. *Maimonides' Treatise on Logic (Millot ha-Higgayon).* Edited and translated by Israel Efros. New York: American Academy for Jewish Research, 1938 (= *PAAJR* 10 [1938]).

———. *Mishnah im Perush ha-Rambam.* Edited and translated by J. Kafiḥ. Jerusalem: Mossad ha-Rav Kook, 1963.

———. *Pirqe Mosheh be-Refu'ah.* Edited by S. Muntner. Jerusalem: Mossad ha-Rav Kook, 1982.

Malter, Henry. "Medieval Hebrew Terms for Nature." In *Judaica: Festschrift zu Hermann Cohens Siebzigstem Geburtstage,* 253–56. Berlin: Bruno Cassirer, 1912.

Manekin, Charles. "Gersonides: Logic, Sciences, and Philosophy." In *Studies on Gersonides,* edited by Gad Freudenthal, 285–303. Leiden: Brill, 1992.

———. "Logic and Its Applications in the Philosophy of Gersonides." In *Gersonide en son temps,* edited by Gilbert Dahan, 133–49. Louvain: Peeters, 1991.

———. *The Logic of Gersonides.* Dordrecht: Kluwer, 1992.

Marcus, Ivan G. "The Song of Songs in German Ḥasidism and the School of Rashi: A Preliminary Comparison." In *The Frank Talmage Memorial Volume,* edited by Barry Walfish, 1:181–90. Haifa: Haifa University Press, 1993.

Mashbaum, Jesse Stephen. "Chapters 9–12 of Gersonides' Supercommentary on Averroës' *Epitome of the* De Anima: The Internal Senses." Ph.D. Diss., Brandeis University, 1981.

Matter, E. Ann. *The Song of My Beloved: The Song of Songs in Western Medieval Christianity.* Philadelphia: University of Pennsylvania Press, 1990.

Midrash Shir ha-Shirim. Edited by E. H. Greenhut. Jerusalem: Ktav Yad Vasefer Institute, 1971.

Midrash Shir ha-Shirim Rabbah. Edited by S. Dunsky. Jerusalem: Dvir, 1980.

Möbuss, Susanne. *Die Intellektlehre des Levi ben Gerson in ihrer Beziehung zur christlichen Scholastik.* Frankfurt am Main: Peter Lang, 1991.

Pines, Shlomo. "Appendix: Problems in the Teachings of Gersonides," appended to his "On Certain Subjects Included in the Book *Ezer ha-Dat* . . . " In *Meḥqarim be-Qabbalah . . . Mugashim Le-Yeshaiyah Tishby,* edited by J. Dan, 447–57. Jerusalem: Magnes, 1986 (Hebrew).

————. "Truth and Falsehood Versus Good and Evil: A Study in Jewish and General Philosophy in Connection with the *Guide of the Perplexed* I.2." In *Studies in Maimonides,* edited by Isadore Twersky, 95–157. Cambridge: Harvard University Press, 1990.

————. "What Was Original in Arabic Science?" In *Scientific Change,* edited by A. C. Crombie, 181–205. London, 1963. Reprint, Pines, *Studies in Arabic Versions of Greek Texts and in Mediaeval Science,* 329–53. *The Collected Works of Shlomo Pines,* vol. 2. Jerusalem: Magnes, 1986.

Pope, Marvin. *Song of Songs.* Garden City, N.Y.: Doubleday, 1977.

Qimḥi, David. *Sefer ha-Shorashim.* New York: n.p., 1948.

Rabin, Chaim. "Hebrew and Arabic in Medieval Jewish Philosophy." In *Studies in Jewish Religious and Intellectual History Presented to Alexander Altmann,* edited by S. Stein and R. Loewe, 235–45. University of Alabama Press, 1979.

Ravitzky, Aviezer. "*Mishnato shel R. Zeraḥiah ben Shealtiel ben Yiṣḥak Ḥen vi-ha-Hagut ha-Maimonit-Tibbonit bi-Me'ah ha-Yod-Gimmel.*" Ph.D. Diss., Hebrew University, 1978.

————. "Samuel ibn Tibbon and the Esoteric Character of the *Guide of the Perplexed.*" *AJSReview* 6 (1981): 87–123.

————. "The Secrets of the *Guide of the Perplexed:* Between the Thirteenth and Twentieth Centuries." *Jerusalem Studies in Jewish Thought* 5 (1986): 23–69 (Hebrew); English translation in *Studies in Maimonides,* edited by Isadore Twersky, 159–207. Cambridge: Harvard University Press, 1990.

————. "The Study of Medieval Jewish Philosophy." *Jerusalem Studies in Jewish Thought* 1 (1981): 7–22 (Hebrew).

Ravitzky, Israel. "R. Immanuel b. Shlomo of Rome, *Commentary to the 'Song of Songs'—Philosophical Division.*" M.A. Thesis, Hebrew University, 1970 (Hebrew).

Rosenberg, Shalom. "Bible Exegesis in the *Guide of the Perplexed.*" *Jerusalem Studies in Jewish Thought* 1 (1981): 85–157 (Hebrew).

————. "Philosophical Hermeneutics on the Song of Songs, Introductory Remarks." *Tarbiṣ* 59 (1990): 133–51 (Hebrew).

Rosenthal, Erwin I. J. "Anti-Christian Polemic in Medieval Bible Commentaries." *Journal of Jewish Studies* 11 (1960): 115–35.

————. *Averroës' Commentary on Plato's* Republic. Cambridge: Cambridge University Press, 1966.

————. "The Concept *Eudaimonia* in Medieval Islamic and Jewish Philosophy." In *Storia della filosofia antica e medievale,* 145–52. Florence, 1960. Reprint, Rosenthal, *Studia Semitica 2: Islamic Themes,* 127–34. Cambridge: Cambridge University Press, 1971.

————. *Political Thought in Medieval Islam.* Cambridge: Cambridge University Press, 1968.

Rosenthal, Yehudah. "The Anti-Maimonidean Controversy in the Perspective of the

Generations." In *Meḥqarim u-Meqorot,* ed. Y. Rosenthal, 1:126–202. Jerusalem: Rubin Mass, 1967 (Hebrew).

Roth, Norman. "The 'Theft of Philosophy' by the Greeks from the Jews." *Classical Folia* 32 (1978): 53–67.

Rudavsky, Tamar. "Individuals and Individuation in the Thought of Gersonides." In *Gersonide en son temps,* edited by Gilbert Dahan, 185–97. Louvain: Peeters, 1991.

———. "Individuals and the Doctrine of Individuation in Gersonides." *The New Scholasticism* 56 (1982): 30–50.

Salfeld, Siegmund. *Das Hohelied Salomos bei den jüdischen Erklärern des Mittelalters.* Berlin, 1879.

Samuelson, Norbert. "Gersonides' Account of God's Knowledge of Particulars." *Journal of the History of Philosophy* 10 (1972): 399–416.

———. "On Knowing God: Maimonides, Gersonides, and the Philosophy of Religion." *Judaism* 18 (1969): 64–77.

———. "The Problem of Free Will in Maimonides, Gersonides, and Aquinas." *Central Conference of American Rabbis Journal* (January 1970): 2–20.

Saperstein, Marc. "The Conflict over the Rashba's Ḥerem on Philosophical Study: A Political Perspective." *Jewish History* 1 (1986): 27–38.

———. *Decoding the Rabbis: A Thirteenth-Century Commentary on the Aggadah.* Cambridge: Harvard University Press, 1980.

———. *Jewish Preaching, 1200–1800.* New Haven: Yale University Press, 1989.

———. Gersonides' On God's Knowledge.

Schwartz, Dov. "Rationalism and Conservatism: The Philosophy of R. Solomon ben Adreth's Circle." *Daʿat* 32–33 (1994): 143–82 (Hebrew).

———. "The Tension Between Moderate Morality and Ascetic Morality in Medieval Jewish Philosophy." In *Bein Dat le-Mussar,* edited by Daniel Statman and Avi Sagi, 185–208. Ramat Gan: Bar Ilan University Press, 1993 (Hebrew).

Septimus, Bernard. *Hispano-Jewish Culture in Transition: The Career and Controversies of Ramah.* Cambridge: Harvard University Press, 1982.

Shapiro, Herman, ed. *Medieval Philosophy.* New York: Modern Library, 1964.

Sherwin, Byron L. "The Human Body and the Image of God." In *A Traditional Quest: Essays in Honour of Louis Jacobs,* edited by Dan Cohn-Sherbok, 75–85. Sheffield: JSOT Press, 1991.

Sirat, Colette. *A History of Jewish Philosophy in the Middle Ages.* Cambridge: Cambridge University Press, 1985.

———. "*Mar'ot Elokim* by Hanokh ben Shelomoh al-Constantini." *Eshel Beersheva* 1 (1976): 120–99 (Hebrew).

Solomon ben Abraham (Rashba), *Teshuvot ha-Rashba.* Edited by H. Z. Dimitrowsky. Jerusalem: Mossad ha-Rav Kook, 1990.

Spanier, Ehud, ed. *The Royal Purple and the Biblical Blue: The Study of Chief Rabbi Isaac Herzog and Recent Scientific Contributions.* Jerusalem: Keter, 1987.

Staub, Jacob. *The Creation of the World According to Gersonides.* Chico, Calif.: Scholars Press, 1982.

Steinschneider, Moritz. *Die hebräischen Übersetzungen des Mittelalters und die Juden als Dolmetscher.* Berlin, 1893. Reprint, Graz: Akademische Druck, 1956.

Strack, Hermann L. *Introduction to the Talmud and Midrash.* Philadelphia: Jewish Publication Society, 1931.

Strack, Hermann L., and G. Stemberger. *Introduction to the Talmud and Midrash.* Rev. ed. Edinburgh: T&T Clark, 1991.

Strauss, Leo. *Philosophy and Law.* Translated by Fred Baumann. Philadelphia: Jewish Publication Society, 1987.

Toomer, G. J. *Ptolemy's Almagest.* New York: Springer-Verlag, 1984.

Touati, Charles. *Les Guerres du Seigneur, III–IV.* Paris: Mouton, 1968.

———. *La pensée philosophique et théologique de Gersonide.* Paris: Editions de Minuit, 1973.

———. "Le problème de l'inerrance prophétique dans la théologie juive du moyen âge," *Revue de l'Histoire des Religions* 175 (1968): 169–97. Reprint, Touati, *Prophètes, Talmudistes, Philosophes,* 257–71. Paris: Cerf, 1990.

———. "Le problème du *Kol Nidrey* et le *responsum* inédit de Gersonide." *REJ* 154 (1995): 327–42.

Twersky, Isadore. "Did R. Abraham ibn Ezra Influence Maimonides?" In *Rabbi Abraham ibn Ezra: Studies in the Writings of a Twelfth-Century Jewish Polymath,* edited by Isadore Twersky and Jay M. Harris, 21–48. Cambridge: Harvard University Press, 1993 (Hebrew).

———. *Introduction to the Code of Maimonides.* New Haven: Yale University Press, 1980.

———. "Joseph ibn Kaspi: Portrait of a Medieval Jewish Intellectual." In *Studies in Medieval Jewish History and Literature,* edited by Isadore Twersky, 231–57. Cambridge: Harvard University Press, 1979.

———. "Some Non-Halakic Aspects of the *Mishneh Torah.*" In *Jewish Medieval and Renaissance Studies,* edited by A. Altmann, 95–119. Cambridge: Harvard University Press, 1967.

Urbach, Ephraim. "The Homiletical Interpretations of the Sages and the Expositions of Origen on Canticles, and the Jewish-Christian Disputation." *Scripta Hierosolymitana* 22 (1971): 247–75.

Vajda, Georges. *L'amour de Dieu dans la théologie juive du moyen âge.* Paris: Vrin, 1957.

———. "An Analysis of the *Ma'amar Yiqqawu ha-Mayim* by Samuel b. Judah ibn Tibbon." *Journal of Jewish Studies* 10 (1959): 137–49.

Van Engen, John H. *Rupert of Deutz.* Berkeley: University of California Press, 1983.

Vermes, Geza. "'Lebanon'—The Historical Development of an Exegetical Tradition." In G. Vermes, *Scripture and Tradition in Jewish Haggadic Studies,* 35–39. Leiden: Brill, 1961.

———. "The Symbolical Interpretation of 'Lebanon' in the *Targums.*" *Journal of Theological Studies* n.s. 9 (1958): 1–13.

Walfish, Dov Barry. "Annotated Bibliography of Medieval Jewish Commentaries on Song of Songs." In *Ha-Miqra be-Re'i Mefarshav: Sefer Zikkaron le-Sarah Kamin,* edited by Sarah Yafet, 518–71. Jerusalem: Magnes, 1994 (Hebrew).

Weil, Gerard. *La bibliothèque de Gersonide d'après son catalogue autographe.* Louvain: Peeters, 1991.

Weil-Guény, Anne-Mary. "Gersonide en son temps: Un tableau chronologique." In *Studies on Gersonides: A Fourteenth-Century Jewish Philosopher-Scientist,* edited by Gad Freudenthal, 355–65. Leiden: Brill, 1992.

Wirszubski, Chaim. "Giovanni Pico's Book of Job." *Journal of the Warburg and Courtald Institutes* 32 (1969): 171–99.

Wolfson, Harry A. *Crescas' Critique of Aristotle.* Cambridge: Harvard University Press, 1929.

———. "The Internal Senses in Latin, Arabic, and Hebrew Philosophical Texts." In *Studies in the History of Philosophy and Religion,* edited by G. Williams and I. Twersky, 1:250–314. Cambridge: Harvard University Press, 1973.

———. "Maimonides and Gersonides on Divine Attributes as Ambiguous Terms." In *Studies in the History of Philosophy and Religion,* edited by G. Williams and I. Twersky, 2:231–46. Cambridge: Harvard University Press, 1977.

———. "The Terms *Taṣawwur* and *Taṣdiq* in Arabic Philosophy and their Greek, Latin, and Hebrew Equivalents." In *Studies in the History and Philosophy of Religion,* edited by G. Williams and I. Twersky, 1:478–92. Cambridge: Harvard University Press, 1973.

Zinberg, Israel. *A History of Jewish Literature.* Vol. 3. Translated and Edited by Bernard Martin. Philadelphia: Jewish Publication Society, 1973.

INDEX

157